Beyond Malthus

BEYOND
MALTHUS
Population and Power

NEIL W. CHAMBERLAIN

Basic Books, Inc., Publishers

NEW YORK : LONDON

© 1970 by Basic Books, Inc.
Library of Congress Catalog Card Number: 70-126947
SBN 465-00661-2
Manufactured in the United States of America
DESIGNED BY VINCENT TORRE

Preface

THIS BOOK had its origin in the Dryfoos Conference on Collective Bargaining in the Public Service sponsored by Dartmouth College in the spring of 1968. One of the conferees, a municipal official of some forty years standing, offered his judgment that unionization of public employees was unnecessary in his city because he believed in following an "open door" policy, so that any employee had ready access to him to discuss whatever was on the employee's mind.

I was sufficiently taken aback to speculate, as he continued to talk, how an intelligent individual could adopt such an anachronistic point of view. It occurred to me that quite possibly he was still looking at the public service through the same eyes with which he had viewed it when he first entered on his duties four decades earlier and that his thinking, in this respect at least, had been unaffected by the growth in the size of his city and the increase in the scale and specialization of its services. From this my mind was led on to contemplate other respects in which growth in the size of a population, an increase in its density, or a shift in its composition might affect social relationships in ways which might easily be overlooked.

As an economist, I had always regarded population from a Malthusian perspective, as a pressure of people on resources. This new and quite accidentally inspired line of inquiry opened my interest to a different set of effects stemming from population changes, the pressures of people on people. This new interest, I soon found, was not unrelated to my long-standing concern with bargaining power relationships, since a major part of the problem seems to be encompassed in the broad question of the ways in which population pressures tend to redistribute power within a society or between societies.

I have found very little literature explicitly addressed to this question, except for discussion of the *Lebensraum* thesis in international power politics and, from an earlier date, of the influence of numbers on forms of government. I have found a large number of relevant paragraphs in studies directed to other issues, a number which I am sure could be increased by whatever multiple of time one chose to put into the search. My explorations have been enormously aided by James Berson, who showed a sensitive intelligence and keen perception in combing through a vast number of journals and books. I am grateful to the faculty research fund of the Graduate School of Business, Columbia University, for its financial support.

For a good many years I have envied those authors who could sign their prefaces at some exotic location to which they had repaired to write. I am enormously pleased to be able now to join that select company. The whole of this book, including this preface, has been written in a small village a few kilometers outside of Asti, in northern Italy. Here I have sat before my typewriter on a third-floor balcony overlooking an incredibly beautiful, almost voluptuous hillside, terraced in grapes, atop which a few miles away sits perched the neighboring village of Camerano, its compact red-tiled roofs glistening in the sun, dominated by the steeple of its church, an appearance which is characteristic of all the hilltop villages in this Monferrato area. On a clear day the snow-covered peaks of the Pennine Alps are plainly visible. It is from this serene perspective that I have been able to contemplate the monumental and turbulent issues with which this book is concerned.

NEIL W. CHAMBERLAIN

Cinaglio d'Asti

Contents

Beyond Malthus

CHAPTER 1

Framing the Issue

SINCE *The First Essay on Population* by Thomas Malthus, the population question has commonly been viewed as an arithmetical one. It was the English minister who, in the pursuit of his intellectual inquiries, conceived the necessary disproportion between the rate of growth of population and the rate of growth of food and other produce. He thereby introduced into the study of economics, still in its infancy, a note of gloom and pessimism that earned for it the name of "the dismal science." Not that Malthus was the first to take a theoretical approach to the subject, but as Lord Robbins has said, "it was Malthus who really put this on the map."

Malthus makes his point so pithily that it is best to let him speak for himself. In the first chapter of his Essay he asserts:

I think I may fairly make two postulates.

First, that food is necessary to the existence of man.

Secondly, that the passion between the sexes is necessary and will remain nearly in its present state. . . .

Assuming then, my postulates as granted, I say, that the power of population is indefinitely greater than the power in the earth to produce subsistence for man.

Population, when unchecked, increases in a geometrical ratio. Subsistence increases only in an arithmetical ratio. A slight acquaintance with numbers will show the immensity of the first power in comparison of the second.

By that law of our nature which makes food necessary to the life of man, the effects of these two unequal powers must be kept equal.

This implies a strong and constantly operating check on population from the difficulty of subsistence. This difficulty must fall somewhere and must necessarily be severely felt by a large portion of mankind.[1]

"A strong check . . . severely felt by a large portion of mankind." What did the English parson have in mind?

The germs of existence contained in this spot of earth, with ample food, and ample room to expand in, would fill millions of worlds in the course of a few thousand years. Necessity, that imperious all pervading law of nature, restrains them within the prescribed bounds. The race of plants, and the race of animals shrink under this great restrictive law. And the race of men cannot, by any efforts of reason, escape from it. Among plants and animals its effects are waste of seed, sickness, and premature death. Among mankind, misery and vice. The former, misery, is an absolutely necessary consequence of it. Vice is a highly probable consequence. . . .[2]

And later, in the seventh chapter, he comments:

The different modes which nature takes to prevent or repress a redundant population, do not appear, indeed, to us so certain and regular, but though we cannot always predict the mode we may with certainty predict the fact. . . . We may be perfectly certain that unless an emigration takes place, the deaths will shortly exceed the births; and that the increase that had taken place for a few years cannot be the real average increase of the population of the country. Were there no other depopulating causes, every country would, without doubt, be subject to periodical pestilences or famines.[3]

Malthus followed his analysis to its rigorous conclusions in a way that earned him, at best, a bitter respect. He became a foe of the family allowance system of welfare which was very much under debate at the time of his writing (1798).

I entirely acquit Mr. Pitt of any sinister intention in that clause of his poor bill which allows a shilling a week to every labourer for each child he has above three. I confess, that before the bill was brought into Parliament, and for some time after, I thought that such a regulation would be highly beneficial, but further reflection on the subject has convinced me that if its object be to better the condition of the poor, it is calculated to defeat the very purpose which it has in view. It has no tendency that I can discover to increase the produce of the country, and if it tends to increase the population, without increasing the produce, the necessary and inevitable consequence appears to be that the same produce must be divided among a greater number, and consequently that a day's labour will purchase a smaller quantity of provisions, and the poor therefore in general must be more distressed.[4]

Professor Sam B. Warner has provided striking empirical illustration of the operation of Malthus's "imperious" natural law.[5] He notes that because the poor have always been the most numerous category in any country, "the history of populations is the history of the responses of the common people to slight gains and losses in their opportunities and environment. The sheer number of the poor magnify these slight adjustments into changes of huge dimensions and often violent outcomes." The case of the Irish from shortly before the time of Malthus's writing onward constitutes a bleak example.

The combination of high farm rents and competition from English textile manufacturers precipitated a considerable migration from Northern Ireland to America even before the Revolution. With the end of the Napoleonic wars, Dublin's cotton and silk mills suffered a similar decline, stimulating a fresh migrant movement. For the next thirty years a growing number of peasants and village craftworkers found the opportunities in the young egalitarian United States more attractive than in their more feudally organized homeland. Meanwhile, the introduction of the potato, which required less land and a minimum of cultivation, led to an increase in population which has been estimated at 179 percent over the period 1779–1841. "As Ireland became a potato country, the shadow of starvation lifted slightly. . . . Early marriages became invariable: girls were usually married before they were sixteen, . . . and by their early thirties they were grandmothers. Thus the population spread with the rapidity of an epidemic."[6]

Then in 1845 and for the following four years, disaster struck in the form of failure of the potato crop, which had become the national staple. A population which had climbed to 8.5 million was cut to 6.5 million in the space of four years. Over a million died of starvation or disease. Another million fled to English slums or sought to escape to America, at £4 to £5 a head, though some 200,000 died of starvation or cholera at ports of embarkation or in transit on the "coffin ships" or "fever ships" as they came to be called. Continued emigration to the New World and a lower birth rate persisted for the next forty years, gradually restoring the peasant standards of the preceding century. But the reduced birth rate has continued to the present, and Irish population is now only half its peak of more than a hundred years ago.

What emigration, pestilence, famine—Malthus's three equalizers of the unequal powers of procreation and cultivation—did for the Irish has also been evident in the internal population patterns of the United States, as the high population-growth areas of Appalachia, the rural south, and the mountain states demonstrate. The poor of these regions have populated the expanding cities of other areas and have themselves constituted the object of public assistance programs under the administrations of various presidents from Franklin D. Roosevelt on. On a more massive, world-aggregative scale, the pattern repeats itself in the declining status of the more rapidly growing underdeveloped countries, whose populations are rising at an average rate of 2.6 percent per annum as against 1.6 percent for the developed economies, thereby forcing a division of

income (growing in the less developed countries at only a slightly
lower rate than in the industrialized areas) among a swelling number of people.[7] Standards of living, even when rising absolutely if
slowly, fall relative to the advanced economies with each passing
year, providing little margin for disaster and a declining inducement
for those who can leave to remain.

For all the apparent evidence supporting Malthus and his inexorable ratios, dissenting voices have never been stilled. Is the population problem really one of man against nature, with nature always
in control? Is misery man's necessary lot, a consequence of too
many mouths (with not enough food) or too many feet (with not
enough standing room)? Is a natural limitation on the expandability
of food and space the only effective curb on man's procreative
passion?

One persistent rebuttal has asserted man's control over nature.
Through technological innovations, with respect both to production and social organization, the specter of starving masses can be
exorcised, it is said. Indeed, Malthus himself jousted with one of
the earliest believers of this view, a fellow clerical philosopher,
William Godwin, who maintained in a running debate that when
men learned to live together in a kind of primal communism without limitation of such social perversions as private property and
the marriage institution, an Eden-like balance between man and
nature would assert itself. Malthus scoffed at such utopianism, falling back on his arithmetic disproportions to prove that however
optimistic Godwin might be, he could at best only defer for a
brief time the evil day when population would outrun subsistence.

But a more formidable foe followed Godwin in the person of
Karl Marx. Like Godwin, but with far more sophistication and
logic, Marx held that social reorganization and technology were the
parallel instruments by means of which the tooth and claw of primitive nature could be blunted. This has remained a cardinal tenet of
Marxian socialism down to the present day. Max Ways, a *Fortune*
editor, reports a conversation with Russian physicist Gersh I. Budker, director of the Institute of Nuclear Physics, during a journal-
istic tour of Siberia. Ways quotes Budker as commenting that
"men tend to underrate what science and technology can already
accomplish. He poured scorn on timid people who worry about the
'population explosion.' They seemed to him like 'tired, frightened
civilizations, huddled behind the walls of ancient cities, deploring
the barbarian hordes outside the gates.' "

In Way's account, Budker observes that people who are afraid of population growth "look at a baby and see only a mouth to be fed. They do not see the hands, which will be more than capable of feeding the mouth. If the population of India fell to the level of the population of the U.S., each Indian, instead of being as well off as an American, would be poorer than Indians are now. When the population of the U.S. reaches the level of the present population of India, each American will be much richer than Americans are now. That is because Americans, like other progressing peoples, know how to work together, to help one another."[8]

But one need not be a socialist to take the position that changes in social organization and technology can accommodate unchanged human procreative tendencies. Joseph Fisher, the eminently respectable economist who presides over Resources for the Future, a nonprofit research institution, reported in 1968 that resources are or can be made available to sustain any foreseeable population growth to the year 2000. Nor is this a case of saying, after then, the deluge, as Malthus accused Godwin, but rather simply the scientific way of saying that one's knowledge permits prediction to the end of the century but not prophecy beyond that point.[9]

That global resources will accommodate global population growth in the foreseeable future waives a number of serious problems, as Fisher noted. It says nothing about the political difficulties of distributing the world's resources. Nor does it take into account the dangers that exist in using resources on the required scale: excessive amounts of carbon dioxide that would be pumped into the atmosphere by the increasing use of fuel oils, or the threat in the disposal of atomic wastes, or an increase in the heat of the earth beneath the thermal blanket. But these are either problems of social technology whose solution is not outside the realm of feasibility or a surface of physical dangers on which mankind skates, as on thin ice, but which like thin ice may yet sustain him.

The argument on this score has been nicely summarized by Maurice Halbwachs in his notable elucidation and extension of Durkheim's foray into social morphology:

Thus the industrial and economic organization to which men turn and whose products they demand is not like land exploited to the limits of its fertility, and that at some point is no longer productive. Industry responds to these appeals and even solicits them. It is never out of stocks, reserves, materials (often procured at great distances), and technical inventions which turn up at the right time. The more we receive from it, the more it is prepared to produce; as if taxing, pushing, and harassing it, far from exhausting industry, only releases new forces in it and gives it new vigor.[10]

The special significance of this trait of industry—in contrast to the less tractable limitations on the fruits of the land—is that industry has shown itself to be an amazingly fecund source of supply, apparently capable of taking over provision of the necessities of existence if the natural barriers imposed by a mythical Mother Ceres assert themselves.

A second riposte to the Malthusian position is offered by what is known as the theory of the demographic transition. In this approach not only is technology at work, but also changing patterns of social behavior which act to limit the growth of population *before* it is rudely cut back by famine and disease. This thesis pictures a three-stage demographic evolution.[11] Stage One characterizes preindustrial societies. A high birth rate (four to six or more children per child-bearing woman) is offset by a high death rate, producing a relatively stable population.[12] Fertility and mortality rates are the consequences of traditional modes of behavior rather than any conscious decision. Indeed, the notion of controlling births and deaths is little entertained, since these are viewed as acts of God's will rather than human will.

In Stage Two modern sanitation begins to make its entrance on the scene, a technological advance rather easily diffused. Other forms of disease prevention assist in curtailing the mortality rate. At first the greater number of surviving children helps to swell the population and to evoke Malthusian concern, but then the rising urban industrial and commercial middle class sprouts a number of social innovators—people who, responding to the opportunities and challenges of worldly success, begin to experiment with family planning. They purposively limit the number of children as a means of improving their own status and securing the future of those fewer children whose further progress they actively push. These practices too are diffused to the lower economic groups, particularly as society becomes more and more urban, and spatial pressures put limits on the desirable size of families if standards of living are to be maintained.

At this point industrial (or postindustrial) society has entered Stage Three. Social planning limits both the number of deaths and births to a level consciously selected in accordance with people's preferences. Once again population growth achieves a kind of stability, with only minor fluctuations, but now the balance between nature and man is a consequence of man's improved mastery over nature, both in terms of technology and procreation, rather than of nature's imperious control over man.

Malthus confounded again! The habits of earlier centuries give way to new behavioral patterns adapted to a changed culture, aided by a new technology of contraception. Nor is it new techniques of birth control that initiate the change, but rather people's desires that lead to the development of new techniques that make possible the way of life that is wanted.

Indeed, so enthusiastically did twentieth-century urbanites take to the new way of life that Gunnar Myrdal, in the 1938 Godkin lectures at Harvard, took as his theme the proposition that depopulation should be checked. The "slow but steady development of birth control has become a truly serious peril for the reproduction of people,"[13] and while it may be too much to hope for a population policy that provides for some increase in numbers, at least the western industrialized societies should strive for a stationary population, one that would maintain its size.

Time has dispelled such fears and reintroduced concern that the rate of population growth may be excessive in some sense, even in the United States. But the sense in which it may prove excessive no longer relates to subsistence levels, even when subsistence is viewed in terms of changing cultural standards. It relates to a whole style of life that includes such ingredients as recreational room, urban space, educational levels, and purity of air, all of which can diminish indefinitely in accommodating population pressures but in diminishing will take with them a preferred way of life. Such a prospect puts in question just how much control a society does in fact exercise over itself when one speaks of population policy, but it raises such an issue not in a Malthusian natural law context but in a context of political philosophy, just as a person might question how much control a society actually exercises over its crime rate or its military involvements.

Let us consider still another way of looking at "the population problem." It has been argued that the reduction in physical amenities such as space and in the quality of social life that comes from congestion (whether of theaters, transportation facilities, schools, hospitals, highways, or restaurants) comes not so much from an increase in numbers of people as from an increase in their incomes. Even in the industrialized economies, even with a stationary population, if per capita income is rising, more and more people can afford the luxuries which society offers. They thereby bring pressure to bear on resources which are limited, whether of parks or health facilities, airways, or universities. Not the pressure of numbers but the pressure of wealth jeopardizes not a natural balance but a preferred balance of people and resources.

This approach stands Malthus on his head. As the case is argued by Professor Jean Mayer of the Harvard Center for Population Studies: "Malthus was concerned with the steadily more widespread poverty that indefinite population growth would inevitably create. I am concerned about the areas of the globe where people are rapidly becoming richer. For rich people occupy much more space, consume more of each natural resource, disturb the ecology more, and create more land, air, water, chemical, thermal, and radioactive pollution than poor people. So it can be argued that from many viewpoints it is even more urgent to control the numbers of the rich than it is to control the numbers of the poor."[14]

Professor Mayer catalogues the deteriorating style of American life by pointing to the vast increase in rubbish disposal disfiguring the landscape, including the abandonment of nine million motor vehicles every year; the shortage of water in many cities attributable not to more people drinking and bathing but to the increased use of airconditioning, private swimming pools, and industrial uses catering to consumers' wants; a one-decade increase (1950–1960) in attendance at state parks of 125 percent, compared with a population increase of less than 20 percent.

That the air is getting crowded much more rapidly than the population is increasing is again an illustration that increase in the disposable income is perhaps more closely related to our own view of "overpopulation" than is the population itself. From 1940 to 1967 the number of miles flown has gone from 264 million to 3,334 billion (and the fuel consumed from 22 to 512 million gallons). The very air waves are crowded: the increase in citizen-licensees from 126 thousand to 848 thousand in the brief 1960–1967 interval is again an excellent demonstration of the very secondary role of the population increase in the new overpopulation. I believe that as the disposable income rises throughout the world in general, the population pressure due to riches will become as apparent as that due to poverty.[15]

This income approach to population problems has the advantage of a broader perspective. It emphasizes that population policy is something pertinent not only to the underdeveloped economies but to the industrialized and wealthier societies as well. But it is difficult to follow it to the conclusion reached by Professor Mayer, that "a rational policy may entail in many countries not only a plateauing of the population to permit an increase in disposable income, but a decrease of the population as the disposable income rises."[16] For in the same way that science, technology, and industry have combined to overcome the dangers of food shortage in the advanced economies (and potentially in the world at large), so are they likely to meet the problem of space and facility shortage. The rising incomes which Professor Mayer sees as the source of the problem could be also its cure, as they are allocated, for example, to the development of new forms of recreation, perhaps embodying the *illusion* of space in a way that will satisfy contemporary tastes, to improved forms of transportation economizing on time and lessening the discomforts of congestion, and to expanded and innovative educational facilities.

Granted that the means of meeting the needs may not be available at the time the need arises, but only with a lag that permits the need to be translated into effective demand (whether political or economic), there is no apparent reason why overpopulation in terms of wealth cannot be met in the same way as overpopulation in terms of numbers. Indeed, once one has abandoned subsistence as a limitation on population growth, at least in those countries that have affected the demographic transition to Stage Three, it is hard to separate the effects of increasing numbers from increasing wealth, since the two are likely to go hand in hand except for brief periods such as had Gunnar Myrdal worried.

But that is not to say that there is no population problem or problems. If it were, there would be no reason for this book. The intent of the analysis contained in these pages is not to take issue with Malthus but to extend the realm of his inquiry. Even if the Malthusian traps were not sprung, in the sense that total resources expanded, through technological advances, to accommodate the human swarm, population problems would still haunt mankind. They would be problems of scale and proportions.

Like Malthus, this book is concerned, in major part, with disproportions in rates of change, not, however, between numbers of people and nature's yield but between numbers of people and other people, and between numbers of people and social institutions. These changing relationships are confounding in their intricacy and pervasive in their effects.

In part, this aspect of the population problem emerges because of differential rates of population change among people, among the subgroups of a nation, or among nations in the world. Regardless of what happens in the aggregate, within a nation or within the world, the component groups or nations will grow or maintain themselves at different rates. The consequence is almost certain to be changes in group relationships and international relations over time. This book is concerned with how such population changes among groups and nations affect their relative positions, relationships, and bargaining power.

If we conceive of each significantly differentiable group as having a stake in the larger society of which it is a constituent, then we can also conceive of its seeking to preserve that stake or to enlarge it over time. The compulsions on it will vary (as will its success) with its size, among other things. It may enter into alliances or live compliantly or adopt new methods of asserting its power or any of a number of other stances, depending on the needs and potentials of the particular time; we can only be sure that over time change will take place in its relations with other groups that reflect the relative changes in populations. As the total population changes in size and composition and location, a regrouping permits some blocs to improve their position at the expense of others, or at least relative to others.[17]

Not only differential rates of population change are involved but also the social context within which population change takes place. Even if the Moslem minority of Ahmadabad were expanding at a somewhat lower rate than the Hindu majority of the same city, it would feel the pressures more because of the tighter social space in which it is confined, relating to such matters as the availability of housing, schools, and jobs. While both groups might suffer from the fact that their population growth outstripped economic development (the Malthusian curse), the Moslems would suffer disproportionately more. In every society there are such differentially disadvantaged groups, on whom the effects of population changes (either of their own people or of the peoples by whom they are surrounded) fall more critically. Over time, social and political consequences may emerge.

In approaching this major theme, Chapter 2 begins by developing a few conceptual building blocks, necessary for construction of the later analysis. *Social organization*, the *distribution of the social advantage*, and the *structure of authority* combine to determine how effectively and how acceptably the effects of population change will be met. Since these institutions are themselves changing at different rates, pressure points are created. These may be contained by various devices or they may expand and produce social fission. Pressures may be accommodated or they may explode.

With some elaborations, the same may be said of the world at large. Differential rates of population change among nations occur within differing contexts of resources and social organization, determining how the effects of population change are internationally distributed. Again, social and political consequences are unavoidable.

But how disentangle the effects of population change from those of technological change in examining shifting group and national relationships and relative bargaining powers? Does technology operate as an exogenous and indirect influence on population by affecting the social organization, the distribution of social benefits, and the authority structure in ways which accommodate larger populations (as Marx argued)? Or is technology itself at least partly responsive to population changes, being guided in its own development by the kinds of wants which a society, changing in numbers and density, effectively expresses? The latter position is the one presented in Chapter 3.

The density aspect of population change just referred to has its own special consequences. Density effects show up most vividly in the urbanization trend, producing functional changes in the social organization, modifying the culture, and affecting conceptions of the respective spheres to be accorded individual freedom and government regulation. Density effects in the national unit also have their influence on the form of government, necessitating simultaneously the centralization of certain governmental powers and the decentralization of other functions to local units. The very meaning and substance of democracy are called into question in the process.

As populations increase in size, the broad base of low-income and largely nonpropertied individuals and families likewise expands, raising challenges to traditional notions of private property and income distribution. Can popular governments protect islands of personal privilege from the turbulent sea that would erode them? In the face of economies made more complex by population increase and the consequences that entails, will the pressure for organized and contrived solutions drive countries ineluctably toward forms of economic planning that take precedence over private purpose?

These issues—raised by the pressures of people on other people, affecting the acceptability and survivability of social institutions— are aspects of the population problem which have been accorded only passing attention. In our preoccupation with the Malthusian trap, we have neglected systematic examination of major social consequences stemming from shifts in population numbers, location, and composition. Most population analysts have centered their attention on the demographic factors of fertility, mortality, and rates of growth, rather than their persistent and pervasive social consequences. Although numbers of individuals have noted certain effects or presumed effects, these commentaries have seldom become the basis for any sustained inquiry leading to conceptual enrichment of social theory.

Population need not be the core of social theory for it to assume a significant role. Its relationship to social change may still permit some theorists to emphasize technology as the kingpin (as Marx did), or religion (as Weber and Tawney have done), or a *Zeitgeist* (as Spengler), but certainly population changes have their part to play in any social theory, more systematically and conceptually than has been the case. This book aims at a modest contribution to this desirable end.

NOTES

1. Thomas Malthus, *Population: The First Essay*, paperback edition (Ann Arbor: University of Michigan Press, 1959), pp. 4 and 5. I cite this edition because of its ready availability to any reader interested in reading or rereading this seminal work. This edition also contains a nice preface by Professor Kenneth Boulding.

2. *Ibid.*, pp. 5–6.

3. *Ibid.*, p. 45.

4. *Ibid.*, p. 47.

5. Sam B. Warner, "Population Movements and Urbanization," in Melvin Kranzberg and Carroll W. Pursell, Jr., eds., *Technology in Western Civilization* (London: Oxford University Press, 1967), especially 533–538. In summarizing the Irish case, I have also drawn on chapter 6 of Cecil Woodham-Smith's remarkable history-biography, *The Reason Why* (London: Constable, 1953). For a more extended treatment of the subject by the same author the reader is referred to *The Great Hunger* (New York: Harper & Row, 1962).

6. Woodham-Smith, *The Reason Why*, p. 107.

7. The point is graphically made by Professor J. E. Meade in "Population Explosion, the Standard of Living and Social Conflict," *Economic Journal* 77 (June 1967): 233–255.

8. Max Ways, "The 'House of the Dead' Is Now the Liveliest Part of the U.S.S.R.," *Fortune*, August 1968, p. 187. Budker, in this interview, strangely belittles the role of technological development. Ways writes: "Did Budker mean that Malthus had been outdated by advanced technology? No, he said, Malthus was wrong when he wrote, wrong in terms of the technology available in his own day. The Malthusian argument . . . never had any scientific basis." And again: "The problem is not population. The problem is not technology. The problem is social justice." This approach seems to discount the principle of

diminishing marginal productivity. Each new pair of hands is believed capable of producing as much food and other subsistence as the last pair of hands. But if one wishes to avoid some mystical social optimism, this would be possible only with technological innovation, at a minimum innovation in social organization.

9. Fisher spoke at a Conference on Population convened at Princeton September 27–30, 1968, under the sponsorship of the Interdisciplinary Communications Program.

10. Maurice Halbwachs, *Population and Society*, trans. Otis D. Duncan and Harold W. Pfantz (Glencoe: The Free Press, 1960), p. 175.

11. From among a number of statements of this view, the interested reader is referred to F. Lorimer, *Culture and Human Fertility* (New York: UNESCO, 1954), Chapter 6, "The Nature of the Demographic Transition," or James M. Beshers, *Population Processes in Social Systems* (New York: The Free Press, 1967).

12. Actually, recent historical research suggests that over the centuries population has tended toward a slow secular growth, cut back at intervals by wars, plagues, and other catastrophes. Prof. K. F. Helleiner, in "The Vital Revolution Reconsidered," in D. V. Glass and D. E. C. Eversley, eds., *Population in History* (London: Edward Arnold, 1965), p. 86, writes:

> The opinion, still widely held, that before the eighteenth century, Europe's population, though subject to violent short-run fluctuations, remained stationary over long periods, or was growing only imperceptibly, is, I believe, no longer tenable. There is sufficient evidence to indicate that those oscillations were superimposed on clearly recognizable "long waves." At least two periods of secular increase can be tolerably well identified in the demographic history of medieval and early modern Europe, the first extending from about the middle of the eleventh to the end of the thirteenth, the second from the middle of the fifteenth to the end of the sixteenth, century. . . . *In this sense the demographic development of the eighteenth century was not unique.* What was unprecedented about it was the fact that the secular upward movement started from a higher level, and that it was able to maintain, and for some time even increase, its momentum. Population growth in the eighteenth and nineteenth centuries, unlike that of previous epochs, was not terminated or reversed by catastrophe.

13. Gunnar Myrdal, *Population* (Cambridge: Harvard University Press, 1940), p. 18.

14. Jean Mayer, "Toward a Non-Malthusian Population Policy," *Columbia Forum* 12 (Summer 1969): 5.

15. *Ibid.*, p. 13.

16. *Ibid.*

17. The geographical aspect of this proposition has been suggested by Florian Znaniecki, *Cultural Sciences* (Urbana: University of Illinois Press, 1963), p. 410. "Every inhabitable territory on the surface of the globe, every section of this territory is a possession of some social group, often a joint possession of several groups, and is subjected to its or their control. Nobody can live in any portion of space or even move across it without the explicit or implicit permission of the group which controls it or tends to gain control over it. The struggles between social groups for territories as common values are well-known factors of demographic changes."

CHAPTER 2

Population and the Distribution of Privilege and Authority

BEFORE exploring the effects of population change, let us set the stage by examining certain general social phenomena.

The Distribution of the Social Advantage

At any point in its history, a society has certain preferential conditions which it bestows on its members in unequal manner. The unequal distribution arises out of its very organization. It must have some form of government, however rudimentary, and government requires executives, administrators, and functionaries who stand above the undifferentiated citizenry. A society must have some form of economic organization, which implies that some individuals have power to decide how the available resources get used. There must also be some form of reward structure related to the participation of individuals in carrying out society's tasks, with rewards distributed according to some principle such as the scarcity of needed capabilities or a presumed importance of certain contributions which affects individuals differentially.

Over time, familiarity and custom underwrite what hereafter we shall call the distribution of the social advantage. Certain classes are sanctioned in their claim to preferential social status, political position, and economic power. These are the "elites." Outside these privileged circles the excluded groups accept their inferior roles. It is they who do the "dirty" work or get the short end of the civic budget.

Every society distributes its social advantage unequally, but the manner of distribution varies among societies. More primitive or less developed peoples tend toward a two-class organization, a simple division among a controlling elite and a controlled mass of peasants and laborers. In his essay on "Civilization," John Stuart Mill noted more than a hundred years ago:

> In the more backward countries of the present time, and in all Europe at no distant date, we see property entirely concentrated in a small number of hands; the remainder of the people being, with few exceptions, either the military retainers and dependents of the possessors of property, or serfs, stripped and tortured at pleasure by one master, and pillaged by a hundred. At no period could it be said that there was literally no middle class—but that class was extremely feeble, both in numbers and in power: while the labouring people, absorbed in manual toil, with difficulty earned, by the utmost excess of exertion, a more or less scanty and always precarious subsistence. The character of this state of society was the utmost excess of poverty and impotence in the masses; the most enormous importance and uncontrollable power of a small number of individuals, each of whom, within his own sphere, knew neither law nor superior.[1]

If Mill's words sound hyperbolic, one need only recall the harsh impact of privilege on yeomen of the enclosure movement in England itself in the period preceding Mill. As to the general position of England's landed aristocracy in Mill's own time, one author has this to say:

> It is almost impossible to picture the deference, the adulation, the extraordinary privileges accorded to the nobility in the first half of the nineteenth century. A peer was above the laws which applied to other men. He could run up debts, and no one could arrest him. . . . He could commit a criminal offense and no ordinary court had jurisdiction over him. . . . Flattered, adulated, deferred to, with incomes enormously increased by the Industrial Revolution, and as yet untaxed, all-powerful over a tenantry as yet unenfranchised, subject to no ordinary laws, holding the government of the country firmly in their hands and wielding through their closely knit connections an unchallengeable social power, the milords of England were the astonishment and admiration of Europe.[2]

On the contemporary scene, one can collect examples almost at random from among the underdeveloped countries. Of Iran, for example, it has been said:

> . . . Only about five percent of the farmers own the land they till. Villages are owned by landlords and about 10 thousand villages belong to people who own at least five villages. It is customary for Iranians to

state that their country is owned by 200 families, and these are identified as the major landowners. Over one-third of the members of Parliament are members of the 200 families or are relatives of this group. Most of the land is controlled by absentee owners who live in the cities, and some of the feudal aristocrats possess a hundred villages they have never seen. Landlords feel little responsibility for the land or the people who work one it and frequently the landlord seels to the highest bidder the right to collect the rents from the peasants. Since the landlords or their relatives are able to dominate Parliament, efforts have failed to increase the peasant's share of the crop, to eliminate absentee ownership, or to limit land holdings.[3]

The elite of Guatemala have been similarly portrayed:

The Government and the economy have always been in the hands of a segment of the population culturally alienated from and therefore in-different to the fate of the peasant majority. A tenth of 1 percent of the farms in Guatemala cover more than 40 percent of the total farm area, with 2.1 percent covering more than 70 percent of the total. More than 88 percent of the farms account for only slightly more than 14 percent of the total farm area and average five acres or less. Concentra-tion of land has meant more than just concentration of power and wealth; it has meant a subsistence living, at best, for the majority of the people.[4]

With economic, political, and social development, requiring a more complex form of organization of society, the distribution of the social advantage also becomes more complex. Privileges are shared by more than one elite; the number of groups which accept their lower positions in the social hierarchy also increases, and they are differentiated among themselves. Indeed, in a highly developed industrial society, it may become difficult to identify the elites, though everyone takes their existence for granted. In the United States, for example, they have been linked loosely to those who control "big business"; in France they may consist of the graduates of the École Polytechnique and other *grandes écoles*. But along-side these privileged groups others claim and are granted their special position in the society, their extra cut of the social advan-tages, even if the cut is not so large. Leaders of "big labor," for example, can be viewed as another elite.

David Riesman has suggested that in the United States interest groups have taken over from an earlier more clearly defined elite. In his view we have now substituted for the clear leadership, privilege, and imperative of the business ruling class of an earlier day "a series of privileged groups, each of which has struggled for and finally attained a power to stop things conceivably inimical to its interests and, within far narrower limits, to start things."[5] However one may label such groups, the principle remains: that society is allocating its social advantages of status, political position, and economic power unequally, benefiting some more than others, in a way that more or less conforms to the requirements of its present stage of organization, though sometimes with a lag that can create pressure points in the organizational surface.

Beneath the thin layer of its elites, a developing or a developed society breaks down into a number of subpopulations. These need not be exclusively economic in their orientation. Religion may be a divisive factor, even to the extent of splitting a country (as Pakistan separated from India) or becoming the basis for political process (as in Lebanon political position has been allocated by legal convention between Christians and Moslems). Ethnic groups may persist rather than assimilate, as the Chinese and Indians in Malaya, the French in Canada, the Walloons in Belgium.

One of the sharpest cleavages often occurs along race lines. Here the United States, almost from its inception, has provided a conspicuous example. In the period of slavery, the unequal distribution of social advantage on racial lines was built into the organization of society. "At the present time the descendants of the Europeans are the sole owners of the land and the absolute masters of all labor; they alone possess wealth, knowledge, and arms. The black is destitute of all these advantages, but can subsist without them because he is a slave."[6] With the termination of slavery the inequality of advantage between black and white assumed other forms, ranging from systematic exclusion from the vote and skilled employments to systematic exclusion from white schools and residential neighborhoods. The suburbs of major cities became the privileged possession of whites, confining migrating Negroes to urban ghettos. All this is too familiar a story to require repetition; it serves only to remind us that whether or not racial categories are considered the sociological equivalent of classes, they do constitute subpopulations which are sometimes significant in terms of the distribution of the social advantage.

In this last case, the whites as a whole constitute an elite group relative to the blacks as a whole, but within each of these two large and encompassing subpopulations there are of course other breakdowns of privilege. As previously noted, the modulation of the privilege scale becomes finer with the degree of development.

For our purposes, any such breakdowns, of whatever kind, are relevant only insofar as they are related to the distribution of the social advantage. In almost any contemporary society of any size it is possible to distinguish groupings of one sort or another for various definitional or analytical purposes—political parties, cultural groups, religious sects, service organizations—which are unlikely to have any significant relation to how the social advantage gets distributed. These do not concern us. Although such associations may involve elements of social status, if only in membership eligibility, they are at most reflections of other more significant groups or classes, and not themselves breakdowns of subpopulations that count in determining how a society's advantages get allocated.

Geographical divisions, for example, may assume importance in helping to form the literature of a country, or its sports competitions, but may (or may not) be ignored in determining the composition of those classes or groups which are relevant to the distribution of the social advantage. In the United States, the West does not compose a social class with privileges and benefits differing from those accorded the East. By contrast, East Pakistanis constitute a significant class or group because they have been underprivileged relative to West Pakistanis. The foreign exchange earned by their agricultural exports has been ploughed into the development of West Pakistan industry, benefiting disproportionately a small elite group of families who can be identified by the knowledgeable. Such industrial development as has occurred in East Pakistan, more often than not, has been the offshoot of West Pakistan companies and operated under West Pakistan management, to the point where the Bengalis of the eastern wing have been demanding, if not separation, at least the "Bengalization" of East Pakistan industry. Here the distribution of social advantage is clearly at stake in a geographic division which happens also to be ethnic.

An Aside on Nationalism as a Basis for Social Organization

In a modern industrialized society the social advantage is distributed to a good many definable groups claiming and granted their rated share. In earlier societies, and in underdeveloped economies at the present, the two-class distribution was and is more characteristic, as we have had occasion to observe, consisting of a small elite and "all others."

This latter classification is not very satisfactory, implying as it does an amorphous and undifferentiated aggregate. As Ralf Dahrendorf has pointed out in his penetrating study of classes, it reduces the nonelite population to a residual, defined only by its exclusion from the marks of privilege. It would be preferable to define it by its own characteristics, if only as "working class population" or "peasantry." This has the further advantage of reminding us that small groups may lie somewhere in the social territory separating the elite from the mass (as Mill said, the middle class has never wholly been absent), groups which may conceivably be the nucleus for the more extensive group differentiations which come with more complex social organization. Nevertheless, for ease of expression we shall sometimes use mass to stand in opposition to elite in speaking of societies which are essentially binary. We shall examine the concept of the masses more fully later.

Dahrendorf resists viewing the "subjected conflict groups" of industrial societies as "essentially unorganized masses without effective force."[7] He sees interest groups, even when low in the social hierarchy, as having their own organization and specific membership, perhaps overlapping with the membership of other interest groups. Since we do not limit our attention to industrialized societies, as this would exclude some in whose population problems our interest is keen, we need have no reluctance to think of a mass which is essentially unorganized. Nevertheless, we can accept the fact that some form of organization of a general population, however undifferentiated, is necessary in effecting the transition to a more sophisticated form of society. To a degree in the past and more importantly in the present, nationalism is just such an organizing instrument. A sense of nationalism becomes the means for making cohesive an otherwise loosely associated population. It acts as an integrative device helping to bind the elite and the mass into a functional whole. It provides a geographical unit within which development is to be sought, if at all.

Granted that this is organization at an elementary level, it is also organization that is elemental. Without a sense of nation, encompassing elite and mass alike, the only basis for justifying the unequal social distribution is one of personal relationship of a feudal and rudimentary nature. But a sense of nation provides or necessitates some higher justification for the prevailing system of privilege.

Nationalism is not a faith or a point of view which one either has or does not have. It comes with differing degrees of conviction, measured in large part by the emotional pull of the nation as against one's own locality. It involves transference of one's attention and concern in varying degree from the parochial to the national. The villager or farmer starts by regarding his local community as the center of his universe: for him this *is* nation. Other villages with which he comes in contact involve him in a system of foreign relations. As these associations deepen and widen, the sense of nation also expands. It is *never* static, but the big leap comes when a network of provinces or states ("little nations") pool their sovereignty to create an entity which to the combined masses still has a large element of artificiality about it. It is when this sense of the unreal and abstract gives way to a sense of substance and reality that nationalism serves as an organizing device for the masses, integrating them into a social system whose constituent functions must be more rationally and consciously defined and organized than in a smaller unit.

The Structure of Authority

But let us now return to the main thread of our argument. The distribution of the social advantage necessarily carries with it an allocation of authority and power. Authority implies the existence of certain rights of action and reward, capacities which are provided for under customs, rules, and laws. Power implies a capacity to act autonomously in situations not provided for in the framework of authority. Indeed, one may go further and conceive of power as the capacity to take action without respect to the system of authority, overriding that if the occasion seems to warrant. If power is exercised frequently in this manner, however, it undercuts the system of authority, robbing it of its force. If authority and power are to exist side by side, then power must recognize the force of authority and confine itself to actions outside authority's sphere.

The authority sanctioning the prevailing distribution of the social advantage is thus in reality an institutionalized description of the functional roles and rights of all those composing the society. Authority in this sense always limits the need for the assertion of power and is far more effective than the exercise of power could be, since it operates by consent rather than imposition. The institutionalization of roles and rights over time creates a sense of social stability; individuals, whatever their position in the society, develop

expectancies as to how other people will and should behave toward
them in a variety of situations, and what their own obligations are
to others.[8] These rights of expectancy (a system of *mutual* obligations) become charged with value for each person, as he asserts the
authority over others that the system allows him. However little
that may be, it could always be less.

It is by such time-honored systems of authority that the distribution of the social advantage, however unequal, becomes ratified.
Even privileges which seem grossly disproportionate to us, at a different time and place, become explicable once we appreciate the
force of arrangements which have won acceptance long enough to
have become embedded in the instinctive reactions of everyone in
society, whatever his position. Thus Tocqueville, himself a tentative
democrat, commented of feudalism:

> As the noble never suspected that anyone would attempt to deprive
> him of the privileges which he believed to be legitimate, and as the serf
> looked upon his own inferiority as a consequence of the immutable
> order of nature, it is easy to imagine that some mutual exchange of
> goodwill took place between two classes so differently endowed by fate.
> Inequality and wretchedness were then to be found in society, but the
> souls of neither rank of men were degraded.
>
> Men are not corrupted by the exercise of power or debased by the
> habit of obedience, but by the exercise of a power which they believe
> to be illegitimate, and by obedience to a rule which they consider to be
> usurped and oppressive.[9]

Everett Hagen, in writing of the system of relationships prevailing
in traditional societies, comments that the peasant tends to take an
ordered view of the social, governmental, and business elites, who
inhabit "a world far beyond his ken." "He looks on the statuses of
these groups in his society as higher and lower, but also as not
merely appropriate but proper. It never occurs to him to think that
he might act so as to change things. The world is as it is. He thinks
the concept of his trying to change it to be ridiculous, shocking, a
little indecent, and immoral."[10]

In modern industrialized countries where the notion of actions to
redistribute the social advantage is taken for granted, it is also taken
for granted that such efforts must operate through appropriate, that
is, prescribed channels, and these channels themselves are part of the
authority system. In advanced countries no less than in underdeveloped, there is an institutionalized set of customs, rules, and laws
which establish rights of expectancy, embracing the whole of the

population and sanctioning the distribution of the social advantage. No society could operate without them.

The institutionalized authority structure, characterized by persistence and continuity, often defeats efforts to modify it. The role and rights of Negroes in the United States, for example, change slowly even in the face of legislation providing for change, because people whose behavior must change if the new laws are to have their effect are still operating on the basis of certain rights of expectancy which have molded their actions for years—rights which embody the discriminatory treatment of people whom they consider inferior. To grant Negroes equality in the distribution of the social advantage would leave whites relatively lower on the social totem pole; understandably, many resist.

India provides an almost classic case of the complexity and persistence of the authority structure. British rule for several centuries built up a caste of white privilege superimposed on the traditional Indian castes. At independence, an Indian political elite simply slipped into the seats and privileges formerly occupied by the British.

In New Delhi, the lavish palace of the former Viceroys, which Gandhi had wanted to turn into a hospital for the poor, became the residence of the Indian President. Nehru, as Prime Minister, moved into the sumptuous residence of the former British Commander-in-Chief. The state governors were also housed palatially and were given a civilian and military staff whose functions were mainly ceremonial and social. . . . The right to ride in cars marked with flags was eagerly sought as a symbol of authority, and the official trips of governors and ministers were conducted with pomp and protocol.

. . . Such resplendence emphasized the new government's role as the successor to the British raj; it also encouraged the view that political independence had done little more than displace a foreign with a native privileged group.[11]

Despite official concern for accelerating development, little was accomplished that had any impact on the Indian mass. "There has as yet been no important rise in average income, and inequality is generally assumed to have increased." Despite unanimous passage in the 1955 Parliament of an act outlawing the caste system, "the caste system is probably stronger today than it was at the time when India became independent."[12]

Myrdal has documented the process by which the old system has persisted. The new central government, committed to effecting economic change, has no effective means of administering the sprawling Indian economy except through the rural elite of landowners, merchants, and moneylenders—the very groups which have been reaping their unequal share of the social advantage under the time-honored authority structure which the central government is presumably seeking to change. "These small upper strata see to it that policies averse to their interests are not put into effect or are turned to the benefit of themselves or their dependable 'clients' alone."[13]

An Indian sociologist has characterized this group:

> The rural elite are, as a group, aggressive, acquisitive, and not burdened by feelings of guilt towards the people they exploit. Hierarchy and exploitation are so deep-seated in rural India that they are accepted without questioning. Neither the urban politician nor the administrator can do without the rural elite and the latter know it.[14]

"No wonder, then," comments Myrdal, "that the evaluative studies invariably conclude that these [development] programs have helped mainly those in the rural population who were already well off."[15] Moreover, the rural elite, whose authority and power reside in the villages, districts, and states, use their enormous political influence over the dispossessed to further policies in support of provincial (rather than national) rights and powers, in favor of disunity rather than central control. Their relative success is indicated by the preservation of the old order. The central government, composed chiefly of the urban elite, is locked into a mutual dependency relationship with the rural elite: the former must depend on the latter for the execution of governmental policy, and the latter are protected from a redistribution of the social advantage by their alliance with the former. A stronger sense of nationalism would strike at this parochial control, but so far it has been inhibited by the powers of the local elite to manipulate opinion.[16]

Containing Pressures for Change

Even in industrialized societies, accustomed to rapid technological change and characterized by democratic institutions, that any significant modification of the distribution of benefits proceeds at a viscous pace should not be so surprising. If most everyone in the society is provided for in the status quo, only the greatly dissatisfied are likely to press for change. Others may complain, but few will act. They have their place in the system to defend, their role and rights to be protected from invasion by others. Any major change involves unfreezing the presently frozen structure of privilege; it is often better to stick with what is known, perhaps tinkering with it a bit in an effort to get a little something extra. "Better leave well enough alone" becomes the slogan of conservative caution.

Thus it is not generally the case that a small entrenched elite presides over a society from which it is ruthlessly extracting rich rewards at the expense of an overburdened mass. That may indeed characterize certain traditional societies. But the notion of a structure of authority supporting an unequal distribution of the social advantage is a far more general phenomenon, applicable to advanced as well as backward economies, to democracies no less than authoritarian societies. Its essence lies in the fact that its distribution of privileges is institutionalized in such a way that redistribution is difficult. Those who feel frozen out of the present structure, or who deeply feel, on abstract principles of justice, that the distribution is excessively disproportionate, are likely to be the only voices raised for radical change. They will be listened to, however, only under circumstances which we shall shortly explore.

In this kind of a situation, even organizations which are usually thought of as contesting or protesting in nature are likely to find their role and rights within the prevailing authority structure, so that they too become part of the established order. This is true, for example, of labor unions, which in most advanced societies have won for themselves a secure place from which to bargain for further advantage, and whose leaders enjoy a considerable measure of status and privilege. A French observer commented at the time of the 1968 worker uprisings, which had moved with a greater spontaneity than the unions liked: "They have built up solid organizations designed to oppose the regime within the framework of its institutions. They remain steadfastly on the side of law and order and tremble at any call to armed insurrection which would sweep them away along with the regime. They did not want to create agitation but to quell it and keep control over their restive troops."[17]

Even those members of a disadvantaged group who have made their way out of it are just as likely to be found on the side of existing allocation of privilege. Negroes who have secured an education, a good job with middle-class income, and have been able to move into newly opened areas of good housing are likely to resent and resist the infiltration of lower-class Negroes into their preserves. Upper-class Indians who have inherited British status following independence are just as likely to resist excessive democratization.

Having made one's way with difficulty up the ladder of privilege, one does not like to have an escalator installed for the general public. The effort to contain those who would revise the authority structure thus has many adherents.[18]

A number of techniques have aided the elites, whether small and concentrated or more numerous and dispersed, in maintaining the prevailing distribution of privileges. One method is to maintain control over the election machinery, limiting use of the ballot to effect change. Property as a prerequisite to voting continued down to modern times and constituted an effective way of giving political voice only to those groups who had most at stake in the status quo. Even without a property qualification, it remains true that wealth and position permit unequal influence on the political process.

More subtle has been control over the educational process. Until relatively recently, higher education was a preserve of the aristocratic and well-to-do. It was not valued for any utilitarian reason but viewed as a luxury to be afforded by the few, just as the culture which it spawned. The opening up of educational opportunities for the less privileged may be viewed, from one aspect, as an equalizing tendency, reducing the disproportionate benefits of the upper classes. From another point of view it also served as a means of containing middle-class pressures for a redistribution of the social advantage by transmitting elite values to some of the ablest sons of the middle class. Even though diluting the scarcity value of a college education, it partially succeeded in narrowing the leadership of nonelite groups to those who had "proved themselves" by acquiring a degree, in the process acquiring an appropriate sense of the appropriate.

A more general technique for containing pressures for change is to admit the contesting groups to a larger position in the authority structure; the prevailing distribution of social advantage is pulled and hauled a bit but left largely intact. This can be done by cooptation, with the ablest of the opposition incorporated into government. A majority political party can absorb an insurgent group by adopting either enough of its leadership or enough of its objectives to attract enough of its members to make its survival difficult, if not impossible. Personnel of a regulatory agency whose assignment is reform may have their zeal diluted by favors extended by the interests they are presumed to regulate.

The technique of containment by involvement has been tried in situations as varied as the Community Action Agencies of the War on Poverty, where the "poor" were to be given "maximum feasible participation," the *panchayat raj* or "democratic decentralization" of

India, and the basic democracies of Pakistan, all of which presume to give a measure of participation in government even to the most lowly. To a hard-line conservative this may represent retreat, but to the strategist it may be an effective way of blunting teeth before they bite. President De Gaulle's principal recipe for handling the aftermath of the student riots in France in 1968 was "participation" by students, parents, and community leaders in deciding local school policy within the framework laid down by the Ministry of Education, producing a cynical student response in the form of a conjugation exercise, "I participate, you participate, he participates, we participate, they rule."[19] An observer of the Pakistan scene wrote of its system of 120,000 basic democracies: "The bitterly disappointed and virtually disenfranchised clerks, students, and professionals of East Pakistan's towns and cities tend to see it all as one gigantic patronage system with the Basic Democrats, representing the traditional landed interests, as the main beneficiaries."[20]

The extension of the right to vote is the most general form of enlarged participation. The consequences have been neither as radical as the forces of change had anticipated nor as the forces of conservatism had feared. After enlargement of the electorate in England in 1867, between 30 to 75 percent of the working class have supported the Conservative party.[21] In India, because the rural elite so largely dominate the "poor, unorganized masses, democracy itself thus plays into the hands of petty plutocracy."[22] One British sociologist concludes that what seems to have taken place in the democratic countries up to the present time is not so much a reduction in the power of the upper class as a decline in the radicalism of the working class.[23]

Without attempting any more complete catalogue of devices for containing pressures for a change in the authority structure, let us simply note that resort can also be had to physical repression. On a national level, it may be by a coup d'état which ousts a government too responsive to dissident groups or, on a local scale, by vigilante groups seeking to preserve their community's immunity to forces threatening change.[24]

If some concessions are made to those seeking an enlarged share in the social advantage, this may be sufficient to permit a slow and orderly reconstruction of society over an extended period of years. Robert Dahl has provided an excellent picture of this process at work in New Haven, Connecticut.[25] An initial elite based on church and property maintained social, economic, and political control of the city far into the nineteenth century. It then was forced to relinquish economic and political control to a rising business class, retaining its social privileges, including control over church, schools, and cultural institutions, thus bifurcating the elite advantage. With the further passage of time and the introduction into the expanding community of large numbers of immigrants to man the local factories, a swelling Italian subpopulation asserted its right to political influence, electing several mayors and numbers of councilmen, state representatives, and congressmen. The upper levels of the business community still remained out of reach to this group, however, as well as admission to upper social circles. The elite were trifurcated. Concession and containment went hand in hand.

In traditional societies where privilege has been intrenched for centuries, the pressures of a growing population with a changing composition are less easily met. In Iran, for example, the Shah has been an exponent of reform, but he must contend with an elite which is not.

Since the parliament is controlled by landowners, the Shah and his supporters must balance rewards granted to each of the major classes and in so doing, partially satisfies but does not endear himself to any group. Because of this precarious alliance, many Iranians are convinced that social and economic development is not being seriously pursued and it appears that the basic goals of development are being discarded in order to please both the individual and institutional demands. Since the aristocracy has never served the country selflessly and religious leaders are afraid of democratic social and economic change, many Iranians believe that any attempt to combine all these elements into one "legitimizing formula" can be achieved only by compromise and inconsistency. The basic problem is the gulf between the expectations of the growing middle class and the intelligentsia and the ability of the government to meet these demands.[26]

Once a delayed change in the distribution of the social advantage and the authority structure which underlies it begins, it may be difficult to contain the movement. American Negroes again provide an example. When the wave of riots in major cities throughout the country, beginning in 1967, had evoked a public concern which began to find expression in concessions, militant Negro groups began pressing harder on all fronts. Events which would have evoked only mild reaction from them only a few years earlier were met with extreme actions, such as the closing of a Ford Motor Company plant by 500 Negroes in protest over an alleged racial epithet directed by a supervisor to one of them. The United Automobile Workers, part of the plant's authority structure, found itself embroiled and contested when it sought to obtain a return to work.[27] Beginning in 1968, militant Negro students sought a share in the authority structure of colleges to the extent of appointing professors, admitting students, and determining curriculum, and in some instances met with partial success.

Effects of Population Change on Social Organization

Let us recapitulate briefly. The social advantage gets distributed in unequal proportions, reflecting, however imperfectly, the way in which a society is currently organized. A structure of authority in the form of customs, rules, and laws grows up justifying the distribution of the social advantage and justified by the social organization. Minor modifications may be made in the authority structure and the distribution of the social advantage to accommodate changing social organization, but significant changes are unlikely to be made by the principal beneficiaries of the present system. Moreover, they have a number of devices by means of which pressures for change may be contained, at least for a time. In any event, it is seldom that pressures for major change will be forthcoming on a sustained and aggressive basis since a degree of inertia is generalized throughout the system by reason of the fact that in the distribution of the social advantage most groups have been allocated certain advantages which they seek to preserve and fear to risk by overtly challenging the system.

There are thus a number of variables in the picture, all of which are subject to change but not necessarily at the same rate. First, there is the social organization itself; second, the distribution of the social advantage, which follows from it; third, the authority structure supporting the distribution of advantage. Fourth, and the one in which we are most interested but which we have not yet discussed, is population: its size, composition, and location.

Because our interest is in the effects of population change, we shall make this the independent variable. We ignore for the moment the impact of concomitant changes which are likely to be at work in the system, such as technological innovation and the spread of education, and ask, what happens to the social organization, the social advantage, and the authority structure when a population is growing?

Of course, the answer may be that nothing happens. For one thing, the *rate* of growth is significant. Even if a population is increasing, if its rate of increase is very slow the added numbers can more easily be accommodated. There is no way of saying how fast a rate of growth is necessary before it has its effects; the answer will depend on a society's stage of development, its prior growth rates, its available resources. Since we are concerned with the effects of population growth generally, in any society, this means that we must take the history, institutions, and resources of a society as they are given at the point in time and analyze the impact of greater numbers given those circumstances. The differences will certainly be great as between, for example, a society which limits the incidence of education and suffrage and one which extends both to all in certain age categories.

Let us first take the aggregative case, where the population as a whole is increasing. The Malthusian effect, operating unalloyed via the law of diminishing returns, would in time subject the population to want and misery until disease and starvation cut back the increase in numbers. But already we can make several important modifications in this formulation, aside from those qualifications concerning technological advancement and contraception which we noted in Chapter 1. First, the produce of a country is not distributed equally among its people. Certain groups, the privileged or the elite, are granted a disproportionate share. Moreover, the disproportion applies not only to material substance but also to social status and political position, which collectively are subsumed under the term the social advantage. This distribution is underwritten by the authority structure. There is no reason to believe that any adverse effects of the pressure of numbers will be distributed any more equally than the benefits flowing from the social organization. If there is a pressure on resources, then, we can say that those groups whom we speak of as contained by the authority structure will be disproportionately disadvantaged. The diminishing returns from resources will fall on them most heavily.

Recognizing that we are dealing with societies in various stages of development, we have to avoid any connotation that the resource whose fixed supply gives rise to diminishing returns must always be agricultural land. In the United States, for example, population could increase rapidly for an extended duration before the country would face a food shortage. But in every society at any time there must be some factor whose fixity is unable to cope with rapidly increasing numbers. The fixity may be only short run, as in the case of transportation facilities or industrial capital, but it may also be of a long-run nature, requiring some major scientific or technological achievement or a change in tastes before the shortage is overcome. Urban space is a good example. As it becomes scarcer per capita because of expanding populations, it is the contained groups which most feel the pressure, while the elite are able to offset the effects by continuing to buy the scarce commodity even at sharply rising prices or by supplementing urban space with a second home in the country. Recreational facilities provide an obvious parallel. Education offers still another example: if the pressure of numbers leads to a deterioration of standards, because of the limitation of educational resources, the elite are in a position to offset this effect by resort to institutions of more selectivity and expense.

But now enters a different kind of fixity, the fixity of social organization. As a population expands and redistributes itself, it can no longer function effectively under new circumstances by using old organizational forms. The point can best be made by gross example. The United States in the third quarter of the twentieth century cannot rely on the same economic and political structure that suited it a hundred years ago. A doubled population concentrated in metropolitan centers simply cannot function efficiently using the same institutions that fitted a largely agricultural population half that size. Indeed, many would argue that the country is inhibited from functioning more effectively precisely because it has not changed enough.

The solution of physical problems that cut across local political boundaries seems to require a degree of common coordinated action that is extraordinarily difficult to obtain in the absence of a general local government to effectuate it. The federal government, after spending billions in shoring up the local status quo and having a powerful unintended impact on the nation's urban areas, is increasingly concerned to coordinate that impact in the service of rational, planned goals. . . . Indeed, the creation of the Department of Housing and Urban Development was viewed by many as a step toward creating a national ministry of local government that would use its carrot and stick to bring about metropolitan planning that would become in effect metropolitan government.[28]

The same point could be made with respect to society's constituent institutions. Business enterprises, universities, hospitals, labor unions cannot function effectively today with the same organizational forms that suited their much smaller predecessors of a century ago. Even without the advancement in knowledge and technology which has occurred in that time, the pressure of added numbers alone requires modification of functional forms. As an organization grows, its manner of functioning must take account of that growth or it is impeded from performing its function, a case of diminishing returns flowing from a fixed factor.

Compounding the problems of change in social organization is the need for entirely new institutions. The density of present urban populations, for example, has required the organization of entirely new systems of public relief, public health, sanitation, law enforcement, and education. The rise of large metropolitan centers, in the words of Philip Hauser, "forces the substitution of rational for traditional ways of doing things."[29]

There are difficulties, however, in effecting change in the social organization. As we have noted previously, the structure of authority in a society reflects, even though imperfectly, its social organization, and the structure of authority supports the distribution of the social advantage. A change in social organization would require a change in the authority structure, thereby threatening the allocation of privilege. New functionaries would have to be provided for, power and authority to deal with changed situations would have to be redistributed, virtually necessitating some dilution of existing power and authority and introducing a revised system of rewards and benefits appropriate to the new organization. No wonder that for those who are the chief beneficiaries of the existing system, the status quo is preferred. But by exercising their position to frustrate change, they thereby inhibit the effective functioning of the society. And the effects of that malfunctioning are disproportionately distributed, falling most heavily on those who are already disadvantaged.

Potential Effects of Population Change on the Structure of Society

But why should the disadvantaged groups who, after all, constitute the largest part of society put up with this state of affairs? The common explanation is the "apathy of the masses," a matter which we shall examine in greater detail shortly. But even assuming for the moment that such apathy exists there must be some limit to it. It is true that starvation does occur in economically depressed countries without provoking political revolt, and that unemployment sometimes reaches substantial proportions in the industrialized economies without creating a groundswell of unrest. The larger numbers of people still possessing some stake in the distribution of the social advantage which they fear to lose normally assures a stability and order in society, barring major upheaval. Nevertheless, at some point a deteriorating condition, either absolutely or relatively, may lead those who have been contained by the structure of authority to threaten that structure. An increase in population which presses on some limited resource to the significant disadvantage of substantial numbers always creates a potential danger of political instability and sometimes an imminent threat.

A report on Calcutta provides an example. Joseph Lelyveld, correspondent for the *New York Times*, describes the city as a "catchall" for the countryside's surplus labor.

With the glut of the unskilled, Calcutta's industrialists long ago became accustomed to paying the lowest industrial wages in India and reaping the highest profits. But in times of scarcity the price of rice is the highest in the country.

Last year [1967] it went higher than at any time since the Bengal Famine of 1943. Labor unrest and what the industrialists call "indiscipline" then reached floodtide. No doubt, Communist agitators could claim some credit. But what made the agitators effective was the sheer desperation of the workers. Communist trade-union leaders soon found they could ride the emotional wave, but couldn't be sure of their ability to control or channel it when it served their purpose to do so. . . .

For months factories and offices were paralyzed by go-slow movements and wildcat strikes. Anyone traveling about the city on errands was almost certain to be delayed by processions of workers angrily chanting revolutionary slogans and waving red banners. Industrialists went to work not knowing whether their workers would allow them to return to their homes at the end of the day. Soon they stopped wearing ties and jackets. "The workers cannot stand to see you wearing good clothes or driving a good car," a shaken employer explained at the time. "They hate it."[30]

The burst of agitation and violence burned itself out, and workers returned to their jobs. ("The industrialists have their jackets and ties back on now, but they don't imagine they've seen the end of anarchy here.") But even if such an outburst is short-lived, it serves as a reminder that deprivation can lead to insurgency and attempted surgery on the prevailing structure of authority. If the reminder goes unheeded, at some future date the blow may fall.

This does not imply that resistance to the existing distribution of the social advantage must occur when a people is most depressed. The evidence has indicated again and again that it is usually only after the lowest point has been reached and some improvement in conditions has been experienced that the spirits of a depressed people are raised high enough to support an attack on the existing distribution of privilege. Such relative terms—"some improvement," "high enough"—are the despair of the social analyst who presumes to scientific precision, but they can be disregarded in real life only by the politician who presumes to be rash.

The case of Calcutta also illustrates that it is likely to be in the cities, created by population growth and redistribution, that the disadvantaged mass develops into a political force which must be taken into account. Pressures for change are most to be expected where the presence of numbers permits a more frequent exposure to and a readier exchange of ideas. There is a lesser risk to one's social advantage, however pitiful it may be, by being anonymous in the crowd. The conviction of being right is stronger for being one of many (that tyranny of the majority over men's minds which both Tocqueville and J. S. Mill so much feared). There is ampler opportunity to demonstrate, even to riot, and in the process to gain a feeling of political power. Even if such actions are episodic and impulsive, over time they have the effect of educating the people involved in the exercise of behavior which is political in nature and is certainly not apathetic.

So far only the differential effects of population pressure between the elite and the less privileged groups, the latter considered as a class, have been considered. In some cases, however, segments of the population at large are differentially affected. This would normally require that they have shared unequally in the social advantage, or are in some respect competitive with each other. Or disparate rates of growth among subpopulations, due either to differential fertility or migration, may leave them in different relative positions, or threaten previous relative positions.

For example, a subpopulation may have been allotted only certain kinds of jobs considered undesirable for others, as in the case of Negroes in the United States or the untouchables in India. An increase in the numbers which are so contained will carry a disproportionate disadvantage to that group, as against all other groups, since its job opportunities are restricted. More of them will be contending against each other for the limited employment opportunities available, thereby depressing each other's position and the position of all of them relative to the rest of the population.

The same result may flow from restricted housing. If some segment of the population, perhaps Negroes or Jews, is confined to a particular sector, viewed as undesirable to others ("ghettos"), any increase in their numbers, whether differentially greater or not, will have a disproportionately adverse effect on them as long as they are tied to a particular locale and others have greater freedom.

In these situations the opportunities for effective political protest or threat may be limited to repudiation of a political party or alliance with a larger opposition party. Nevertheless, even in such instances the potential effects of a population (in this case, a subpopulation) increase cannot be disregarded. Canada provides an example. In 1835, Tocqueville could write of the French Canadians that they constituted "the remnant of an old nation lost in the midst of a new people," and add: "A foreign population [the English] is increasing around them unceasingly and on all sides, who already penetrate among the former masters of the country [the French themselves], predominate in their cities, and corrupt their language."[31] By the turn of the century, however, the French had become a majority in the Province of Quebec. By the 1960's, remembering their long-time exclusion from top positions of most English-dominated firms and other expressions of an imposed inferiority, they were waging an effective campaign for greater autonomy within the Confederation, if not actual independence. The long-held sense of a disproportionate disadvantage in the distribution of privilege was given its effect.

America's Negro population provides another example of how a depressed minority can react politically. Subjected to social humiliation, allotted the meanest employments, and often deprived of their vote, the black subpopulation declined from about 19 percent of the total to about 10 percent by 1930. By 1950 it was still only 10.5 percent. During the 1950's, due to increased birth rates and decreased death rates, the nonwhite population gained almost 2.9 percent per year, compared with 1.8 percent for the whites. "The nonwhite population growth rate, 60 percent greater than the white, has risen, then, to a level at which a doubling is achieved in about twenty-five years."[32]

Nor is this all. Some 92 percent of all Negroes in the United States lived in the South at the time of the 1860 census. Fifty years later, this was still true of 89 percent. Then followed the several migrations to the North, peaking at the time of the two world wars. By 1960, about 40 percent were residing outside the South. It is estimated that by 1970 or soon after, half the Negro population will be distributed between the North and the West. Superimposed on this geographical relocation went a movement from the rural areas to the cities. In 1910, only a little more than one-fourth of the Negro total lived in urban places, as defined by the census. The proportion is now close to three-fourths.

The consequences of this movement have been seen in the civil rights activities of the 1960's. A population expert could write in 1953, "Racial composition will be treated very briefly at this point because it is a matter of but little concern in many, perhaps in most, communities even in the United States,"[33] but only ten years later came the start of an agitation that turned the race problem into the foremost issue confronting the country, with Negro mayors elected in two major cities, Negro representation increasing on governing bodies of many private and public agencies, a national businessman's organization committed to provide jobs, a coalition of urban interests seeking to upgrade the status of Negroes in virtually all aspects of life, and a "black power" movement gaining widespread recognition. In this instance too it was undoubtedly the concentration of Negro population in major cities that escalated its political influence. Scattered throughout the countryside they could have mobilized much less power.

There are other cases where differential fertility rates among subpopulations have endangered the distribution of political power within a country. In Lebanon, there is a delicate balance of power between Christians and Moslems. "The Muslims undoubtedly have a higher birth rate than the Christians, and a Muslim majority could change the relationship of Lebanon with other Arab countries and the West."[34] The situation in Malaya is far more complicated, involving as it does a division of the population into the three main groups of Malaysians, Chinese, and Indians. The Chinese are as numerous as the Malaysians, each with perhaps 45 percent of the total; the Indians comprise the remainder. Each of these communal groups has struggled for position, with the Chinese attaining economic superiority and the Malays retaining political advantage. "The fear that a politically dominant Malay community in an independent Malaya might threaten the economic interests of other ethnic groups prompted the wealthier sections of the Chinese and Indian communities to form their own political organizations."[35] Numbers of Chinese also supported an indigenous Communist party not out of ideological orientation but because they saw in it an instrument for the improvement of their own political position. At the same time, each of the three communal groups is itself divided between a wealthy controlling elite and a disadvantaged mass. The three controlling elites have managed to effect an uneasy compromise which allows for a federal government, but because the compromise allots the Chinese a somewhat inferior political status—the citizenship laws of the new Federation were drawn to insure a Malaysian voting majority—it has promoted partisan Chinese activity. Moreover, since all those born after the date the Federation came into existence automatically acquire citizenship, and since the Chinese are increasing at a more rapid rate, the Malaysian majority can be retained, if at all, only by manipulation of voting districts. The general Chinese restiveness is further complicated by the fact that the Chinese elite is anxious to protect its own dominant advantage in the economy by promoting political stability, which means its substantial support of the status quo in contrast to the desires of its own communal group, which is achieving majority status and is anxious to remove the political disadvantages from which it has suffered.

In general, if a subpopulation is growing at a greater rate than other groups, and is enfranchised, it appears to endanger the interests of those other groups, especially if it itself is dissatisfied with its own participation in the social advantage. If a subpopulation is growing at a differentially greater rate and is disenfranchised, this can only augment its discontent with its inferior position and increase the threat of future political action. Actually, a differentially greater growth rate may not even be necessary; it may be enough that it is increasing as fast as other constituent groups. The significant consideration may simply be that it attain some critical mass, which can more effectively register its impact. Just as the relocation of a scattered population into an urban mass increases its political effectiveness, without any increase in numbers, so may the growth of a dissatisfied group in absolute terms, without any proportionate increase, be the means for it to press more vigorously for amelioration of the causes of its discontent. Depending on the strategy of protest, there is likely to be some critical size—some absolute number of people—necessary to make the protest effective, whether this takes the form of the concentration of votes on a particular candidate, the launching of a campaign of propaganda, seizure of offices, or a program of sabotage. An increase in absolute numbers thus increases the range of effective political protest. It also provides some greater measure of security, since it becomes more difficult to penalize a large group in contrast to a small one.[36]

Perhaps the most important consideration lies in the fact that a group which feels itself unfairly disadvantaged relative to other groups and at the same time is increasing in size sets up conditions which can be exploited by a leader. The group becomes, to use the expression which the law has coined for other purposes, an "attractive nuisance," large enough to make itself felt, disadvantaged enough to provide the basis for arousing militant discontent, the vehicle by means of which an ambitious individual, whether idealist or demagogue, can ride to public prominence. Its growth makes it more inviting to the incipient leader from outside; its added numbers also increase the possible leadership resources which it is generating within its own ranks.

An increase in political sensibility by a growing subpopulation which already is dissatisfied with its share of the social advantage, or which suffers because its share in the social advantage is restricted in a way that requires it to parcel out its limited share among a larger number of its own people, is likely to lead to a diminished sense of integration of that group with the larger society. The structure of authority, the system of values, which it had more or less accepted in the past may become a target of attack. The more dissident Negroes in the United States have flaunted their alienation from white society by belligerently disregarding the petty rules of conduct which make a city a civilized place, such as those relating to refuse disposal, respect for recreational facilities and public property, and courtesies on public transit vehicles. The piece of paper carelessly tossed aside under a "Don't litter" sign is a symbolic rejection of the rules of a society which has rejected them. This loss of social cohesion is a further warning of the possibility of a future political confrontation. It can be more easily and flagrantly engaged in as the numbers who participate in it grow.

The same phenomenon is discernible in countries moving from traditional ways toward industrialization. In the process, some groups or individuals discover the extent of their disadvantage. Their resentment at the structure of authority which benefits an elite so disproportionately disposes them favorably toward extremist groups, promoting radical change. The unskilled and often unemployed groups massing in the cities and the aspiring radical leaders become attractions for each other. Traditional values and respect for authority become eroded. "The social classes emerging or being transformed are being driven by the sheer force of numbers . . . towards the more radical . . . political alternatives."[37]

Aside from numbers, the political effectiveness of a suppressed group depends greatly on the depth of their conviction of wrong. The rawer the sense of grievance, the greater the power even of small groups, since they will be prepared to be more extreme, less yielding, more persistent, less contained by the existing structure of authority. The political strength of a group also depends on how clearly understood and how widely shared are their objectives, the demands which they make on those who are more content than they with the present distribution of the social advantage.

The Rise of New Classes and New Leaders

Let us turn now from the effects of changing numbers on the position of groups already existing within a society to the rise of entirely new classes. We earlier saw how population growth by itself carries its own compulsions. Even with resistance from those who fear that any tampering with the authority structure will dilute their social advantage, at some point the increase in numbers, their concentration in cities, perhaps also political discontent of the sort we have just examined, all will impel some change in the organizational structure of society. This change in social organization along with the increases in numbers opens up new opportunities: for those who newly participate in the revised organization, or for those who see the occasion for new specialized functions. This will be the case in societies of whatever stage of development, so that the new function may relate to something as elemental as an expanded civil service to conduct an increased official business, or it may involve a reorganization of agriculture with small family farms giving way to larger commercial farms in order more effectively to supply expanding urban populations. This would provide opportunities not only for enterprisers on the land but also for a new breed of middlemen to transfer and distribute the produce.

The new opportunities thus created by changes in the social organization—changes which, whether or not also occasioned by other influences, are impelled by population movements—may in fact create a *demand* for new technology which is forthcoming from another innovative group, the inventors. The rise of expanded urban and national markets, for example, creates its own demand for new industrial and agricultural equipment capable of mass production, as well as for new forms of transportation and communication. We shall examine this phenomenon in a later chapter. For the moment, it is enough to observe that change in social organization breaks open a range of opportunities in a kind of linked sequence or chain reaction, in the process augmenting the numbers of the "new breed."

A new class of interests thus begins to form, seeking a larger cut of the social advantage. If it is accommodated, the prior distribution of privilege becomes modified. If there is resistance from those who prefer the status quo, a new dissatisfied class has been created. Thus it was with the rise of the business class in England, as it later was with the development of a labor union bureaucracy both in England and the United States. In each instance the new forces sought social status, economic benefit, and political influence within an authority structure that resisted them. In each case, alliance was sought with larger groups which were also disproportionately disadvantaged in the system: the disenfranchised working class in England, who helped the middle class secure political power, and the artisan class in England and the United States whose loss of independence following specialization of labor and the expansion of the competitive market provided the membership base for the rise of a union officialdom. In time, both groups found their acceptance and won an expanded share of the social advantage.

This same creation of a new class can be observed in more traditional societies, both in the past and at present. The eleventh century offers another instance of an emerging group driven to alliance with a lower-class population in support of its own cause. The upper-class burghers of the reviving cities, seeking their own autonomy from the lords to whom they were nominally beholden, championed free status for the entire population of the city. In the thirteenth century, with those same patrician burghers restricting the rise of merchants to political and economic position, the merchants joined the oppressed workers of the city in seeking a redistribution of privilege.[38]

The pattern of a relatively small group of "new men" relying on a larger group to increase its political strength is probably a necessary one if what is involved is a genuine reorganization of society, rather than simply the substitution of a rising elite for a declining one or the inclusion of a new class in the ranks of the existing elites—if what is involved is a shift of institutions and authority and not just a movement of people. The reliance on a larger group, in traditional societies, almost necessitates an appeal to the masses of peasants and urban proletariat. In the Middle East, "the Arabian-American Oil Company has an Arab Industrial Development Division which is promoting light industries and has provided technical assistance and loans to persons interested in establishing local industries. Together with the 25 thousand oil workers, these entrepreneurs represent a small middle class which is becoming increasingly resentful of the privileges of the ruling elite, their own low status in the traditional social scale, the wasteful expenditures of the oil revenues and the absence of an adequate welfare program."[39] This resentment is not likely to find effective expression, however, until or unless it seeks a much broader support from those still lower in the social hierarchy.

A rising new class is always a potential threat to the existing order. The shift in the composition of the population which it constitutes reflects the yeast of change at work in the social system; whether simply an expanding population, or an expanding population with other forces accompanying, there are pressures for modification of the social organization. If these pressures break through the crust of containment they will, sooner or later, find at least a partial expression in a redistribution of the social advantage and a shift in the supporting authority structure.

In addition to those who carve out new specialized roles within a changed economic organization, there are others who discover new possibilities in a political role relative to discontented subpopulations. Among salaried professionals, civil servants, and newly minted intellectuals, particularly if drawn from working-class backgrounds, are often to be found those who aspire to mobilize new mass movements. In part this may stem from their own frustration at failure to gain a larger share of the social advantage, in part from an idealistic and sometimes ideological motivation. They too are innovators, but of a different sort, seizing on opportunities which have been created out of a shift in the social structure following on population growth, perhaps facilitated by other influences.

These kinds of individuals are to be found in every society. The Negro subpopulation in the United States has graduated a number in the 1960's, just as have the depressed populations of other continents. Nationalism is often seized upon as a vehicle for organization and reform. (Black nationalism in the United States, or the milder version of black separatism, parallels the national reform movements of more traditional societies.)

One interesting development has been the emergence of military officers as leaders of mass movements in contrast to their usual role as supporters of the status quo. In a number of countries, the army has been an institution through which people from the still impotent middle class have been able to move into positions of authority, in this respect comparing with the Catholic church of medieval times. Among these have been some espousing economic development and an improved position for the peasantry and urban working class. Egypt, Syria, and Iraq provide examples of this type of action, and to a lesser extent Pakistan. Latin America, from time to time, has produced such movements. "The general picture was one in which the young officers, also frustrated in their ambitions, made common cause with the rising popular groups."[40]

A Middle East analyst has observed:

> Probably the most significant development in Middle Eastern politics in the postwar period has been the ascendancy of military governments. When experiments with democratic institutions were unsuccessful, the young middle class army officers who possessed nationalistic ideas, seized the opportunity to initiate social and economic reforms. In most countries the military has become a factor in social change, although in Iran, Jordan and Saudi Arabia, the army still protects the ruling class. . . . In many ways the present military governments are now more representative of public opinion than were those determined by a free-election system. Under the military governments new socio-economic groups have become active in political affairs, such as the proletariat through state-controlled unions, the peasants through agrarian reform programs, and the newly developed technical and administrative class of young men through the increased economic activities of the governments. The military rulers have also expanded education and, through the use of mass communication media, have created a greater sense of community responsibility and, consequently, increased the political participation of these new groups.[41]

In effect, what we are involved with here is a nonpower elite: those who have already moved sufficiently above the mass that they occupy preferred positions but who are nevertheless dissatisfied with their station and prospects. They seek to upset the present institutionalization of power to create new positions of authority for themselves. They would do this by captaining a movement of the masses, not by palace revolt as might have been the case a century or so ago. In an age of urbanization and nationalism, the masses constitute a power base which cannot be ignored.

Such examples should not suggest that a significant change in the structure of authority can take place *only* by revolt and revolution. In the western democracies, the popular vote, even taking account of the fact that it has produced no radical changes, produces a significant shift in the authority structure. The New Deal administrations in the United States provide an example. Nevertheless, piecemeal change may come too slowly; gradualness may be too gradual. Here too the United States provides an example—the civil rights reforms of the 1950's and early 1960's succeeded in arousing Negro expectations without satisfying them, leading to a frustration which erupted into violence and contained the seeds of a genuine race conflict.

No suggestion is being made here that movements of this type may not occur without respect to changing population characteristics. The only point stressed is that when significant changes do occur in the numbers, composition, and location of a population, they are almost certain to have their impact on the distribution of the social advantage, the structure of authority which supports it, and the social organization from which these two follow.

Population Change as an Intervening Variable

The pressures of population change may be exacerbated by other changes occurring concomitantly. Such concurrent changes may even become the means by which insurgent or dissident groups within a society seek a shift in the distribution of the social advantage to their benefit. They may even be the stimulators of group action. What the relative contributions of population change and such concurrent movements are is an unanswerable question. At a minimum, it is unlikely that a group or class which is declining in numbers would become insurgent relative to other groups or classes whose numbers are increasing (though if satisfied with the status quo, it may become defensive), whatever the changes which are occurring around it. But we can, I think, say more.

These changes—in technology, in education, in religion—do not operate in some wholly independent fashion, autonomous from the rest of society. *Only* if they succeed in disrupting the population base by affecting its numbers, composition, or location can they have any influence. Population change, then, is a necessary intervening variable, and in analyzing the effects of such phenomena as technology and education, it is essential to trace the pattern of their influences on the characteristics of the population. How people relate themselves to each other, the focus of the social sciences, involves not simply describing a relationship but also determining how many are affected and what this does to the structure of authority and the distribution of the social advantage over the period during which the new relationship is coming into existence. This must be done in terms which are conceptual and analytical, rather than empirical and descriptive. What it is that triggers a population change is always ad hoc and specific to a society, but the process of population change—in terms of cumulative pressures for social reorganization, for a revised authority structure, and a redistribution of the social advantage—can be given greater generalization.

I shall not here undertake any restatement of the thesis previously presented in order to relate it to specific concomitant changes such as technological change (especially as expressed in industrialization), improved systems of communication and transportation, the spread of education, extension of suffrage, or the introduction of new values whether of an ethical, religious, or ideological nature. A simple stripped-down formulation should serve to suggest the process I envision.

Whatever change occurs in the social system, if it is significant enough to "make a difference," it will do so by creating some dissatisfaction with the existing distribution of the social advantage, remembering that this includes social status and political position as well as economic benefit. The existing distribution of privilege can be modified only through a change in the authority structure, remembering that this includes customs, rules, and laws. The intruding change is usually introduced by a group which is small in numbers: innovators, enterprisers, zealots, the more ambitious or aggressive, the greater risk-takers, those infected with dreams and drives. To secure a modification in the authority structure, it seeks allies. In general, this will not be easy unless there are larger groups which are also dissatisfied. The greatest likelihood is that such other groups are to be found where population density has been increasing. This includes the cases of growth in aggregate numbers, growth in the size of cities, and growth in population segments which have been tightly contained by the existing authority structure.

The Role of Youth

At this point let me introduce a parenthetical note of a speculative nature. It seems to me that the youth of a society, for a number of reasons, are likely to play a peculiarly important role as an agent of change.

Taken as a category, without respect to subpopulations, the young are often disproportionately disadvantaged. Unemployment rates are highest for them, whether one looks at an advanced economy like the United States or the underdeveloped economies of Asia. The better jobs are filled by older people who got there first, and often they are not anxious to allow the younger and usually better-trained subordinate to show them up by granting him discretion. Thus they frequently impose the weight of their authority and make the young recruit "toe the line" until he becomes bitter with frustration. Where housing is short, whether in Sweden or Latin America, it is the young who must naturally wait in line for a room or apartment, often deferring marriage as a consequence.

It is not, then, just the matter of a "generation gap"—a difference in the way they see things—that leads to conflict between young people and their parents. It is also a difference in their attitude toward the prevailing authority structure, how they distribute themselves between support of the present system and a radical change. The older people are likely to have more of a stake in the existing distribution of the present advantage; young people are as yet still largely excluded and feel mainly the restraining effect of authority.

Moreover, if idealism strikes it is most likely to strike the young. As they look about their society, unencumbered by the weight of inuring experience, they see institutions and customs that seem ripe for change. They also commonly see governments and administrations moving to correct these, if moving at all, with caution and compromise.[42] With the impatience and impetuosity of youth they are more likely to enlist in reform causes and champion radical candidates.[43] Granted that with the passage of time they will take over the greater conservatism characteristic of older years, in the period of their youth their political influence is not without its effect on both policies and attitudes. Here is a group which is likely to hold its beliefs with great conviction and is more disposed to action when it throws up leaders from among its own numbers.

Perhaps because of their idealism, perhaps also because of a cynical realism, the young radicals are more often than their elders likely to make common cause with those of other class origin than their own in opposing the existing structure of authority. Sanche de Gramont has preserved an ironically amusing exchange between middle-class student radicals and striking older workers in the French uprising of 1968. Outside the plant gate, student leaders asked the workers:

> "Aren't you and your co-workers discussing politics?"
> "No. We're not concerned with politics here."
> "What are the workers inside doing?"
> "Playing cards."
> "Couldn't you be doing something more useful?"

"We're not used to working for nothing."

"What do you think of the union order not to join us in street demonstrations?"

"We've got enough to do here. We haven't got time to throw paving stones. And anyway, we don't feel at ease with the children of bourgeois."

"Sure, we're the children of bourgeois, but we repudiate what our parents stand for."

"Where are your parents right now?"

"Spending the weekend in the country."

"I wish I had the money to go to the country."

"What good would it do you if we're still being exploited by the capitalist system? You've got to think beyond a 10 percent wage increase."

"First, I'd like to have the wage increase. I've got three kids."[44]

It is a long cultural step from France to Communist China, but it would appear that youth there play the same role as the agent of change, except that there change goes by the name of revisionism. In reporting his conversations with Mao Tse-tung, André Malraux illuminates some of the obscure and seemingly mercurial changes of official policy. Mao sees the future of China as bound up in an "uninterrupted revolution," not unlike Trotsky's view of a "permanent revolution." The character of that revolution lies in its fidelity to the masses, conceived of no more as coolies than as mandarins, but with whatever degree of economic development still conceived of as the masses. "Equality is not important in itself," says Mao, "it is important because it is natural to those who have not lost contact with the masses." Out of this is to emerge, as a product of continual struggle, culture and customs "as different from the traditional customs as yours are from feudal customs."

But in this youth plays a dangerous part. In its enthusiasms and impulsiveness it can threaten the emerging culture. In a society where "more than two hundred and eighty million Chinese under seventeen years of age have not a single memory prior to the capture of Peking," there may be a waning sense of the significance of the very revolution which is to be continued. Mao expresses his reservations to Malraux: ". . . the survivors of the old guard [of the army] have been molded by action, like our state. Many of them are empirical, resolute, prudent revolutionaries. On the other hand, there is a whole generation of dogmatic youth, and dogma is less useful than cow dung. One can make whatever one likes of it, even revisionism. Whatever your ambassador may think, this youth is showing dangerous tendencies."[45]

It would appear, then, that Mao's launching of the Red Guard, that youth organization which for a time terrorized institutions which Mao might have feared were becoming too settled and administrators who might have been growing conservative, was the old general's way of reinvigorating the youth, of turning them from the "revisionism" of intellectuals, who were all too likely to be infected with western views. But youth was not to be trusted, even with its own salvation. In Mao's words, "The young are not Red by birth; they have not known Revolution." And again, "Youth must be put to the test."[46] The Red Guards who had tasted power were in turn chastised by being subjected, in a subsequent swift shift of official policy, to the dictates of the working proletariat, that is, the masses themselves. The Chinese experience is important as a reminder that in every society, however authoritarian, it is youth with its own special characteristics that represents a threat to the incumbent order.

Another element in this picture of youth as an agent of social change has been provided by an eminent microbiologist, René Dubos, who has written: "The latent potentialities of human beings have a better chance to emerge in a living form when the social environment is sufficiently diversified to provide a variety of stimulating experience, especially for the young."[47] Dubos's comment takes on added meaning if we remember first that cities have always provided the most diversified experience and, second, that an ever increasing proportion of the population of every society is living in cities. The young are thus increasingly exposed to influences conducive to the realization of latent potentials, a result which is likely to have the double effect of exacerbating dissatisfactions with an existing order and producing a greater pool of youthful leaders and mobilizers of change.

Still another ingredient is the increasing spread of education around the world, not only in the sense of embracing more numbers but also of extending for a longer duration. The longer the student remains in school, the more time he has to engage in objective and analytical examination of the society surrounding him. His instructors, at least in western education, ask him to challenge what he is told, to think for himself. In many countries the university has become a training ground for political action and students have precipitated political movements. In writing of India, Myrdal says: ". . . the student agitator, allied to the political bosses, exploits the sense of frustration and insecurity Indian students commonly exhibit. In a more general way, political parties since independence have sought to build up student political movements as training grounds for future party leaders or simply as centers of opposition to the government."[48] The same thing could be said of a number of other countries. Education, in addition to intellectually equipping each new generation of youth to a far greater extent than the preceding generation, also prepares youth for an active role in social and political affairs. In the university society has created not only an instrument for the transmission of cultural values but also a nursery of reform.

Finally, we note a simple and ineluctable fact. In any society experiencing a sustained or increasing rate of population growth, the proportion of youth will also increase. In countries whose rate of population growth is relatively low, such as the United Kingdom, the age group below fifteen may constitute less than a fourth of the total population (22.6 percent in 1963). For countries with rapid population growth, the proportion in the same age category will be double that.[49] As the youngest age group moves into the fifteen to twenty-four year bracket, the proportion of the total population represented by this youth-to-young adult class will also increase. Thus, in Thailand in 1960, the fifteen to twenty-four age group constituted 18.8 percent of total population, in contrast to a figure of 14.1 percent in the United Kingdom in 1963.

Not everyone under twenty-five is a rebel, so that expanding societies do not necessarily sit on a smoldering volcano of youthful discontent. Nevertheless, it would seem a warrantable hypothesis that where youth represents so substantial a part of the population, and in view of its special characteristics which dispose it to challenge the status quo, it becomes a major force for social change. A population's characteristics determine the size of the pool of youth from which both leaders and a potential large-scale following may emerge. As the density of youth rises relative to the total population, it increases both their disadvantage (as they compete with each other for limited opportunities) and their political influence.

Evolution of the Masses

Earlier we had occasion to refer to the masses in considering the possibility that nationalism might serve as an organizing device. Other references to the masses have been sprinkled through these pages. It is now time to examine this concept more explicitly.

There are several ways of conceiving of the masses. In the first instance, they may be regarded as the broad and undifferentiated population base, the aggregative equivalent of "the common man." This would include the rural as well as the urban population. But if we think of the term "mass" as implying some homogeneity of the constituent parts, then in more primitive and traditional societies there could hardly be a single mass combining both urban proletariat and rural peasantry, since their life styles and economic interests would be so disparate. At a minimum, we would have to think of the rural mass and the urban mass.

Obviously, then, the characteristics of the mass change with the stage of development of a society. In more primitive societies there is relatively little organization, and links between city and country-side are limited and casual. As societies develop, the variety of organizational life increases, and communication between town and country becomes constant and varied, so that the rural culture reflects a great deal of urban culture even if not mirroring it precisely. The homogeneity of the population increases, so that we can perhaps more realistically speak of the mass of the population and mass culture than in a primitive society. Paradoxically, this takes place in the very process of a society's expanding its assortment of organizational activity, becoming—as we say—a pluralistic society. The homogeneity of the population increases along with the variety of its activity; not that the masses are identical in all respects or share the same opinions on all subjects, but that there develops a life style and set of values characteristic of the society as a whole.

Historically, over the last five hundred years, and contemporarily, we can discern three major stages in social development. First, traditional society, with what can be loosely labelled a feudal social structure and a culture which is the creation of the elite. Second, an industrializing and nationalizing society, with a middle class pressing vigorously for a redistribution of privilege and loosely related to the increasingly urbanized masses which are more vaguely interested in change. Third, modern society, industrialized and pluralistic, where the masses give rise to the culture not in the sense of creating it but by effectively influencing it.

Let us take a closer look at the characteristics of the masses in each of these stages. In traditional societies the apathy of the common people is proverbial. Writing in 1883, one student of India observed: "I find great populations cowering in abject misery for centuries together, but they do not rise in rebellion; no, if they cannot live, they die, and if they can only just live, then they just live, their sensibilities dulled and their very wishes crushed out by want."[50] Contemporary analysts report the same phenomenon. In the Middle East, for example, the "political indifference on the part of the impoverished masses" has been identified as one of the factors impeding economic development.[51]

One might interpret such apathy as a kind of resigned acceptance of an existing structure of authority; individual oppressors may be resisted but one can hardly hope to overthrow a system. In his visits to the countryside in India, Pakistan, and the Philippines, Myrdal obtained the impression that "there is often a sullen dissatisfaction among the underprivileged in the villages that may be revealed to the sympathetic inquirer but is politically abortive, since there is no avenue whereby the individual can make his protest effective. . . . Where a large proportion of the population is landless, where share-cropping is the pattern of tenancy, and where there are tenants and landowners on very different levels of prosperity and social status, the village is a complex system of human relationships with criss-crossing interest lines that impede concerted action by the poor."[52] With respect to India, Myrdal says of its politicians: "Since the masses are docile and 'amenable,' they need not be approached directly; it is enough to win over the dominant group that controls them."[53]

Another reason for the apparent passivity of the masses in traditional society is their inability to articulate their grievances. Indeed, even in industrialized societies one of the functions of labor leadership is to give expression to dissatisfactions which workers have not effectively formulated for themselves; small wonder, then, if in less advanced countries uneducated masses find difficulty in giving voice to discontent.[54] Moreover, even in societies where the franchise has been widely extended, it takes considerable intelligence and a degree of discipline to exercise one's vote.

In view of these characteristics of the masses in traditional societies, is it reasonable to expect that they can ever be moved to political action or ever organized to force a change in the existing authority structure? At this point, our previous analysis becomes relevant. While it would be unreasonable to expect initiation of action by the masses, they may become responsive to leaders—from their own ranks or from the outside—who have their own interest in fomenting change. In this connection it is enough to remind ourselves that an expanding and urbanizing population is likely to contain substantial numbers who are disproportionately disadvantaged by the increased population density, and who thereby become more responsive to overtures from indigenous or outside leaders. Urbanized masses are also subject to increased exposure to more privileged groups and greater interchange with those having common cause, both effects tending to heighten the sense of injustice.

Moreover, an expanding and urbanizing population provides a greater variety of organizational activity, a greater pluralism at least in a special-interest sense, thereby increasing opportunities for leadership to emerge. The pluralism of traditional and transitional societies is not, of course, the same as that of advanced societies; it lacks their cultural variety. Nevertheless, increasing population density, by impelling changes in social organization, itself encourages a greater diversity of organized activity, which is important as a breeding ground for new classes and new leaders. Out of this is not likely to come a mass movement in any monolithic sense, but more involvement of the masses in social activity.

No two peoples ever evolve at the same rate or in the same way. Nevertheless, the general direction would seem to be clear. As more and more of the common people become accustomed to participate in organized activity, they gradually gain confidence and competence. It becomes more difficult for elites to control their actions. The exercise of the vote becomes a usable instrument for revising the structure of authority, at least in its most restrictive aspects. The political power of the masses gradually moves from being latent and potential to being tentative and then actual.

John Stuart Mill predicted the outcome more than a century ago:

> When the masses become powerful, an individual, or a small band of individuals, can be nothing except by influencing the masses; and to do this becomes daily more difficult, and requires higher powers, from the constantly increasing number of those who are vying with one another to attract the public attention. Our position, therefore, is established, that by the natural growth of civilization, power passes from individuals to masses, and the weight and importance of an individual, as compared with the mass, sinks into greater and greater insignificance.[55]

Mill's conclusion is consistent with that of contemporary analysis. "The rule of the masses is not inconsistent with elite control of the state, for that rule is expressed in the fact that the governing elite is itself formed in the image of the mass."[56] Nor does this conclusion have application only to western democracies. A society's mass develops, just as its economy develops, and just as economic development is not restricted to democracies, neither is the development of a mass culture. The governing elites may be chosen differently and they may govern differently, but they will predictably, in time, all take their cues from their masses.

This says nothing about the quality of the resulting mass culture. There may be good reason to lament consequences such as that "political and educational agencies must adapt themselves to the intervention of the masses by permitting participation on the basis of low standards of knowledge and conduct."[57] Nevertheless, such a movement toward a mass-oriented culture seems inescapable as the mass evolves.

Once again it is necessary to interpose the reminder that other influences besides population change are at work—the spread of industrialization, of education, of suffrage, among others. Nevertheless, these must have their influence through changes in the numbers, composition, and location of population as an intervening variable, as has been noted before. Population change thus constitutes a powerful influence for modification of the distribution of the social advantage and of the structure of authority, sometimes independently and sometimes proximately as a consequence of other forces.

Summary

The organization of a society, whatever its stage of development, is reflected in its distribution of the social advantage, including status, political position, and economic benefits. This is institutionalized through its structure of authority, in the form of customs, rules, and laws. Since most everyone finds himself so situated in the system that he is allocated certain advantages denied to at least some others, there is a general disposition not to risk an attempt at any major overhaul of the system. Marginal modifications seek to mollify those who can make a case for serious inequities. In addition, a number of devices enable those who benefit most to contain dissident groups, preserving the status quo or the nearly status quo.

As population increases, it can function effectively only by changing its organization. But since a change in organization would find its reflection (even though with a lag) in the authority structure and the distribution of the social advantage, a society's elite groups tend to impede change. They thereby frustrate the effective functioning of the society, creating disadvantages which are distributed as unequally as advantages. Nevertheless, at some stage, either social organization is modified to accommodate the larger population or those who are disproportionately disadvantaged attempt an assault on the structure of authority.

The growth of a population is not likely to affect its subpopulations equally. Those which are more contained by the structure of authority will suffer more from the pressure of their numbers against the social walls confining them, whether this relates to jobs or housing or some other social advantage in which they have been limited. Beyond some pressure point, the result is likely to be an explosive effort to revise the authority structure and the distribution of benefits. Their concurrently increasing size and disadvantage set up conditions inviting to a politically ambitious individual who may see the group as a vehicle to public position and prominence. Their increasing alienation from the values of the society which has exploited them disposes more of their number to radical action.

A change in the social organization arising from population growth (or any other reason) creates new opportunities which give rise to new classes, seeking a larger share of the social advantage for themselves. Because their numbers are usually small, they must seek an alliance with larger groups also dissatisfied enough to attack the existing structure of privilege. Such larger groups are most probably those which have been feeling most keenly the effects of increasing population density, whether in terms of aggregate numbers, or urban agglomerations, or subpopulations which have been tightly contained. The new class, a rising elite, provides the leadership which the disadvantaged masses commonly lack. Military officers in the underdeveloped countries are becoming an increasingly important source of such leadership.

Obviously population change by itself is not always, perhaps not often, solely responsible for the disturbances to the social organization which set off a chain of effects. Technological innovation, the spread of education and suffrage, among other influences, are major forces for change. They have their effect, however, only through their impact on the numbers, composition, or location of the population, so that population, if not always an independent variable, is at least an intervening variable.

The youth of a growing population may very well play a major role in pressing for change. They are among those who are usually disproportionately disadvantaged; they have less stake in the existing structure of authority, more idealism, more impatience, and in a society with a steady or a rising rate of growth their proportion of the total population increases. The density of the number of youth relative to the total population may thus be one clue to the strength of pressures for change.

The masses to whom a rising leadership relates itself evolve from a state of feudal dependency in traditional societies to a state of general influence in shaping modern societies. The transition is at least partially effected through population changes: in location (the influence of urbanization), in numbers (the greater pluralism of activity, increasing the social involvement of a people and training more leaders), and in composition (the introduction of new classes following from changes in social organization).

One should refrain from implying that population changes by themselves are the most important formative influence in society, but one would certainly be warranted in concluding that their influence is too great not to be given more explicit attention in any theory of social change.

NOTES

1. John Stuart Mill, *Essays on Politics and Culture*, ed. Gertrude Himmelfarb (New York: Doubleday, Anchor Books, 1963), pp. 47–48.

2. Cecil Woodham-Smith, *The Reason Why* (London: Constable, 1953), p. 8.

3. Joanne E. Holler, *Population Growth and Social Change in the Middle East* (Washington, D.C.: George Washington University Press, 1964), p. 27.

4. Henry Giniger, "Guatemala Is a Battleground," *New York Times Magazine*, 16 June 1968, p. 14.

5. David Riesman, "Who Has the Power?" in R. Bendix and S. M. Lipset, eds., *Class, Status and Power* (Glencoe: The Free Press, 1953), p. 155.

6. Alexis de Tocqueville, *Democracy in America.* (New York: Alfred A. Knopf, 1945), 1:388. Copyright 1945 by Alfred A. Knopf, Inc. Reprinted with permission of the publisher.

7. Ralf Dahrendorf, *Class and Class Conflict in Industrial Society* (Stanford: Stanford University Press, 1959), p. 200.

8. I have discussed the significance of such rights of expectancy in a specialized situation in contemporary society in an earlier book, *Social Responsibilities and Strikes* (New York: Harper, 1953), Chapter 1.

9. De Tocqueville, *Democracy in America*, 1:9.

10. Everett Hagen, *On the Theory of Social Change* (Homewood, Ill.: Dorsey Press, 1962), p. 71.

11. Gunnar Myrdal, *Asian Drama: An Enquiry into the Poverty of Nations* (New York: The Twentieth Century Fund, 1969), 1:273–274. The details on

Indian society all come from this prodigious study. Reprinted with permission of the publisher.

12. *Ibid.*, p. 278.

13. *Ibid.*, p. 292.

14. M. N. Srivinas, quoted in Myrdal, *Asian Drama*, 1:293.

15. *Ibid.*

16. A government need not represent the privileged groups in a society for it to act as a conservator of their interests. Even a reform government inherits the same structure of authority that faced its predecessor governments—a structure that cannot be changed simply by official act, since it goes deep into the habits of a people. In July 1966, after a surprising outpouring of votes from the rural areas, a reform government came to office in Guatemala under Mendez Montenegro. In an interview he described his position as follows:

"My Government is conscious of the difficult political period in which it has to carry out its program. On the one hand, the propaganda of the guerrillas and of the extreme left, which asks for extreme and immediate reform; and on the other hand, the natural resistance of the wealthy classes, who favor an evolution so slow that I would never bring my country out of the considerable backwardness in which the majority of the Guatemalan people finds itself. To the rightist class, which has considerable political and economic power, confidence must be restored that economic and social reforms are not Communist and that agrarian and tax reforms are not confiscatory. But the effort of persuasion cannot and must not prevent action by the Government, which moreover, has been initiated with moderation if it is compared with the agrarian and fiscal reforms of other countries of Latin America."

The correspondent, Henry Giniger, commented ("Guatemala Is a Battleground," *New York Times Magazine*, 16 June 1968, p. 25, © 1968 by The New York Times Company. Reprinted by permission.): "The Government's 'moderation' appears to have been excessive, and efforts to obtain and keep the confidence of the oligarchy have had an almost paralyzing effect on it."

17. Sanche de Gramont, "The French Worker Wants to Join the Affluent Society, Not to Wreck It," *New York Times Magazine*, 16 June 1968. © 1968 by The New York Times Company. Reprinted by permission. What makes de Gramont's comment doubly interesting is that he applied it not only to the French labor unions but also to the French Communist party.

18. Maintaining the status quo may also involve excluding certain immigrant groups, but in this case the excluded groups can seldom marshall retaliatory power.

19. Reported by Don Cook in the *Atlantic*, November 1968, p. 47.

20. Joseph Lelyveld in the *New York Times*, 8 August 1968.

21. Robert McKenzie and Allan Silver have analyzed this phenomenon in *Angels in Marble: Working Class Conservatives in Urban England* (Chicago: University of Chicago Press, 1968).

22. Myrdal, *Asian Drama*, 1:292–293.

23. T. H. Bottomore, *Elites and Society* (New York: Basic Books, 1964), p. 35.

24. In Cairo, Illinois, which maintains a slight but uneasy margin of whites over Negroes, almost all branches of government were entirely in white hands as of 1969. In the face of Negro pressures for change, abetted by a few white clergy both from within and outside the town, following a three-day riot over the hanging of a Negro in jail, along with recurring gunfighting, a vigilante group known as the "White Hats" was formed. Said one leading member: "Our main deterrent value is that we are untrained and dangerous in the streets. The

[National] Guard is trained for restraint and the militants take advantage of it. But ordinary Joes with shotguns are going to defend their property and won't read them a card about their rights. We're going to shoot them. I don't care if it's Father Montroy [a Catholic priest working with the Negroes] or the Pope." *New York Times*, 23 June 1969.

25. Robert A. Dahl, *Who Governs?* (New Haven: Yale University Press, 1961).

26. Holler, *Population Growth and Social Change in the Middle East*, p. 29.

27. *New York Times*, 29 April 1969.

28. Norton E. Long, "Political Science and the City," in Leo F. Schnore and Henry Fagin, eds., *Urban Research and Policy Planning* (Beverley Hills, Calif.: Sage Publications, 1967), pp. 254–255.

The "one man, one vote" decision of the United States Supreme Court (*Baker* v. *Carr*, 369 U.S. 186, 1964) marked a radical change in political influence due to changes in social organization flowing from a shifting, urbanizing population.

29. Philip Hauser, *Population Perspectives* (New Brunswick, N.J.: Rutgers University Press, 1960), p. 133.

30. Joseph Lelyveld, "Can India Survive Calcutta?" *New York Times Magazine*, 13 October 1968, p. 78. © 1968 by The New York Times Company. Reprinted by permission.

31. De Tocqueville, *Democracy in America*, 1:448.

32. Hauser, *Population Perspectives*, p. 58.

33. W. S. Thompson, *Population Problems* (New York: McGraw-Hill, 1953), p. 96.

34. Holler, *Population Growth and Social Change in the Middle East*, p. 38.

35. Gunnar Myrdal, *Asian Drama*, 1:160. An account of the Malaysian situation is found on pp. 157–161, and 381–386.

36. Everett Hagen, *Theory of Social Change*, p. 71, argues that aggression is a personality trait, exercised when one dares. If this is true, the greater security one feels in numbers would increase the expression of the aggression trait.

37. Manfred Halpern, *The Politics of Social Change in the Middle East and North Africa* (Princeton: Princeton University Press, 1963), p. 111.

38. Fritz Rorig, *The Medieval Town* (Berkeley: University of California Press, 1967), pp. 27–28, 89.

39. Holler, *Population Growth and Social Change in the Middle East*, p. 41.

40. Edwin Lieuwen, *Arms and Politics in Latin America* (New York: Praeger, 1960), p. 132.

41. Holler, *Population Growth and Social Change in the Middle East*, p. 16.

42. In writing of Guatemalan reform President Mendez's desire to last his term in office, to establish the precedent of a peaceful succession, and the compromises with influential groups which he had to make in pursuing this goal, *New York Times* correspondent Henry Giniger commented: "More than one Guatemalan has worriedly asked whether young people, particularly those in the schools who already tend to lean toward the extreme left, would not turn to the Communists as the only force with an effective answer to the nation's problems." "Guatemala Is a Battleground," *New York Times Magazine*, 16 June 1968, p. 26.

43. At the time of the student-worker insurrection in France in 1968, an observer, describing the characteristics of the workers involved, wrote: "Finally, there was a small group of politically active young workers who repudiated both

de Gaulle and the traditional parties of the left. 'Elections won't change any-thing,' one of the leaders of the Bouguenais plant occupation said. 'De Gaulle is a paternalist who is defending the interests of a class, while the left-wing parties aren't ready to take power, and even if they did, they would not be able to make the necessary social changes. The only way is to take power by other than legal means. . . ." Sanche de Gramont, "The French Worker Wants to Join the Affluent Society, Not to Wreck It," *New York Times Magazine*, 16 June 1968, p. 8.

44. *Ibid.*, p. 62.

45. From André Malraux, *Anti-Memoirs*, as excerpted in the *Atlantic*, October 1968, pp. 114, 119, 120.

46. *Ibid.*, pp. 113, 119.

47. René Dubos, "Biological Individuality," *Columbia Forum*, Vol. 12 (Spring 1969).

48. Myrdal, *Asian Drama*, 1:294, footnote 4.

49. The effect of population growth on age composition is strikingly evi-dent if we compare data for five countries with high growth rates and five among those with the lowest growth rates.

	Annual Rate of Population Increase (1958–65)	Percentage of Population Under 15
Costa Rica	4.2	47.75 (1963)
Dominican Republic	3.6	47.29 (1960)
Venezuela	3.6	45.17 (1963)
Mexico	3.4	44.42 (1960)
Philippines	3.3	45.69 (1960)
East Germany	nil	23.00 (1964)
Austria	0.5	22.04 (1961)
Italy	0.7	24.24 (1964)
England and Wales	0.8	22.64 (1963)
France	1.3	26.43 (1962)

Sources from N. Keyfiitz and W. Flieger, *World Popu-lation: an Analysis of Vital Data* (Chicago: University of Chicago Press, 1968) and United Nations, *Statistical Yearbook, 1966* (New York, 1967).

50. J. R. Seeley, *The Expansion of England* (London: Macmillan, 1883), pp. 233–234.

51. Holler, Population Growth and Social Change in the Middle East, p. 16.

52. Myrdal, *Asian Drama*, 2:780–781. Myrdal cites Nehru's comment: ". . . the really poor never strike. They haven't the means or power to demonstrate."

53. *Ibid.*, 1:292.

54. In similar vein, Genevieve Knupfer has presented evidence, with respect to the United States, that "the economic and educational limitations accompanying low status produce a lack of interest in and a lack of self-confidence in dealing

with certain important areas of our culture; as a result, there is a reduced participation—a *withdrawal from* participation in these areas." She also cites C. C.
North to the effect that low status produces a kind of mental isolation which
operates to "limit the sources of information, to retard the development of
efficiency in judgment and reasoning abilities, and to confine the attention to the
more trivial interests of life." Genevieve Knupfer, "Status and Power Relations
in American Society," in R. Bendix and S. M. Lipset, eds., *Class, Status and
Power* (Glencoe: The Free Press, 1953), p. 256. If this is true of people in the
United States, how much more likely it is to characterize people in less developed
societies.

55. John Stuart Mill, "Civilization," from *Essays on Politics and Culture*,
pp. 52–53.

56. Philip Selznick, "Institutional Vulnerability in Mass Society," *American
Journal of Sociology* 56 (1951):321.

57. *Ibid.*, p. 322.

CHAPTER 3

Population and Technology

SO MUCH of the behavior of a society appears to be related to the technological changes which it experiences, in particular the process of industrialization, that one may despair at separating out, analytically, the impact of population changes, as we have just been attempting to do. Perhaps the most that can be said is that population changes take their place alongside technological changes in affecting the functioning of a society. Even to say so little would be a significant addition, but we can, I think, say still more.

Instead of attempting a neat separation between the impact of technology and population influences, let us rather explore the ways in which population changes affect technology itself. If we discover that population plays a leading role in shaping technology, we can then impute to the former a larger measure of the proximate influences we now attribute to the latter. In such an exploration there is no intention of crediting population with a primal role in all social relationships, as though from it all blessings and all hardships flow; we are simply seeking to identify such relationships as can be clearly established analytically.

In technological change we will encompass the act of invention of a new product or process, its incorporation into the production process by some innovator, and its subsequent diffusion to others within the society. Let us start at the beginning with invention. What gives rise to it? Is the popular impression correct that invention tends to be an undirected intellectual activity, responding to no discoverable general forces? Or is it directed chiefly by new scientific discoveries, which provide the breakthroughs which the inventor follows up? Or is it shaped chiefly by preceding inventions, which stimulate a flow of succeeding inventions, each one opening up a new path down which subsequent inventors can travel?

In answering such questions we are benefited by the pioneering work of Jacob Schmookler.[1] Obviously, at any point in history, the possibility of a particular invention's being made is dependent on, and limited by, the existing stock of knowledge.[2] But the available knowledge is a permissive condition, setting limits to what *can* be done, to the feasible. It does not determine what invention actually does take place from among the countless possible inventions which conceivably could take place. Schmookler's contribution lies in tracing the determining influence on inventors' activity to the effective economic wants of a society. The inventor is guided by what a society most demands, not necessarily in the crude sense of calculating what people are most willing to pay for and then setting out to supply it, but in the sense of attacking the problems which his society considers important. In Schmookler's words, "inventions, important and otherwise, generally represent creative responses to felt wants."[3] The direction of an inventor's effort is largely determined by his expectations of the value to society of the solution of the technical problem to which he addresses himself.

In terms of the industrial process, this means that inventions tend to be addressed to those industries which are flourishing, for whose products and services a social need is expressed in economic form, by demand and purchase. In effect, the demand for invention is a derived demand, which can arise at any point in the production process, so that it may itself follow from a prior derived demand. Thus the invention of the steel industry's continuous hot strip mill in 1923 was in response to the needs of the expanding automobile industry. The growing demand for automobiles created its own special needs for steel, and the invention met that need.

In general, Schmookler finds that the allocation of funds for inventive activity tends to parallel the allocation of funds for capital investment, not because invention gives rise to investment, but because an industry's level of investment is an indicator (even though imperfect) of its economic importance. The decline of inventive activity in an industry tends not to reflect the exhaustion of technical possibilities but the petering out of economic potential. He cites the case of the horseshoe as an instructive example. One could hardly imagine a simpler product, which could be expected to have early exhausted an inventive potential. But with the westward movement in the United States in the last century the demands on horses—and horseshoes—increased; so did the demand *for* horseshoes. As a consequence, the number of patents for improvements in this simple product rose steadily until the end of the nineteenth century and then fell off, presumably as the use of the steam engine began to displace horsepower, making the production of horseshoes a less profitable (that is, less needful) activity. Why should inventors address themselves to the technical problems of a declining industry?

Schmookler posits that every industry presents almost endless problems to which inventors could turn their attention. How then do they choose among them? Not on the basis of fancy or simple intellectual curiosity, but in anticipation of the value of the end result. Generalizations of this sort cannot be established on the strength of individual cases, but the point of view expressed by Thomas A. Edison helps to convey the flavor of such a commonsense approach. Edison gauged the desirability of an invention by its commercial value, undertaking it only if "there was a definite market demand" for the product.[4] Why should an inventor occupy his time with a problem that few people are interested in?

If we accept, then, that the process of technological change starts with a response to the expressed wants of a society, how does population change relate to this process? We will find at least four streams of influence.

First, an increase in the size of a population increases the market potential (and profitability) of some industries more than others and may also make profitable some industrial operations which would not have been undertaken with a smaller market. In both cases, the expected economic value of the solution of whatever technical problems characterize such industries will increase, encouraging the flow of inventive activity in their direction. Phyllis Deane, who has made perhaps the most exhaustive examination of England's Industrial Revolution, provides supporting evidence.

> The conclusion suggested by this survey of the evidence on innovation in the eighteenth and early nineteenth centuries is that it was only when the potential market was large enough and demand elastic enough to justify a substantial increase in output that the rank and file of entrepreneurs broke away from their traditional techniques and took advantage of the technical opportunities then open to them.[5]

An increase in the size of a market is not solely a matter of population growth, to be sure; it also reflects rising incomes which, even with a stable population, would increase the number of potential customers. Nevertheless, the population factor is too important to be discounted.

An increasing population produces a second influence on technological change. It adds to the number of entrepreneurs or business firms, since the business population increases, even if not proportionately, with population generally. It thereby increases the opportunities for experimentation with new techniques. Those improvements which are most successful (that is, most profitable) are the ones which tend to become diffused to other producers.

A third influence on technology of an expanding population is of special importance. As a society grows, its structure of wants undergoes change. New wants are generated by the process of expansion, thus giving rise to new spurs to inventive activity.

We have already seen in the previous chapter how the increase in a country's size creates pressures for changes in its social organization. Even if these are contained for a time, at some point they must be given at least partial expression. Two types of change which are hard for a growing country to escape, for example, are centralization of authority and specialization of function. These stimulate demands for new techniques. To some extent, the techniques may involve only social reorganization, how people relate themselves to each other, but to some extent they give rise to technological innovation as well. A swelling civil service, for example, will create a demand for new methods of keeping records. The same type of demand will arise concomitantly in expanding private institutions. An economic need will thereby be produced which can be expected to have its outlet in inventions spawning a whole new industry devoted to information taking, information flows, and information keeping. At one level of development, this may mean devising or adapting such instruments as typewriters, carbon paper, and filing equipment. At a more advanced level, such growth creates a demand which makes the computer a focus of inventive activity.

It is not only added numbers, as such, that stimulate new needs which give rise to technological change. Increased density in the form of urban concentrations is also important. Here again Phyllis Deane has given an excellent summation of how population increase, technological change, urbanization, and pressures for change in the social organization all interact. In the latter half of the eighteenth century, England's spinning-mills (spearheading the Industrial Revolution) grew up as self-sufficient company villages, usually located near water power, and dominated by the mill owner. These mills had an expanding market in Continental Europe and in North America, but they also prospered from a growing home market as England's population, which had remained stable over an extended period, began to increase at a surprising rate. Power became a limitation on output, especially uncertain water power. In terms of our preceding analysis, there was a demand for new, more certain and more effective sources of power supply. The inventors Thomas Newcomen and James Watt responded to this need. With steam power, the pattern of owner-dominated mill villages changed completely.

When steam became the main motive power of the spinning-mills it became preferable to build the new factories in towns, where the reserve of labour was large in relation to the requirements of the factories. There the industrialist could . . . callously cast off labour when trade was slack without any fear of losing it permanently. He could leave his workers to crowd into the garrets and cellars of existing tenements and rely on private building-contractors to adjust the supply of housing accommodation to the demand for it by running up jerry-built houses to be let off at exorbitant rents.[6]

With increasing urbanization of industry, the paternalism of the earlier water-based mill owners thus gave way to an impersonal system of recruiting workers from the general labor pool which the city provided. A mill owner was released from any feeling of personal responsibility for his work force. "From this second phase of the factory age emerged the true industrial proletariat, numerous, capable of united action because it was concentrated, increasingly conscious of its political grievances, and working in an environment which became steadily more unwholesome as the towns grew and as the entrepreneur became less and less involved in a personal relationship with his workers."[7]

In this account are represented all the forces we have been discussing, interacting in a complex way but with the population factor never out of sight. Admittedly with other influences present, an expanding population adds to the size of the market and thereby creates a demand for technological innovation. The new technology leads to a shift in the location of industry and an accompanying increase in urban density. The latter elicits a demand for new kinds of goods and a corresponding demand for facilitating technology,[8] and at the same time produces pressures for changes in social organization. One could, if he wished, impute the causative force in this sequence to technology, but population change constitutes both an element in initiating the sequence and the mediating variable through which the influences of technology work themselves out.

The expansion of cities has a further impact on technology by bringing together a more heterogeneous public and providing its members with opportunities for increased contact with and exposure to each other. Out of this changed and charged milieu emerge new wants which help to direct the flow of innovation and technology. Such technological innovations are not, however, necessarily confined to the urban setting which initially gave rise to them. Developments in printing and the graphic arts, for example, have primarily been in response to economic needs expressed by city populations, but once the technological responses have been made the resulting products are also available to those in the countryside. Thus innovations in the form of new products, even if arising in the city, in time fan out and create changes in the consumption patterns of people generally. The desire to purchase new factory-produced products imposes on farmers or peasants a greater necessity for raising cash crops. The cash nexus which previously may have bound them only loosely to the rest of society becomes stronger. But small, diversified, subsistence farms are not capable of providing the cash revenues which such changes in consumption require. Limited small-scale farming tends to become less and less possible as a way of life. The alternative is movement to the city.

This is, in fact, the major explanation for the twelve per cent population decline in Plainville between 1940 and 1950 (seventeen per cent for the county as a whole during the same period), the thirty-seven per cent drop in the number of farms in the county between 1945 and 1954, and the trend toward larger individual land holdings, from an average farm size of 151 acres in 1945 to the 217 acre average in 1954. The modern Plainville farm family seeks, and needs, additional land to expand beef and dairy farms in order to earn more money, and thus, to realize greater advantage from the constantly expanding complex of modern technology which it constantly incorporates into its ideal standard of living. Those who cannot make it are increasingly motivated to leave Plainville, further ramifying kin and kinship bonds, each a potential and intimate avenue of communications with the outside.[9]

As a derivative effect with technological implications, as agriculture becomes more commercialized and more profitable, its effective demand for technical innovation increases. Substitute the name of any small French agricultural town for Plainville and the above statement could be used unaltered except for percentages. Indeed, even some countries not very far along the industrialization road would show this influence already at work.

Another inducement to the expansion of farm size lies in the increasing demand being generated for the commercial supply of food to growing cities. The added demand can only be met by improved agricultural practice, requiring new inputs of chemical fertilizer, improved seed, and power equipment. The new practices generally are characterized by economies of scale, whether obtained by actual consolidation of land holdings or some form of cooperation.[10] This in turn makes farm labor redundant, pushing it off the farm and into the city, where it adds to the consumers of food. The mechanization of agriculture permits larger urban populations, and at the same time the swelling urban populations create a demand for the mechanization of agriculture. This double movement was notably apparent in the United States from the Civil War on. Here again, the complex interaction displays an important population component. Urbanization spawns new products, in time altering rural consumption patterns and imposing a greater dependence on cash farming. At the same time, increasing urban agglomerations (drawing their added numbers in part from rural areas, in part from natural increase, in part from immigration) likewise impose a need for more commercial farming. These combined population influences help to create an effective demand for invention and innovation in agricultural technology.

Some of the most significant technological changes introduced by expanding and urbanizing populations are in the fields of transportation and communication. Obviously the development of canal and rail systems in England and the United States did not arise in some autonomous fashion; it was directly responsive to the needs and wants of a growing population, permitting that specialization of farm and factory, country and city, which we have just noted. With growing cities, urban transport too became a specialized need, giving rise to such technical solutions as the trolley, motor bus, subway, and freeway. We can now foresee the demand for some new technology to meet the continuing need for urban mass transportation. "Adequate mass transit will tend to become regarded as an essential part of urban infrastructure investment, that is as essential to urban existence as piped water and sewerage."[11]

We have so far observed three influences which population change can produce on the structure of technology: (1) an expanding population increases the market potential and profitability of certain industries, thereby directing inventive activity toward them; (2) the business population tends to expand along with population generally, increasing opportunities for technological experimentation; and (3) an expanding and urbanizing population produces changes in social organization which create new wants, which is to say new problems eliciting technologic solutions. There is a fourth consequence which we will label the personnel effect. A larger population increases the likelihood that some individual will have the creative insight to solve the technologic problems presented by intensified or modified social wants, and a larger population, particularly a larger urban population, increases the possibilities for developing specialized skills suited to the new technologies.

As H. J. Habakkuk has pointed out, "The more able men there

are in an industry the more chance the industry will throw up an entrepreneur of genius."[12] Going back one stage, we could add that the more men there are in an industry the more chance that the industry will throw up able men, with the usual caveat that we are talking about men who have been given the same opportunities for self-development. In his anthropological approach to the process of innovation, H. G. Barnett likewise concluded that "the larger the number of individuals involved, the greater will be the certainty that new ideas will appear," providing that the society does not impede the dissemination of ideas or the geographical concentration of people with similar interests.[13] In effect, this is simply the law of large numbers at work.

A similar argument applies to the development of technical specialization. "There are many more chances in a larger group of finding someone with the qualities necessary to make a precision mechanic, an artisan, an artist, an actor, an administrator, or a diplomat."[14] As the size of a population increases, so too does the range of the physical and psychic capacities represented in it, as well as the range of motivation and interests. Thus, in addition to the demand factors stimulating technological development, supply factors are also more conducive in a larger population.

Differences among Societies

If population expansion (its increasing density within cities or within the country as a whole) has such multiple stimulative effects on technology, why does India (to take but one example) lag in industrialization behind a much smaller nation such as Sweden? Is the case overargued?

I think not. It is unreasonable to compare, in terms of technology, two countries at markedly different stages of economic development or two countries with markedly different cultures, as though the only difference between them were one of population size. Whatever the stage of development, or whatever the culture, an expanding population is likely to create both a greater demand for and supply of technological innovation, for the reasons we have explored, than would a smaller population under the same circumstances. It will not, however, necessarily have the same technological impact as a population expanding equally, but under conditions which are significantly different. A growth in numbers in an advanced society will create a different demand for technological innovation than will a growth in numbers in a primitive society, but an increasing population even in a favela in Rio will have its effect on that society's demand for invention, and will increase the chances that the wanted invention will be forthcoming. It is *within a given culture* that an increase in population density creates its own particular demand for change in social organization and its own new wants or needs, thereby directing the flow of whatever inventive talent that people possesses.

A functional relationship between size, the stage of development, and the potential for entrepreneurial activity has been noted by Myrdal in the case of India. The relationship holds equally good if we substitute innovation for enterprise.

Even if India is economically small compared with the advanced countries—having less total monetized demand for non-food products than, say, Norway—its national market is still much larger than that of any other country in South Asia. This advantage, together with its resources of coal and iron ore, has made it possible for India to have proportionately more industry and a larger class of modern or quasi-modern entrepreneurs. In addition, its sizeable market has made possible a type of planning for economic development that in turn helps to bind the country together.[15]

A formulation relating the effect of increasing population on technological development, on the one hand, to a country of given culture and stage of economic development, on the other hand, has analytical appeal. If invention (and technological change generally) are responsive to a people's wants, this allows us to explain the slowness of industrialization in some countries by the difference in the kind of wants fostered by that country's culture.

In recent years it has become fashionable to assert that people in underdeveloped areas (the Middle East and South Asia, for example) show an avidity for the products of western technology that belies their supposed lack of interest in things material. Undoubtedly the spiritualism of the East in opposition to the materialism of the West is a theme which has been overplayed, but it would be overplaying the reaction to say that a basic philosophical difference does not exist. Peoples of these areas may welcome western products without, however, wanting them enough to change their way of life, or to change their ways rapidly. Or the number of people who want such innovations may represent only a small proportion of the whole. The responsiveness to a cash nexus making possible the acquisition of factory-made goods which we noted previously in the case of western farmers may conceivably be present rather generally within an eastern society, but more weakly. The result would be a slower pace of industrialization.

Invention and innovation are products of a people's *effective* wants, determining the direction and amount of their inventive and innovative activity. Some cultures place greater importance on material wants than others, and this is reflected in the shape and pace of their technological development. A Protestant Ethic does not, for example, characterize India.

The cultural factor may help to explain not only the pace of industrialization but also its shape. For example, it has sometimes been said that the influence of transportation on metropolitan development is important in explaining why some cities grow cohesively and "organically" (to use a Durkheimian term), with areas of specialization interacting with each other, while other cities tend to be collections of villages.[16] But from the point of view presented here, the shape of a city's transportation system is responsive to its wants; the city does not simply grow on a pattern imposed by an autonomous transportation network but generates its own demands for a transport system which then has its repercussive effects.

Although it is sometimes contended that the process of industrialization imposes its own imperious forms of social organization,[17] the logic has yet to be presented why a society's effective wants cannot control the shape of its industrialization as well as the pace (the latter is not denied). Industrialization can, of course, be conceptualized abstractly enough that its common elements can be identified (like those of language) in all cultures where it occurs, but this is a different matter from saying that wherever it occurs its less abstract forms, its functioning institutions, themselves create a culture common to all peoples.

We conclude on a grim note this brief section on the significance of diversity of culture and stage of economic development for the influence of population change on technology. It has been argued that the reduction of mortality in the West was a product of the industrial revolution. Now, however, because science is international in character, because the change (from more to fewer deaths) is one which is generally wanted in all cultures, because the technology needed to achieve this end is something easily diffused and the costs are often underwritten by foreign aid programs, a sharp reduction in mortality often occurs unaccompanied by any significant increase in industrialization.[18] The consequence of rapid population increase is thus likely to be a deterioration of living standards among those who are disproportionately disadvantaged.

The orthodox view as to the consequences of such a development is the Malthusian one. Without a decline in fertility, disease and famine must eventually restore some balance between people and resources. There is an alternative. Political upheaval may seek to change the authority structure and the distribution of the social advantage. We have been through this in the preceding chapter and there is no need for repetition. But such a process of political pressure, however repeatedly applied, cannot accommodate a continually rising population unless there are changes in the social organization which include more rapid industrialization and commercialization of agriculture. The significant point here is that this *must* to a large extent be a consequence of a change in *effective* wants on the part of growing numbers within the population itself. A new breed of politicians and entrepreneurs can facilitate the introduction of changed social organization, but without an underlying demand for such change by enough people to make a difference, the "new breed" must wait for the demand to materialize; at best they can encourage it, but they cannot force it. And demand, in this sense, means wants that are felt sufficiently to motivate changes in a way of life.

We observe again that it is not only the elite of a society, seeking to preserve its privileges, who thus impede social change. It is also people scattered throughout the system, at all levels, each seeking to hang onto his own bit of traditional privilege, his limited stake in the scheme of things as they are given, who constitute a bulwark against the unknown and untried. Where resistance is so widespread, where caution and conservatism (born of pessimism) are general, change comes with difficulty. It is usually spearheaded by a relatively small group seeking aggressively to improve its position, bolstered by a larger group of those disadvantaged *enough* to risk change behind such leadership. We have already seen how population changes may produce such a configuration.

Thus population changes influence technology in both an immediate and a remote sense. Increased density modifies the structure of effective wants which largely determine the direction and degree of innovative activity, within whatever limits a country's culture imposes. But that change in *effective* wants itself depends on the degree to which facilitating changes in the social organization are impeded or permitted, in line with the analysis of the preceding chapter.

Population and New Knowledge

The existing stock of knowledge defines the limits within which invention can take place, as we earlier observed. The expansion of knowledge thus widens the possibilities for invention. One need not argue that scientific discoveries create a vacuum of potential invention into which inventors are irresistibly drawn. Indeed, we have discarded that view in favor of the thesis that inventions are a response to a society's effective demand. But the wider the pool of knowledge on which inventors can draw for the solution of technical problems, the greater their possibility of success.

An increase in population contributes to the likelihood of discovery of new knowledge. The number of scientific researchers tends to increase with aggregate population, indeed, in advanced countries disproportionately so.[19] In this case, however, it is the absolute numbers which are important, the fact that more people are researching at more centers and producing more knowledge. As long as the education and training of the larger number engaged in the scientific fields does not deteriorate, the law of large numbers operates here just as in the case of invention.[20]

It is not only an increase in aggregate numbers that is important in the stimulation of new knowledge but also an increase in the contacts among those engaged in scientific investigation. New knowledge is often the product of the interaction among people with specialized knowledge, perhaps less in an organized manner than in an exchange of ideas that stimulates a fresh line of thought. Thus research institutes contribute to such an interchange, as do professional associations, university departments, and other such areas of organized activity. These are most often located in populous centers, the usual locale of intellectual activity. The growth of cities is thus likely to be an additional factor stimulating the production of new knowledge.[21]

Despite these considerations, the proposition that an increase in population stimulates new knowledge carries no implication that an increase in a given country's population is necessary for an increase in its stock of knowledge. Knowledge, once it comes into existence, tends to be the world's property, available to all peoples, regardless of whether their own population is rising, declining, or stable. Of course, the world's stock of knowledge would be reduced to the extent that any country reduced its contribution to it, unless one

accepts the view that what is not discovered today by one country's scientists will be discovered tomorrow by another country's,
in which case only the rate of accumulation of knowledge is affected. But in any event, there would be no special loss to any one
country but to the world generally, and there would be no relative
gain or loss that would follow from the increase or decrease in
knowledge caused by a country's increase or decrease in its population. In what sense, then, if any, can it be said that an expansion
of population (assuming the same standard of education and training) benefits a country by increasing the knowledge available to it?

The answer is given, I think, by the experience of business corporations. The presence of scientists on a firm's staff provides it
with receptors and disseminators of new knowledge, whether or
not generated by the firm itself, who thereby make *available* knowledge which otherwise would be lost to it, in a quite literal sense.
This is particularly true when, as now, the accretions of new
knowledge come with such rapidity that the process of simply sift-
ing what has recently become known is a time-consuming task demanding scientific capabilities. What is true of the corporation is
no less true of a nation. For new knowledge (wherever originating)
to become available to it, it must have scientists of its own keeping
up with their fields, translating the findings of others into language
and terms which are understandable to themselves, to students, and
to applied scientists whose activities are directly responsive to the
effective wants of their country, in the way we have earlier examined.

There is one other respect in which the population growth of a
society, by increasing the number of those engaged in the search
for scientific knowledge, makes a contribution which is specific to
that country rather than to the world in general. Scientific pursuit
may itself be responsive to a society's wants, in the same manner
as invention. This is most likely to be true of the advanced countries, but there is no logical reason for confining this effect to them.
A need gives rise to a technical problem which can only be solved
by some addition to scientific knowledge. As a nation's pool of
scientists grows, it becomes possible to assign some of their number
to such specific investigations, without diminishing excessively the
numbers engaged in teaching and in general research activity.[22]

The effect of population change, an increase in its numbers and
density, thus makes available to a society a larger stock of knowledge than otherwise would be the case, increasing its potential for
technological change, always assuming that its "knowledge people"

are provided with education and research facilities not inferior to what had been the practice in the past. This last proviso cannot be taken lightly, as we shall shortly see.

Population and Education

A country's educational system is essential to its technological potential. It is the chief means by which knowledge is communicated to the young, including to those who will subsequently become its inventors and innovators. It is also the chief means by which habits of disciplined inquiry are instilled. It is likewise a major method of training the specialized personnel—the architects, the electricians, the machinists, the accountants, and other such vocations— involved in effecting technical innovation. Finally, it is often a major source of employment for its scientists, a location for their research activity, and the principal training ground for their successors, all of which are related to the production of new knowledge.

Changes in a country's population relating to both its aggregate numbers and location have their impact on its educational system, and through it, on its technology. Formal educational systems are a function of urbanization. Historically and contemporaneously, rural villages have both a lesser demand for and supply of education. "Under the regime of domestic industry, children were educated by cooperating with their parents on the farm, where the pursuit of both agriculture and the useful arts furnished industrial training, and constant association with adults (especially with the children's parents) provided mental and moral training."[23] With the growth in the size of cities, their increasing specialization of functions, and the development of specialized knowledge, some more formal way was required of assembling and communicating the knowledge which was considered essential for the performance of tasks. With the attenuation of contact between parents and children, as personal employment in the city substituted for family employment on the farm, some more institutional procedure for socializing the young became necessary.

In the handicraft period, young boys could still learn a trade as apprentices and be subject to the parental-like control of their masters. But with the spread of industrialization and its centralization in cities, following the introduction of steam power, new conditions were introduced which further distinguished the educational possibilities of the city as against the country. ". . . country boys have no opportunity to learn trades on the farm or in a village shop. Mental and manual training have been differentiated; the latter cannot be acquired outside the cities, and the former until lately has suffered in village communities from lack of facilities."[24] These conditions still characterize the industrializing economies of today.

As cities have grown, so has the need for formal education. But other influences as well have been at work increasing the burden placed on the educational system and making this a constantly expanding activity in virtually every society around the world. One has been the growth in aggregate populations. Even if the rate of growth is stable, the educational establishment must expand in absolute size to accommodate the larger number of school-age children. A second influence has been the gradual spread of industrialization in the underdeveloped areas, increasing the dependency on acquired skills. Another has been the increasing egalitarianism characteristic of mass societies: a centralized government retains power by reflecting the *generalized* wants of the masses, among which education has figured prominently.[25] Still another has been the fact that knowledge itself has been expanding, necessitating an extension of the educational process if it is to serve its purpose. All of these influences—the increase in aggregate numbers, the growth of cities, the spread of industrialization, the transition to a mass society, and the augmentation of knowledge—derive in part at least from population changes, in ways which have already been discussed. Without exaggerating the influence of population factors on expanding educational activity, the link is obviously a strong one.

Because the educational activity of many societies is expanding at a rate greater than aggregate population and often at a rate greater than economic activity generally, as measured by gross national product (whether the greater rate is due, in underdeveloped countries, to the fact that the educational base is so small or, in advanced societies, that the egalitarian and knowledge factors are so strong), the consequence is to create a serious problem in resource allocation. Every society, however wealthy, is faced with the question of whether it will devote a larger share of its budget to education and training, thereby limiting expenditures in other directions, or whether, within the constraint of an educational allocation maintained at a given proportion of the total budget, it will put proportionately more into the superior training of a smaller number or the lower-level training of a larger number.

The problem facing the underdeveloped economies is particularly acute, since typically they have experienced a rising rate of population growth which adds disproportionately to the school-age group. Thus Puerto Rico, with more than half its population below the age of twenty, and influenced by American educational practices, has found that school expenditures absorb as much as one-fourth its budget, and even then only about two-thirds of its school-age children are in school. Other developing countries, less sheltered and less strongly influenced, can hardly be expected to allocate their resources in the same manner. Particularly if the decision emanates from elite groups or even from development-minded officials who must, however, compromise with elite groups, it is likely to come down on the side of general education as a matter of lip service and higher-level education for a limited number as a matter of practice.

The resource decision in the advanced and mass-oriented economies typically provides for an enlarged share of the national budget going to education, permitting the general education of entire populations and the superior training of a growing proportion. In the United States, for example, if one takes the age group 18–21, the percentage enrolled in schools increased from 22.1 percent in 1946 to 43.9 percent in 1964. Over the same period the number of doctorates conferred tripled.[26] Nevertheless, even in the wealthier economies the budgetary burden of providing constantly improving education for larger numbers has its expression in the form of swollen classes and more impersonal forms of instruction. The result is likely to be an education superior in content but inferior in pedagogical method. And the financial burden of providing "lifetime" or continuing education to working adults—a commitment now in the process of being made[27]—has not even been calculated.

It would be nice if true that the economic returns on investment in education were always such as to "make it pay," so that loans to the underdeveloped countries and prudence on the part of the advanced economies were all that was needed to insure a superior education for all. But waiving all the growing literature on rate-of-return on investment in education, with its dubious conclusions,[28] we can at a minimum conclude that only if a society is prepared to change the character of its effective demands will there be opportunity for the economic employment of all its increasingly educated people. In the underdeveloped countries, this would require more widespread acceptance of a changed style of living as a consequence of industrialization and the commercialization of agriculture. In the advanced economies, this might in time require the controlled stimulation of consumer demands, as Aldous Huxley foresaw in his *Brave New World*. By either route, the general economic relationship between education and technology which we earlier noted would be preserved. The alternative would seem to be an increasing acceptance of education for its own sake, as the justification for expanding budgets, taking it more and more out of the class of an investment good.

Inability to put a specific money value on education does not, however, impair the broader advantage flowing from education, or the desirability of additional education, whatever one's existing stock of knowledge. The broader advantage may be conceived of as a consumer satisfaction, if one chooses to preserve the economic idiom, but that at best only partially covers it. Without respect to the economic utility of particular increments of knowledge, additional education may convey social status, which is part of the social advantage distributed among people. In this connection it has repeatedly been remarked that education today provides the principal avenue of upward mobility in the United States, as in certain other countries. More important, the spread of education, particularly the spread of literacy, becomes an instrument of political position and power, both for a rising new leadership group and the more amorphous masses. John Stuart Mill observed the effects in his own day. Reviewing the English translation of the first volume of Tocqueville's study of the rising American nation gave Mill the occasion for some sympathetic and trenchant remarks of his own.

> For the first time, the power and the habit of reading begins to permeate the hitherto inert mass. Reading is power: not only because it is knowledge, but still more because it is a means of communication— because, by the aid of it, not only do opinions and feelings spread to the multitude, but every individual who holds them knows that they are held by the multitude; which of itself suffices, if they continue to be held, to ensure their speedy predominance. The many, for the first time, have now learned the lesson, which, once learned, is never forgotten—that their strength, when they choose to exert it, is invincible. And, for the first time, they have learned to unite for their own objects, without waiting for any section of the aristocracy to place itself at their head. The capacity of cooperation for a common purpose, heretofore a monopolized instrument of power in the hands of the higher classes, is now a most formidable one in those of the lowest.[29]

If one combines these social and political effects of the spread of education, they would seem to point in the direction of that mass society of the developed nations toward which the inchoate mass of more primitive societies tends to evolve. An elite governs, by definition, but it is an elite responsive to the wishes of a population which is homogeneous with respect to major values: the "opinions" which are held by the "multitude," in Mill's words. Moreover, the elite is a fluid one, admitting to its numbers those who have the ambition to batter their way up, with education as the principal means of ingress; the class distinction between governing and governed is not an odious or onerous one for most component groups.

The consequence would seem to be a very great social stability. Mass society controls, but primarily with respect to the larger issues on which there is general agreement. The interests of lesser groups are compromised within this general framework, creating a distribution of the social advantage in which all have their stake. No more effective containment of dissident minorities or of radical change could be devised.

It is unlikely, however, that such stability can prevail indefinitely. With a growing population, or a shift in its composition, or a relocation (which means principally increased urbanization), certain groups are disproportionately disadvantaged. The pressures for change in the social organization build up, opening opportunities for an aggressive and ambitious breed of "new men." Imperfections or inequities once generally accepted become more obvious and blatant, eliciting idealistic movements for reform, especially among the young. The ingredients are present for an attempted revision of the structure of authority and a redistribution of the social advantage.

It is interesting to note how many reformers, from Plato through Sir Thomas More down to Michael Harrington and John Kenneth Galbraith, have put their faith for an improved society in the increase of an educated class. If their faith has any justification, the spread of education throughout the masses, which so contributes to social stability, may itself generate a threat to that very stability by augmenting and coalescing the youthful idealistic forces pressing for social change. In addition to its contributions to a society's technology, then, its educational system affects its processes of social change.

Summary

Technological change begins with invention, and the amount and direction of inventive activity are responsive to the economic needs which a society manifests. An expanding population increases the market and profitability of certain industries, thereby stimulating inventive effort in solving their technical problems. It also increases the number of business firms in an industry and, hence, the number of opportunities for technical experimentation.

By giving rise to changes in social organization, population growth also creates entirely new needs, which is to say technical problems for inventive solution. Similarly, the increased interactions of an expanding urban society give rise to new wants and their solution in the form of new products, affecting consumer tastes generally and imposing pressures on farm producers to convert to cash crops. Growing cities likewise stimulate the commercialization of agriculture, adding to its attractiveness as a focus of inventive and innovative activity.

The law of large numbers augments the probability that a larger population will produce more people with the creative insight required by invention and innovation than will a smaller population. It also increases the probability of finding the range of psychological and physiological qualities which technical specialization sometimes requires.

Such influences of population on technological change are circumscribed by the stage of economic development and cultural characteristics of each country. The same population changes will not produce the same technological consequences in countries whose effective wants differ significantly.

Invention and innovation depend on a prior stock of knowledge. If the knowledge base increases, the possibilities for the solution of technical problems also increases. Thus, an expansion of knowledge is related to technical potential. An increase in a country's population density improves the chances for discovery of new knowledge, since the population of scientists tends to grow with the general population, certainly in absolute numbers even if not proportionately. This is true for any particular country despite the fact that most knowledge is a free good, and can thus be had from other countries, since even the assimilation and dissemination of new scientific knowledge is a task of constantly increasing dimensions, calling for a growing scientific establishment in every country even if only to assure access to the knowledge generated by others.

A country's educational system also contributes to its technological potential by training the inventors who respond to felt needs, the specialist technicians necessary for converting invention into innovation, and the scientists who enlarge the knowledge base.

Education has been an expanding activity in most countries, for a variety of reasons, often linked to population changes, and frequently raising serious problems of resource allocation. As the price of a good education rises, a country must allocate more to its school budget, or be satisfied with an inferior product, or curtail the numbers provided for; the last two alternatives jeopardize its technological potential.

Nevertheless, it cannot be taken for granted that money spent on education will pay off in technological progress or in any other economic way. But aside from its economic value, education brings social and political advantages which are likely to provide substantial support for expanding budgets, and which are integral to processes of social change.

Thus population considerations affect a country's educational facilities, and these in turn, among other far-reaching influences, affect its technological capacities.

NOTES

1. Jacob Schmookler, *Invention and Economic Growth* (Cambridge: Harvard University Press, 1966).

2. This statement is perhaps more dogmatic than is warranted. Some inventions may themselves bridge gaps in knowledge by creative insight or even by chance, so that it is not quite true that pre-existing knowledge is an absolute prerequisite. Nevertheless, a prior knowledge base is so essential to invention generally that one is probably justified in making the unqualified assertion at least for purposes of exposition. In any event, even granting such leaps over gaps in knowledge, it would still be true that the possibility of a particular invention's being made would depend, figuratively speaking, on the existence of knowledge on each side of the gap, so that available knowledge would still be a necessary permissive condition.

3. Schmookler, *Invention and Economic Growth*, p. 136.

4. Matthew Josephson, *Edison* (New York: McGraw-Hill Book Co., 1959), pp. 136, 137. With respect to a particular invention, Josephson writes (p. 318):

"As was his practice, Edison began by establishing clearly in his own mind a concept of what the popular need and use of an improved phonograph would be, planning his line of development accordingly." Schmookler cites the case of Edison on pp. 108–109 of *Invention and Economic Growth*.

5. Phyllis Deane, *The First Industrial Revolution* (Cambridge: Cambridge University Press, 1965), p. 124.

6. *Ibid.*, p. 148.

7. *Ibid.* As Deane reminds us, "It was the industrious middle class—that comfortable army of artisans, clerks, shopkeepers, merchants, bankers and industrialists—that were the chief beneficiaries of industrialization." This is the class, increasing in numbers and mobilizing working-class sentiment for reform, which became the leading force in wresting from the landed aristocracy a change in the authority structure and a redistribution of the social advantage.

8. Thus Schmookler, in *Invention and Economic Growth*, pp. 181–182, notes with respect to the United States: ". . . the great long-term shift of population from rural to urban areas changed the relative importance of different wants and altered the constraints upon their satisfaction. Thus, the public health problems (in terms of water supply, sewage, and so on) created by the growth of cities are well known. Equally obvious were the effects of higher land rents and urban life on housing, clothing, and transportation requirements." He goes on to argue that "the effect of such gross changes in consumer preferences on the profitability of different industries" had its impact in "the allocation of inventive activity among broad, alternative channels of potential development." We can presently observe this process still at work as city governments (and their constituencies) contend with problems of air, water, and sound pollution, increasing the effective demand for invention and innovation in these areas.

9. Art Gallaher, Jr., "Urbanizing Influences on Plainville," in Philip Olson, ed., *America as a Mass Society* (New York: The Free Press, 1963), p. 191.

10. The Comilla Township cooperative venture in East Pakistan is an outstanding example of this process at work, markedly changing the way of life of those participating in its extensive network of cooperative undertakings in the production and marketing of cereals, poultry, and other produce and in its educational and administrative activities.

11. Hauser, *Population Perspectives*, p. 145. Hauser sees a "return" to mass transport in the form of motor buses or trolley coaches, completing a circle. I would myself expect to see new or at least modified forms of technology emerging to meet conditions (demands) which are different from those obtaining when "trolley coaches" were last in use.

12. H. J. Habakkuk, *American and British Technology in the 19th Century* (Cambridge: Cambridge University Press, 1962), p. 213.

13. H. G. Barnett, *Innovation* (New York: McGraw-Hill, 1953), p. 56.

14. Maurice Halbwachs, *Population and Society* (Glencoe: The Free Press, 1960), p. 38.

15. Gunnar Myrdal, *Asian Drama: An Inquiry into the Poverty of Nations* (New York: The Twentieth Century Fund, 1969), 1:259. He adds:

Then, too, despite its greater poverty and higher rate of illiteracy than any other country of the region save Pakistan, India because it is big has been able to produce an intellectual elite of considerable size and competence and to develop a tradition of public debate on national issues. If we assume that only about 1 per cent of the Indian population has an effective knowledge of English, the language of national communication and debate, India would nevertheless have as large a population base for such an elite as that of Denmark (where the entire population can be reckoned as constituting such a base). The active intellectual elite rising up from this base has fostered enlightened ideas along the lines of the modernization ideology, and has given India a group of competent senior and civil servants with a national orientation.

16. Among others, R. D. McKenzie in *The Metropolitan Community* (New York: McGraw-Hill, 1933) has emphasized this distinction.

17. A position set forth in Clark Kerr, John Dunlop, Charles Myers, and Frederick Harbison, *Industrialization and Industrial Man* (Cambridge: Harvard University Press, 1960).

18. Kingsley Davis presents this argument in Joseph J. Spengler and Otis D. Duncan, *Population Theory and Policy* (Glencoe: The Free Press, 1956), p. 674. He comments: "One fears that more people are being kept alive in order that they may live badly." René Dubos has raised a similar fear with respect to world populations generally in *The Dreams of Reason* (New York: Columbia University Press, 1961). We shall have occasion to consider his position more specifically in a later chapter.

19. Between 1930 and 1965, the labor force in the United States increased approximately 50 percent, the number of engineers by 370 percent, and the number of scientists by 930 percent. From Daniel Bell, "The Measurement of Knowledge and Technology," in Eleanor Sheldon and Wilbert Moore, eds., *Indicators of Social Change* (New York: Russell Sage Foundation, 1969), pp. 201–202.

20. Simon Kuznets has argued along this line in *Economic Growth and Structure* (New York: W. W. Norton, 1965), pp. 127–128, 129: "Since we have assumed the education, training, and other capital investment necessary to assure that the additions to the population will be at least as well equipped as the population already existing, the proportion of mute Miltons and unfulfilled Newtons will be no higher than previously. Population growth, under the assumptions stated, would, therefore, produce an absolutely larger number of geniuses, talented men, and generally gifted contributors to new knowledge— whose native ability would be permitted to mature to effective levels when they join the labor force." He adds that "the possibility of diminishing returns is remote: the universe is far too vast in relation to the size of our planet and what we know about it."

21. ". . . creative effort flourishes in a dense intellectual atmosphere, and it is hardly an accident that the locus of intellectual progress (including that of the arts) has been preponderantly in the larger cities, not in the thinly settled countryside." *Ibid.*, p. 128.

22. The scientific work by western nations on atomic fission and nuclear fusion is a case of such directed investigation, arising under the specialized circumstances of war and threat of war. There are industrial examples as well. "Carothers' basic research at Du Pont which led to nylon was financed by management in the hopes that improvements in the understanding of long polymers would lead to important or new improved chemical products. Shockley's Bell Telephone Laboratories project was undertaken in the belief that improved knowledge of semiconductors would lead to better electrical devices." R. R. Nelson, M. J. Peck, and E. D. Kalacheck, *Technology, Economic Growth and Public Policy* (Washington, D.C.: Brookings Institution, 1967), p. 41.

23. Adna F. Weber, *The Growth of Cities in the Nineteenth Century* (Ithaca: Cornell University Press, 1965), p. 438. First published in 1899.

24. *Ibid.*

25. This does not of course preclude the possibility that a mass society, and the government responding to it, may discriminate against minority groups who are likely in consequence to wind up with an education inferior to that generally provided. The disproportionately disadvantaged are disproportionately disadvantaged in this respect, too. The case of Negroes in the United States is an obvious example, but there are comparable examples in other societies.

26. These figures come from the Organization for Economic Cooperation and Development, *Reviews of National Science Policy: United States* (Paris, 1968), and are cited by Bell in *Indicators of Social Change*, pp. 204–205.

27. As I have argued in "Education and Training: Whose Responsibility?" *American Iron and Steel Institute*, print (New York, 1969).

28. I have expressed my own reservations in "Some Second Thoughts on the Concept of Human Capital," Industrial Relations Research Association, *Proceedings*, 1967, pp. 1–20, and "Some Further Thoughts on the Concept of Human Capital," in G. G. Somers and W. D. Wood, eds., *Cost-Benefit Analysis of Manpower Policies* (Ontario, Canada: Industrial Relations Centre, Queen's University, 1969), pp. 230–248.

29. J. S. Mill, "Tocqueville on Democracy in America" (Vol. I), from *Essays on Politics and Culture*, ed. Gertrude Himmelfarb (New York: Doubleday, Anchor Books, 1963), p. 175.

CHAPTER 4
The Urbanization
Trend

THROUGHOUT the preceding chapters we have had occasion to note the importance of the growth of cities in changing people's habits of thought and action. Few social phenomena have had so pervasive an impact as urbanization. In this chapter we shall concentrate on this aspect of populations.

Background

Let us begin by getting some notion of the extent of the trend to urbanization. In doing so it will be useful to follow Kingsley Davis in making a distinction between urbanization and the growth of cities. The former refers to the proportion of a country's population which is located in cities. It is always expressed as a ratio. On this approach, cities can grow without any increase in urbanization taking place. As a consequence of natural increase, for example, a country's urban population could expand right along with its rural population, increasing the number but not the proportion of people who live in cities. Historically, an increase in urban relative to rural populations occurs through migration. The growth of cities can continue indefinitely, but conceptually at least the process of urbanization has a finite limit—when 100 percent of a country's population lives in cities.

What constitutes a city for purpose of classification is a definitional matter and varies among countries. One common census practice is to treat as urban any town of 5,000 or more. Thus, even if urbanization were complete, in the sense that 100 percent of the population lived in towns of 5,000 or more, the increasing concentration of people in urban areas could continue as people moved from the smaller towns to the larger cities. In recognition of this, more specialized indices of urbanization are sometimes employed, such as the proportion of a population living in cities of 20,000 or larger, or of 100,000 or larger.

Cities first appeared about 6,000 years ago, but for the most part were small islands in a sea of population that was overwhelmingly rural. It was not until very recent times that any *society* could be called urbanized. Even as late as 1900, only one country, Great Britain, could have been so regarded.[1] At least as extraordinary as this slow pace of urbanization in the period before 1900, however, has been its rapid spread since then. A few figures will suffice to make the point. In 1800, the world's population was approximately 900 million. Of this total, only 3 percent lived in some 750 cities having as many as 5,000 residents. In the ensuing one hundred and fifty-year period, world population expanded to 2.4 billion, an increase of two hundred and sixty-five percent. The number of cities with 5,000 or more increased to 27,600 and contained almost 30 percent of the total population. The number of cities of 100,000 or more had risen from 45 to 875 and accounted for more than 13 percent of the world's population.[2]

The same spectacular increase in urbanization is evident in figures for the United States alone. In 1790, when the first census was taken, there were just twenty-four towns with a population of 2,500 or more, representing 5 percent of the nation's total. In other words, the United States was then 95 percent rural. A hundred years later the rural population was down to 65 percent. The 1960 census showed a rural population of only 30 percent.

The accelerated pace of urbanization in recent years shows up in Asia just as in the West. In the forty-year period 1920–1960, Japan's urban population increased about five times; 64 percent of its people now live in cities. In India, 10.8 percent of the population lived in urban places at the turn of the century. By 1961, some 18 percent were urbanized with a rate of increase of over 35 percent in the last ten years.

A few historical facts also add a little perspective to our understanding of the urban phenomenon. If we go back to antiquity, the Greek city-state consisted of an urban enclave surrounded by a countryside which it controlled. In Periclean Athens the total free population numbered about 150,000, divided about equally between urban Athens and the more rural environs. The town also included 100,000 slaves and about 20,000 alien residents. The size of ancient Rome has been variously estimated; perhaps a third of a million comes close to the mark. (By 1500, however, Rome had declined to a population of 55,000.)

Medieval Europe, especially in the northwest, was basically rural.

As late as 1500, a town of 10,000 would have been considered big. The largest city of the late Middle Ages was Venice, which has been estimated as numbering 78,000 in 1363. Other Italian cities were among the giants of those times, with Bologna at 32,000; Florence 55,000; Genoa 38,000; Milan 52,000; Naples 27,000; and Padua 41,000. The Low Countries were represented by perhaps half a dozen major trading towns with populations in the same range. In 1292, Paris numbered 59,000. London in 1377 stood at 35,000. In the late seventeenth century, Paris had increased to half a million, and London had reached almost 700,000.[3]

A variety of forces has given rise to the growth of cities, so that it would be difficult to spell out some general theory of urban development. In many instances, they probably served some combination of administrative, religious, defensive, trading, and manufacturing functions. With the revival of cities in the late Middle Ages, the economic functions of trading and manufacturing became increasingly important. Merchants became a group numerous enough to warrant their own section of the town, designated as the "new burg" to distinguish it from the "old burg," which was the administrative center.[4] The long-distance traders were the elite of this group, and themselves almost a class apart. Towns became specialized in the manufacture of certain types of goods, under the control of local guilds, providing the merchandise for exchange with other localities. Rising mercantile houses established branches in other cities in addition to their home offices. The need for a system of record keeping as well as for exchange of directives and information among these far-flung offices led to business encouragement of a utilitarian education. With the increasing secularization of city life, and particularly with the Reformation, the role of the church in civic affairs receded. With growing autonomy from feudal nobility and often in alliance with the national monarchy seeking to strengthen its central power against the lesser nobility, the city increasingly gained administration of its own affairs.

Urbanization and Industrialization

The rush of urbanization that began in late eighteenth-century England seems to have been compounded of industrialization and general population growth. "Provincial towns and industrialized villages . . . were caught up in the swift advance of industry and population in the second half of the eighteenth century. . . . The semi-agricultural provincial town . . . was transformed into a populous industrial center."[5] The causative influence at work here is not altogether clear. Industrialization has often been regarded as the tinder that lit the explosive growth. Others have emphasized improvements in agriculture, including the enclosure movements of that period, as having permitted urban expansion by reason of greater farm productivity and of propelling displaced farmhands toward the industrializing cities. Still others have pointed to the marked expansion in population which took place concomitantly. It would be idle to attempt to fasten on some sequence of cause and effect; the fact is that all these influences were interacting. Within the set of cultural values which characterized England of the early industrial age, the general increase in population of that period created pressures for technical innovations, along the lines we examined in the preceding chapter. As we also saw, among the innovations resulting was the steam engine, which had its own enormous effect of centralizing industrial production in the larger cities in contrast to the "industrial villages" and "semi-agricultural provincial towns" of the earlier period.

Thus Chambers writes of Nottingham in the years just preceding 1750:

> . . . the adult population—perhaps the group from fifteen to fifty-five—was being rapidly reinforced both by natural increase and by immigration, and the effect was reflected in the rising marriage rate and birth rate. Here was the new industrial army in full spate of self-recruitment; marrying and competing for jobs and houses; stimulating the local economy by their production and consumption; creating new markets for their products by their own inventive genius. . . .[6]

Something of the same effects were discernible in the United States some fifty years later. The westward expansion has often been pictured as an agricultural one, with homesteaders rapidly filling up the open spaces. But along with that movement went the growth of interior cities, partly serving as trading centers but also giving rise to their own manufactures. By 1807, Pittsburgh was described as having an atmosphere "choked with soot." By 1809, Cincinnati was operating two cotton mills.[7] These interior cities also provided new markets for the older more established cities along the eastern seaboard, which began competing with each other for the trade of the new inland centers. Such expanded trade opportunities, along with the competition thereby generated, created pressures for improvements in production techniques, which often took the form of breaking down operations into their component parts, setting workmen (often the less skilled, such as immigrant peasants, women, and children) at more specialized tasks. The rise of modern labor unions in the United States has been attributed in major part to this appropriation of the journeyman's skill by segmenting the total production process into its component parts. It constitutes another example of how an expanding market growing in profitability directs effective demand to technical innovations.[8]

The same phenomenon of expanding population, urban growth, and industrial change can be observed in the developing economies, though on a far more limited scale. As urbanization proceeds, it becomes the basis for expanded trade and production. In the Middle East, for example, "along with the development of an urban proletariat has come a new middle class, made up of members of the traditional craft guilds and merchants who were able to adapt their products to fit new consumer needs. . . ."[9] In these contemporary settings, however, with a markedly different set of cultural values serving to blunt the effective demand for change, industrialization plays a much lesser role in the life of the cities.

Indeed, the differences between the industrializing West of the nineteenth century and the developing areas of the twentieth century are greater than any similarity, with respect to the trend to urbanization. The pace of urbanization in South Asia, for example, is fully comparable to that of England when it was in the midst of its technological revolution, but the technological revolution is lacking. Rapid urbanization proceeds without the galvanizing effect of rapid industrialization. The movement of rural dwellers to the larger cities contributes to the urbanizing movement, without being absorbed by expanding industry. "Urban growth in under-developed areas is not a function of the industrial base but an expression of the severity of the agrarian crisis."[10] Even so, although migrants to the city may not be absorbed in an industrializing process there is evidence that they do improve their economic status. "In India, and probably elsewhere, migration to the town certainly raises money income. In Delhi, a survey suggested that the average inmigrant improves his wage by 170 percent."[11] This is perhaps less surprising when it is realized that the typical migrant to the city tends to be young, better educated, and a cut above the "very poor" of the villages.[12] Nevertheless, the ineluctable fact remains that in the less developed economies of today we find rampant urbanization unaccompanied by any significant degree of industrialization.

The "Middle Class"

We turn now to consider the effects of urbanization. In view of the fact that the term "urban" may refer to places with as small a population as 2,500, at one extreme, and great metropolitan agglomerations like New York and London, at the other, it would be well to keep in mind the general observation of Louis Wirth: "The larger, the more densely populated, and the more heterogeneous a community, the more accentuated the characteristics associated with it will be."[13]

As a point of departure, the city creates a distinct class. The city dweller has been distinguished from the rural and village type in both folk and scientific literature. He is more sophisticated, more current with the world of ideas, more given to rational calculation than to traditional rule. John Stuart Mill phrased the point nicely:

> In populous towns, the mere collision of man with man, the keenness of competition, the habits of society and discussion, the easy access to reading—even the dullness of the ordinary occupations, which drives men to other excitements—produce of themselves a certain development of intelligence. The least favoured class of a town population are seldom actually stupid, and have often in some directions a morbid keenness and acuteness. It is otherwise with the peasantry. Whatever is desired that they should know, they must be taught; whatever intelligence is expected to grow up among them, must first be implanted, and sedulously nursed.[14]

But we can say more. From the late Middle Ages on, the city has been peculiarly identified with the middle class. The term itself is an interesting one, with its simplistic designation of a group interposing itself between the traditional upper class and lower class. As an economic category, business-oriented and change-creating, it sought a redistribution of the authority structure and of the social advantage which authority supported. It carried with it a periphery of white-collar workers, intellectuals, and, in time, government officials. The city was of course the home of a far larger group than the middle class—the industrial working class outnumbered it —but the city was peculiarly the home of the middle class. There were upper-class landed gentry and rural nobility, there was a rural as well as an urban proletariat, but the middle class has commonly been regarded as distinctively an urban group.

It is also the class which has acted as an homogenizing influence in western societies, diluting the social status, political position, and economic power of the upper strata and over time drawing more and more of the working class into its orientation. It has thus laid the basis for the type of modern mass society we noted earlier, and which Tocqueville and Mill saw in the making in the United States more than a hundred years ago. Whether more traditional societies will follow the same route remains to be seen.

Cities and Specialization

A city puts pressure on its inhabitants to specialize their activity, particularly in the matter of earning a living. The density of its population forces people into competition among themselves, as each seeks his economic survival. But unremitting competition is exhausting, and if one is bested by a competitor it is also punitive. One effective means of shielding oneself from competition is through specialized service or production, where specialization connotes differentiation from others. As a city grows in size, it both forces specialization (out of self-protection) and permits specialization (by enlarging the possible market for one's specialty).

It was Emile Durkheim who emphasized the importance of this aspect of urbanization.

From the time that the number of individuals among whom social relations are established begins to increase, they can maintain themselves only by greater specialization, harder work, and intensification of their faculties. From this general stimulation, there inevitably results a much higher degree of culture. From this point of view, civilization appears, not as an end which moves people by its attraction for them, not as a good foreseen and desired in advance, of which they seek to assure themselves the largest possible part, but as the effect of a cause, as the necessary resultant of a given state.[15]

The growth of cities thus reflects an increasing differentiation of functions. Trade functions become split into retailing, wholesaling, warehousing, and transporting. Financial facilitation of trade and manufacture expands into an increasing variety of banking, credit, insurance, and brokerage activities. Merchants specialize in particular lines of goods. Producers differentiate their products in terms of quality, style, price, and service. No function seems to be so finely specialized but that it can be specialized still further.

The city itself typically is specialized by geographical area. The wholesale market area is separate from light manufacture. The financial district has its own center. Theaters cluster together. Such concentrations further facilitate specialization, making possible the servicing of a given type of activity by those who make it their function to attend to its special needs.

Cities themselves become specialized, known for particular services or goods. The largest cities tend to be the innovators of new lines of activity or new products, drawing on their wider range of talents. "In national perspective, industries filter down through the system of cities, from places of greater to lesser industrial sophistication. Most often, the highest skills are needed in the difficult, early stages of mastering a new process, and skill requirements decline steadily as the production process is rationalized and routinized with experience. As the industry slides down the learning curve, the high wage rates of the more industrially sophisticated innovating areas become superfluous. The aging industry seeks out industrial backwaters where the cheaper labor is now up to the lesser demands of the simplified process."[16]

The study of the New York economy undertaken by Raymond Vernon illustrates this process.[17] One after another industry has departed the city as its functions have been taken over by smaller, lower-wage communities. Parts of certain industries have moved out, leaving behind those functions still demanding high talent. In the garment industry, for example, the cheaper clothing (such as men's work shirts) has moved elsewhere, but clothing dependent on style has remained in New York. The same separation has been made between the printing end of the publishing industry (now largely removed) and the editorial side which remains.

"The entire progress of civilization is a process of differentiation, and the city is the greatest differentiator."[18] "If the city is, on the one side, a jungle of potentially infinite and destroying competition, on the other, it shows a nearly infinite capacity of its members to differentiate themselves, to become useful to one another, to become needed."[19] Such testimony to the role of the city in eliciting special talents and stimulating innovative activity has been repeated again and again. And yet the experience of the expanding cities of the underdeveloped areas seems to offer a sharp contrast to a sociological analysis largely based on western observation. Crowded with people lacking much by way of education, special skills, tools or any other assets, the large cities of South and Southeast Asia, for example, often appear to break down into a kind of village existence within the city.[20]

The distinction between the experience of West and East is a real one. It reflects in major part the differences in cultural values among peoples, which causes sharp divergences in the style of living which is *effectively* wanted. Nevertheless, for all the distinction between the industrialized centers of the West and the poverty-ridden cities of the developing areas, within the limits of cultural values it is the city which gives rise to such specialization and innovation as does occur. In the Middle East,

> New types and patterns of industry and trade are slowly producing a new urban middle class and an urban proletariat. The proliferation of civil service jobs with an expansion of government functions, the increase in the number of technically trained and supervisory personnel required by the oil industry, and the growth of commercial employment has helped to create a new elite. Manpower planning studies are being made and technical and trade schools are being established. . . . Social change is gradually having an influence on every aspect of life in the Middle East and, although some of the effects are not readily discernible, they are nevertheless comprehensive.[21]

The Culture of Cities

Urbanization is not only marked by the rise of a new class but also by the creation and spread of a new way of life. If, from medieval times on, the town emphasizes its economic functions, it also becomes the culture-creating unit in society, taking over from the church in this respect and secularizing social behavior. As we have already noted, in advanced western societies, integrated by communication and transportation systems, the hegemony of urban culture reaches into the smaller towns and rural areas. Indeed, with urbanization proceeding at the pace of the last hundred years, urban culture has become pervasive.

What form does that culture take? In the first instance, it seeks a refinement of human behavior, in part as the social expression of that same process of individual differentiation that takes place in the economic arena, in part as the prerequisite to numbers of people inhabiting the same limited space without imposing on them the discipline of a military camp. The words "civility" and "civilization" have the same Latin root as city. They illustrate the necessity of a consciously mannered way of life conducive to peaceful coexistence in a locale where denseness of numbers guarantees a high degree of competitiveness, however muted by specialization. The civilization of the city is one of keen competition contained, even if never wholly successfully, by generally accepted manners, the fashioned rules of etiquette.

At the same time, urbanites are exposed to heterogeneous ways of thinking and behavior patterns, unencompassed by any common codes of conduct. They develop a tolerance and a taste for novelty. Competitive insecurity, never wholly allayed by differentiation and specialization, creates a sense of impermanence and tentativeness. These two streams of influence, along with the drive to specialization, combine in producing that fascinating phenomenon known as fashion or style, which finds its expression in clothing, home furnishings, the arts, education, amusements, even to a degree in religion and government.

With style comes stimulation to the imagination, to creativity, to innovation. These are qualities of the individual who is free to express himself, unencumbered by tradition, suspicion, or hostility. It is the city which uniquely gives the individual his chance for expression. It was not coincidence but consonance that individualism paralleled the trend toward urbanization. But along with individualism goes the proliferation of institutions serving as extensions of a person's special interests, each meeting a need relevant only to some one segment of his total range of activity. Such institutions help to relate the individual, unaided or uncontrolled as he is by the folkways of a closely knit society, to his social environment, but because each deals only with some segment of his life they do not rob him of his sense of freedom and individuality.

Finally, in this cursory survey, urban culture is a money culture. There is little that is produced for one's own use; whatever is to be had can be had only by payment. The impact of this on western society has been enormous, creating as it did a market society, where all goods and services are for sale, where people are dependent for their very living on the pecuniary value which others put on them.[22] The extended family can no longer provide the goods which are wanted or needed; younger members quickly spin off to make their own way. Specialization, essential as a shield against the fiercest competition, both depends on and gives rise to this pecuniary nexus.

It is not just industrialization which gives rise to the market system, even though it adds its own special impact, but the process of urbanization as well. The industrial village or the semi-agricultural industrial town would have stimulated exchange for money, to be sure, but their influence in this regard would have been far less pervasive. Only with the coincidence of industrialization and urbanization does the pecuniary society come into full bloom.

The Individual in the City

"Every man in the world knows that isolation and solitude are found in a much higher degree in the crowded city than in a country village, where one individual's concerns are the concern of all. The cities, then, are favorable to free thought and the sense of individual responsibility."[23] It was in a double sense, then, that the German medieval proverb, cities make free men, was true. The serf or villein who escaped to the city and resided there for a year and a day could not be returned to servitude without formal trial in courts controlled by the burghers. The urban resident was his own man and no bondman. He was also free in the sense of escaping from the surveillance of a largely closed village society. The larger the city, the less the limitation on the individual imposed by a prescribed way of life.

But this latter freedom is not without its price. The larger the city, the more the individual is assaulted by a bewildering variety of casual contacts with an almost intolerable number of individuals on whom he has to rely for the specialized services which only make life possible. "[If] the unceasing external contact of numbers of persons in the city should be met by the same number of inner reactions as in the small town, in which one knows almost every person he meets and to each of whom he has a positive relationship, one would be completely atomized internally and would fall into an unthinkable mental condition."[24]

The only defense is withdrawal, retiring into one's own shell and emerging only as necessary to make the brief essential contact with those on whom one personally relies. Thus the individual is emancipated from the control by others that goes with the integrated life of a small closed society, but he is emancipated into a shell of loneliness, without any identity other than he is capable of providing for himself, given only a shadow's definition by his relations with others, rootless in a society composed of other individuals rootless like himself. This is the state to which, when carried to excess, Durkheim gave the term "anomie," a loss of individual spontaneity resulting from the absence of a sense of social integration, a symptom of social disorganization.

The city dweller's associations tend to be in organizations and institutions formed for special purposes, as we have already noted, to which some segment of his life is loosely attached. But the withdrawal characteristic of city life means that control of such institutions in time passes into the hands of a few who see it as a vehicle for their own advancement, who regard their institutional roles as a form of specialization giving them a protected foothold in the city. Thus there arises, out of special needs, a degree of uncontrolled or loosely controlled organizational power. The labor unions, trade associations, taxpayers leagues, parent-teachers associations, religious institutions are capable of wielding the influence of numbers without their active involvement.

The feeling of *anomie* or alienation carries additional consequences. It leads, on the one hand, to a disinclination to become involved with others even when others are in distress. The dehumanizing aspects of city living are reinforced by repeated refusal of aid or even sympathetic attention. This pathological condition gained widespread attention in 1964 when at least thirty-eight people saw or heard the slaying of a young woman in the Kew Gardens section of New York City without offering any assistance, even to the extent of notifying the police.[25] ". . . there is so much humanity packed up in these streets, so much friction, so much hatred, that we are haunted by the screams we hear in the night—the screams against which we close our windows, our ears, our minds."[26]

At the other extreme, the same conditions which encourage withdrawal from scenes of violence on the part of some may induce violence on the part of others. In one experiment conducted by a Stanford University psychologist, a car with raised hood and without license plates was left parked at the curb in a middle-class neighborhood, first in the small California city of Palo Alto, then in the Bronx section of New York City. In the small town the car was left untouched for more than a week. In New York, twenty-three separate depredations had reduced the car to "a battered useless hulk of metal." The experimenter, Philip Zimbardo, concluded on the strength of this and other evidence that big-city dwellers were becoming "deindividualized" through the attenuation of social controls over their behavior.[27]

Forms of "flash" violence such as riots are sometimes the sporadic outbursts of unrelated and unintegrated individuals who, given some provocation, coalesce briefly into an expression of undisciplined frustration. In the face of such possible consequences of anomie and the general lack of strong social constraints on individual behavior, the city must provide its own substitute in the form of more formal systems of law enforcement, not found in a village and often not even in a small town. The police systems of the present metropolis were unknown and unneeded when those same cities were in their early stages of growth.[28]

Social Discontent in the City

The anonymity which the city provides, the release from traditional controls, and the possibility for individual development combine to make cities the locus and focus of social change. They permit the presence and activity of deviant personalities, including reformers, as well as new classes, dissident masses, expatriates, and migrants. It is the cities, not the countryside, which spawn radical programs and liberal causes.

The receptiveness of cities to those who are discontented elsewhere increases their own exposure to social unrest. As numbers of the uprooted and unhappy congregate together, they reach a magnitude which permits and sometimes touches off a mass explosion. In 1835, Tocqueville remarked on this danger:

The United States has no metropolis, but it already contains several very large cities. Philadelphia reckoned 161,000 inhabitants, and New York 202,000 in the year 1830. The lower ranks which inhabit these cities constitute a rabble even more formidable than the populace of European towns. They consist of freed blacks, in the first place, who are condemned by the laws and by public opinion to a hereditary state of misery and degradation. They also contain a multitude of Europeans who have been driven to the shores of the New World by their misfortunes or their misconduct; and they bring to the United States all our greatest vices, without any of those interests which counteract their baneful influence. As inhabitants of a country where they have no civil rights, they are ready to turn all the passions which agitate the community to their own advantage; thus, within the last few months, serious riots have broken out in Philadelphia and New York. Disturbances of this kind are unknown in the rest of the country, which is not alarmed by them, because the population of the cities has hitherto exercised neither power nor influence over the rural districts.

Nevertheless, I look upon the size of certain American cities, and especially on the nature of their population, as a real danger which threatens the future security of the democratic republics of the New World; and I venture to predict that they will perish from this circumstance, unless the government succeeds in creating an armed force which, while it remains under the control of the majority of the nation, will be independent of the town population and able to repress its excesses.[29]

Between 1830, roughly the time when Tocqueville was observing America, and the Civil War, riots broke out recurringly in all the major cities, usually having an ethnic or racial basis. The worst occurred in Philadelphia in 1844, when the Irish were the target of the action, and in New York in 1863 (the "Draft Riots") when the Irish were largely cast as the aggressors. But perhaps the most spectacular way in which American cities have played host to dissident groups and reaped a reward in the form of social disorganization has been the movement of Negroes from the rural areas of the South into cities throughout the nation; in 1968, only about a million of the 22.3 million Negroes in the United States still lived on farms. Although statistical evidence for the proposition is not persuasive, it is often said that when the Negro population of a city passes a certain percentage, violence erupts.[30] However much credence one may put in such a formulation, it is certainly the case that some critical mass of such a disproportionately disadvantaged group is necessary to promote a flare-up of violence. It is also instructive in this respect that while the young and the young adults (ages 15–44) are increasing in the nation at large at a rate which projects a 57 percent gain by 1985, the increase in urban nonwhites in this same age group is expected to reach 124 percent.[31] Since we have already hypothesized that the young constitute a major force for social change, the potential for violent eruptions from Negroes protesting the present distribution of the social advantage would seem to be increasing rapidly.

A further coincidence of urban characteristics also points to the greater possibility of radical social action in the large cities in contrast to small communities. We have already noted the important role which specialization plays in the life of the city. From research undertaken by James C. Coke, it appears that smaller towns are often beset with some of the same problems attending the larger cities, even though on a lesser scale. Housing blight, for example, is a prevalent condition. But it is only in the larger cities that one finds formal organizations manned by experts agitating for action.[32] Size permits specialization in the conduct of social action programs no less than in economic activity.

It is of course not only through its permissiveness of action-oriented dissident groups that the city invites pressures for social change, but also through the fact that rapid urbanization itself creates particular need for a modification of the social organization, along the lines we earlier explored. Expanding cities make their own problems as well as import them, distributing their advantages and disadvantages with inequality, and seeking to contain by one means or another those who are discontented enough to be led into action. This leads us to the consideration of the impact of urbanization on its governmental forms.

We have been talking chiefly of western cities, but most of what has been said applies, even though not with the same force, to cities in the developing parts of the world. To quote from one study to which frequent reference has already been made,

. . . the family previously provided economic security and protection in return for the loyalty it demanded, but in contemporary Middle Eastern society where population is increasing rapidly and modern means of communication have eliminated the isolation of the group, the individual finds the extended family unable to provide the things he needs and wants. Urbanization and industrial development have further intensified the internal strains that have always existed in the extended family since they offer alternative means of support for those who eventually decide to establish conjugal households of their own. The pressure toward independence is reflected in the desire to select one's own mate and have a household of one's own. The young man who obtains employment on the basis of his own merits does not wish to remain dependent upon his father, and among the modern, urban population such a household is becoming a normal aspiration.[33]

Even though the sprawling cities of Asia lack the dislocating effects of rapid technological change, which have contributed to urban upheavals in the industrializing West, they nevertheless create a culture which is peculiarly urban, more responsive to and creative of forces for social change, even if at a slower pace, drawing to themselves those individuals (however few in number) who are least tolerant of tradition, who find in the city an opportunity to carve out their own differentiated role, including perhaps one of leadership in organizations directed to shifting the structure of authority.[34]

Urban Government

The rapid growth of cities necessitates governmental action. In 1800, Philadelphia with a population of 70,000, New York with 60,000, and Boston with 25,000 were already experiencing growing pains—at a time when garbage removal was left to the pigs, New York and Boston were dark at night, Boston was still without sidewalks, a police force was still to be organized, filth gathered everywhere and often enough led to epidemics, and New York was just laying down the wooden pipes for its water supply. Problems like these were confronted by governments which had not yet evolved much beyond the village stage, with tax systems that could not begin to bear the burden.

In the contemporary world, cities, now vastly swollen in size, confront a different range of problems, including adequate mass transit, adequate housing, adequate school facilities, and crime control. But though the problems differ, present-day cities in the industrialized countries face the same lagging adjustment of governmental form to changing functions and the same inadequacy of revenues to constantly rising expenditures. It is safe to say that as long as urbanization proceeds it will manufacture its own diseconomies of scale, whatever the offsetting values.

The cities of the developing economies are in much worse plight. They have mushroomed into metropolitan centers at an even faster pace than their western predecessors, without time or resources to meet their needs along the way. In Calcutta, for example,

proposals for a mass transit system have been under discussion for nearly 20 years with absolutely no result. Meantime at least one-third of the city's buses and trams can be relied on to be out of service at any given time. . . . transportation being so near to hopeless, little can be done to relieve the overcrowding of the center of the city where approximately one-third of the population lives in *bustees* and considerably more than half in conditions of extreme urban squalor. . . . Only in the best *bustees* are there solid walls between one such—apartment? domicile? pen? stall?—and the next. Usually there are just a few boards, a strip of corrugated iron or a curtain fashioned from an old gunny sack. . . . The simplest way to describe conditions of sanitation in the *bustees* is to say there aren't any. Narrow lanes, often no more than a couple of yards wide, are half given over to open drains whose moldering, putrefying contents run past every doorstep . . . two-thirds of the city's sanitation trucks are normally out of commission, so [garbage] collection is weekly, bimonthly, or virtually unknown. The problem is complicated by the need to remove human wastes from more than 40,000 fly-breeding open privies. . . . With offal everywhere and the ancient pipes rotting, little can be done to insure the purity of the drinking water . . . two-thirds of Calcutta's water comes unfiltered direct from the polluted Hooghly River. Only in recent years has the unfiltered water been chemically treated to reduce the constant menace of epidemic cholera . . . not a single new public school has been added to the system for a generation, with the result that it now serves only one-fourth of the children of school age.[35]

Admittedly, Calcutta is perhaps as bad an example as one could find of the compounding problems of rapid urbanization in the slowly industrializing but still underdeveloped economies. Its catalogue of miseries can, however, be reproduced in many another city with only a difference of degree.[36]

Whether in the advanced or developing areas, such big-city problems can only be adequately met through the development of a highly articulated urban government, with a network of departments, bureaus, boards, administrators, superintendents, inspectors, each performing its specialized function. But the political aspects of city government, in contrast to its service functions, present an even more complex affair. In some countries, as in England and France, provision and administration of important local services has come under the national government. In other countries, as in the United States, the cities have been left largely to themselves or have come under a general state or provincial supervision. Still elsewhere, as in India, the cities are self-governed unless they are incapable of self-government, at which point the central administration imposes its own regime, as occurred in Calcutta in 1967.

Whatever the manner of governing, the large city is such a maelstrom of competing and conflicting interests that it can be effectively governed only through a workable compromise among them. The structure of authority favors certain interests, to be sure, as we observed in an earlier chapter, and others are disproportionately disadvantaged, but if the process of containment is to succeed it must allow for some recognition or expression of the major interests, to avert explosion, interference, or disinvolvement. A workable political compromise is far more difficult to effect when the groups involved are in active contact with each other, within a circumscribed area, than when they are separated by space. The political problems of city government are, for that reason alone, often less susceptible to resolution than those of the national government.

Perhaps largely for that reason there has always been an active advocacy of small towns rather than large agglomerations, and concomitantly of decentralized (small unit) government even within the denser areas. The underlying rationale is explainable in terms of our earlier analysis. If big-city government is rendered unworkable by the heterogeneity of its population, small-unit administration of more homogeneous populations would appear to be the answer. If the city dissolves the social controls which smaller societies impose on their members, creating anomic individuals and irresponsible and segmental power blocs, the return to or preservation of community-size populations would presumably reinforce social order.

There is an undeniable element of validity in such arguments. As cities expand, the structure of authority becomes more removed from those who are supposed to respond to it. As central governments intervene in urban matters, the same result occurs. In order to encourage respect for authority (the orderliness on which any society and especially a big-city society depends), there must be some understanding by those subject to it of the reasons for the way it is exercised. In 1968, local protests over the administration of the school system in such separated localities as New York City and metropolitan France provided examples of that need manifesting itself.

Nevertheless, any notion that small-scale administration can substitute for big-city government is a false one. The essence of a city *is* its heterogeneity; it cannot be decomposed into a mosaic of self-governing neighborhood units, each with its own village-like exclusivity and social particularism, without sacrificing the urban culture which is the city's greatest contribution.

Indeed, in some areas, one of the main problems connected with effective city government is that it is not extensive enough. The city is itself contained by a ring of suburbs and small towns, each self-governing and independent of city control. These benefit from the presence of the city without contributing proportionately to its costs of operation. Privileged groups, seeking to escape direct contact with the swelling masses of the more disadvantaged elements of the population, withdraw to the outskirts of the city, enjoying the best of both worlds: the world of the segregated suburb and the world of the heterogeneous city. This is notably the case in the United States, as the middle-class white population has moved from the central cities to their own suburbs, leaving the cities to the less privileged, especially to the Negroes. As the National Advisory Commission on Civil Disorders emphasized, this course of action, if continued, "would lead to the permanent establishment of two societies: one predominantly white and located in the suburbs, in smaller cities, and in outlying areas, and one largely Negro located in central cities."[37] The same phenomenon has been observed in the major cities of Latin America.[38]

One consequence of such a development is the further erosion of the city's already inadequate tax base, as its population comes to reflect predominantly lower-income groups, while the needs of the cities, already neglected, become more pressing. If ever there was a formula for social explosion, it is here. The workable political compromise which is needed cannot be achieved in the cities because their unit of government does not embrace the suburbs. If sought in the national government, the pressure for compromise will be relaxed as the special problems of the large cities are blended into the broader spectrum of problems of a generally urbanizing society.

Perhaps the answer lies, as some have suggested, in expanding the area of the city to embrace the suburbs. Some solution along this line—an effort to restore the heterogeneity of the city rather than the homogeneity of the small town or village—would seem desirable. But where does the process end? As urbanization proceeds and the space between towns and cities fills up, will merger succeed merger until only a few metropolitan governments encompass the whole of a nation? Or until a single city becomes coextensive with the nation, under a single government, requiring the reintroduction of subordinate local administrative units, which would start the whole process over again . . . and again and again?

In some societies an alternative to suburbanization for the privileged may be simple withdrawal from the active life of the city. As population mounts, unemployment and poverty become more prevalent, social unrest becomes more frequent and more violent, and the city deteriorates, those who still benefit from the prevailing distribution of the social advantage may retreat rather than become more deeply involved in the proliferating problems. The industrialist maintains his investment but does not add to it. The government official becomes immersed in complying with existing regulations but not in confronting new issues. As long as the structure of authority continues to reflect their interests, such a policy is tenable. After them, the deluge. If the deluge comes sooner, there is always the possibility of flight, financed, perhaps, by a Swiss bank account or a family member abroad.

What all of this suggests is something we have already encountered: that as population expands, it requires new forms of social organization. Growing cities, changing in composition too, require new forms of government. What their shape will be is not immutably dictated by abstract processes like "urbanization" or "industrialization" but by these operating within particular cultural settings which have their own influence, especially in terms of the structure of wants which are *effectively* wanted.

The Effect of the City on Its Own Growth

Historically in the West, cities brought an early death to their inhabitants. As late as the mid-nineteenth century, life expectancy was twenty-six in Liverpool and Manchester and thirty-six in London, in contrast to forty-one for England and Wales as a whole. Cholera epidemics visited the major cities with depressing frequency. Even in the first decade of the twentieth century, the death rate of the urban counties of England and Wales was a third higher than in the rural counties, after making allowance for age structure. Improvements in water purification, sewage disposal, and other forms of epidemic control began having their effect, however. By 1950, differences in urban-rural mortality had largely been eliminated.

Historically in the West, urbanization has resulted in lower fertility rates over rural residence: 36 percent lower in the United States in 1800, for example, increasing to 41 percent lower in 1930. In later years the size of the differential has declined, but a significant differential persists. It has been said that "the existence of a rural-urban fertility differential must certainly rank as one of the most widely validated and accepted generalizations in the demographic literature of the Western world."[39] The reasons for this probably include the greater intensity and diversity of urban as against rural life, a more calculated approach to the value or desirability of raising children in the city as against the country, and a more highly educated female population.

In the West, then, with higher death rates and lower birth rates, during their period of most rapid expansion, cities were drawing their numbers from rural migration. As farms became more mechanized and more commercial, they pushed their surplus labor off to the cities. As cities industrialized, they absorbed the displaced farmhands. Higher wages in the cities constituted an added inducement for the excess rural population to seek its fortunes there, along with that hospitality to minority and disadvantaged groups which we have noted.

Nowhere has this farm-to-city movement been more marked than in the United States, as a consequence of its more intense mechanization of agriculture and more advanced industrialization. Although migration had gone on for more than a century, it reached its peak in relatively recent years. Stimulated in part by World War II with its need for food, factory workers, and soldiers, 6 million people were drawn from the land between 1940–1945. But the pace of technological change in agriculture did not slacken with the end of the war and, by 1967, another 13.6 million people had made the switch. By that year, the farm population in the United States had declined to about 5 percent of the total population. A similar movement, if not quite so rapid, has been taking place in the other advanced economies.

The consequence is that the rate of urbanization in the advanced economies is slowing to a virtual standstill. The rural population is no longer large enough to make any significant contribution to the growth of urban areas. A movement from the smaller towns to the larger cities may still continue, adding to the density of the latter, but an outward flow from the larger cities to their suburbs has an offsetting effect. The end of urbanization does not, of course, mean that cities of all sizes will not continue to grow; it simply means that the proportion of the country's population living in what are defined as urban areas has reached a peak. Whatever growth in cities occurs, will occur chiefly from within. To the extent that urban fertility tends to be lower than rural, the over-all rate of population growth will presumably be lower in such an urbanized society than it otherwise would be.

If we turn to the developing areas, we find a different story. There, since 1940, populations have been growing twice as fast as in the industrialized economies, and "their increase far exceeds the growth of the latter at the peak of their expansion."[40] What gives rise to this amazing growth?

In the first instance, the natural increase of these swelling cities is not impeded by adverse mortality rates, as was the case when the West was industrializing. Profiting from western experience on the public health front, and despite conditions in major cities such as Calcutta, the developing nations are preserving life as effectively in the metropolis as in the village. Mortality, at least as shown by crude death rates, has declined to the extent that it does not compare unfavorably with the West.

At the same time, that difference in fertility rates between farm and city which has characterized the West has been virtually eliminated in the developing countries. Although migration from rural areas does add to city size, it "now does little more than make up for the small difference in the birth rate between city and countryside."[41]

The consequence of this is that an over-all rate of population increase is adding to both rural and urban populations in these poverty-stricken areas. Rural population and poverty grow right along with the cities, and are largely unrelieved by cityward migration. "The poor countries thus confront a grave dilemma. If they do not substantially step up the exodus from rural areas, these areas will be swamped with underemployed farmers. If they do step up the exodus, the cities will grow at a disastrous rate."[42]

In the underdeveloped economies, the urbanization process still has a long way to go. In India, for example, perhaps 20 percent of the population now lives in urban areas, which substantially means places of 5,000 or more, compared with about 75 percent in the United States and 80 percent in England and Wales. Fed by high fertility rates, their already large cities are likely to become gargantuan, and the rural countryside will become increasingly urban. And, as yet, urbanization by itself, in these areas, does not operate to lower birth rates.

With no appreciable, certainly no comparable, expansion in economic opportunities, the pressure will build for relief of distress as the disadvantages of rapid growth are distributed as unequally as the advantages. The need for changes in social organization to accommodate the increased numbers will be greater than is already the case, and resistance to change can be predicted from those whose privileges would be inundated by a redistribution of the social advantage and the supporting authority structure.

But no change short of Malthusian catastrophe can relieve the continuing pressures unless there is some modification in the structure of effective wants of the population at large, not all at once by conversion, but increasingly, through those innovating groups which are the cutting edge of change and those larger groups which are sufficiently dissatisfied that they are willing to risk their own limited, but perhaps shrinking, stake in the privilege system to support a demand for change.

The swollen but still swelling cities are almost certain to be the focus of frustration leading to sporadic violence and probably to radical action designed to restructure authority. But the latter will have no therapeutic effect unless it succeeds in altering cultural values of long standing. The pressures of population are thus likely to give rise to internal conflict in the underdeveloped areas, made all the more bitter because it involves an intrusion of foreign industrial ideology confusing (and perhaps unwanted) even to those who might benefit from it.

Summary

Although cities existed 6,000 years ago, only in the last few hundred years has a process of urbanization taken place. Beginning in western Europe, it appears both to have produced and itself been the product of a major cultural shift toward secularism and individualism, in the early phase, and of industrialization and rapid population growth in its later stage, beginning in the last half of the eighteenth century in England. A causal sequence cannot be given with assurance. Clearly industrialization with steam power contributed greatly to the growth of cities, but just as clearly an expanding population, migrating from the rural areas to towns, was itself a stimulus to industrialization. In the twentieth century, and especially since its midpoint, urbanization has been proceeding at a rapid pace in the underdeveloped economies, unaccompanied by any significant industrialization.

One marked effect of urban growth is to encourage specialization of activity. With large numbers of people competing with each other for a toehold in a limited space, there is strong inducement for each to try to differentiate his function from those of others. The larger the city, the finer the specializations which can be supported. Cities themselves specialize in trying to insure themselves a more secure economic position in the larger society. This aspect of urban life is much more evident in industrialized than in underdeveloped countries, but even in the latter, within the constraints of a different culture, specialization takes place.

The city creates its own special class—the middle class—and its own culture. That culture, which characterizes the mass society of the advanced economies, lays stress on civil manners, innovation (particularly as represented by style), individual expression (within broad areas of conformity), institutionalization of specialized aspects of social life, and commercialization of a far greater number of relationships and activities.

The opportunity for the individual to express himself, free of the constraints imposed by a small, integrated community, has its bleaker side. The very number of human contacts to which he is exposed in the city obliges him, for his own sanity, to treat contacts casually and objectively, without intimacy or involvement. He tends to withdraw into his own world, his associations occurring in formal and special-purpose institutions which represent segments of his life. Carried to an extreme (in part a function of city size), the individual experiences the rootlessness of Durkheim's anomie. This may be expressed by rejection of any sense of responsibility for others, even those in distress, or in forms of violence perpetrated against the impersonal community.

The permissiveness of the city draws to it those individuals who are most out of accord with society, including deviants, reformers, and dissidents. The congregation of numbers of those who are discontented with their place in the social scheme may give rise to violent action, such as riots. The concentration of Negroes in American cities over the years is a notable instance of this phenomenon.

The problems generated by urban growth require governmental action, but, given the heterogeneity of a city's population, action on most fronts is possible only with some form of workable compromise among the diverse groups affected. Where these are in direct competition with each other, within a limited space, achieving a workable compromise is difficult. As numbers and heterogeneity increase, the political problem sometimes seems insurmountable: it is popularly said, for example, that New York City is "ungovernable."

The solution which some have urged has been to encourage small-scale units and to decentralize the cities which have become impossibly large. By this device, more homogeneous communities could impose their own social controls over their more integrated populations. While some decentralization may be necessary to give people a greater stake in the authority structure, any major move in this direction would be at the sacrifice of that culture which derives from the cities and is rooted in the diversity of their composition.

As a matter of fact, in some societies a more basic problem may be that cities do not encompass a large enough area, allowing privileged groups to escape to the suburbs, from which they can freely enjoy the benefits of the city without sharing its burdens, including its mounting financial load. In other societies, the prevailing authority structure permits the privileged groups to withdraw from active involvement, including financial responsibility, while remaining residents of the city. Both situations are evidence of the pressing and persistent need for accommodating governmental forms to changing needs as population expands.

The urbanization process has displayed a markedly different pattern in the advanced economies as against the underdeveloped countries. In the former, rapid urban growth was associated with higher mortality rates and lower fertility rates than in rural areas, and their added numbers came from a massive and continuing migration from farm to city. That migration is now largely concluded, so that urbanization has in effect almost run its course. Cities will continue to grow, but only through overall population growth.

The underdeveloped countries are now urbanizing at a faster rate than the West even in the full tide of industrialization. But city growth comes only very little from rural migration. Urban mortality rates are low as these countries draw on the world's accumulated knowledge in the public health field, while urban fertility rates are almost as high as in the rural areas. The process of urbanization still has a long way to go, but the distance is not likely to be covered as a result of rural migration to the cities. Both cities and countryside will increase in population as a consequence of a high over-all rate of population growth. The pressures for accommodating the more tightly packed masses of the large cities may with good reason give rise to a brooding concern for violent eruption.

The problems thereby generated will not be the exclusive concern of the countries immediately involved. The effects are bound to spill over into the world at large, becoming a force for the attempted international redistribution of the social advantage and the system of international authority supporting it. But that is a matter we shall examine in a later chapter.

We have observed numerous and profound effects arising from urbanization. Urbanization is a demographic phenomenon, part of the so-called population problem. It does not, of course, occur autonomously or in isolation, but has its relationships to other trends and movements, interacting with them so that it becomes part cause and part effect. Without imputing to urbanization any wholly independent influence on society or erecting it into a self-sufficient social force, we can nevertheless recognize that this demographic phenomenon is pervasive enough in its influence to be given its conceptual role in any general theory of social process.

NOTES

1. Kingsley Davis, "The Urbanization of the Human Population," *Scientific American*, September 1965, p. 41.

2. Figures are taken from Ralph Thomlinson, *Population Dynamics* (New York: Random House, 1965), p. 276.

3. *Ibid.*, pp. 274–275. By way of contrast, at the time of the Spanish Conquest, Mexico City was estimated at some 300,000. It was believed that perhaps four to six Mayan cities had populations of at least 200,000. The largest cities in the late Middle Ages were probably in China and India.

4. The classic study is Henri Pirenne, *Medieval Cities: Their Origins and the Revival of Trade* (Princeton: Princeton University Press, 1925). A more recent and valuable treatment is Fritz Rorig, *Medieval Towns* (Berkeley: University of California Press, 1967).

5. J. D. Chambers, "Three Essays on the Population and Economy of the Midlands," in D. V. Glass and D. E. C. Eversley, eds., *Population in History* (London: Edward Arnold, 1965), p. 335.

6. *Ibid.*, p. 349. Phyllis Deane, in her very careful study, *The First Industrial Revolution* (Cambridge: Cambridge University Press, 1965), pp. 33–34, writes:

It is clear that there was a complex two-way relationship of cause and effect shaping these two trends—population on the one hand and output on the other—even if it is not clear exactly what form that relationship took at all times . . . it seems reasonable to suppose that without the growth of output dating from the 1740's the associated growth in population would eventually have been checked by a rise in the death rate due to declining standards of living. It seems equally probable that without the population growth which gathered momentum in the second half of the eighteenth century, the British industrial revolution would have been retarded for lack of labour. It seems likely that without the rising demand and prices which reflected, *inter alia*, the growth of population, there would have been less incentive for British producers to expand and innovate, and hence that some of the dynamism which powered the industrial revolution would have been lost. It seems equally likely that the expanding employment opportunities created by the industrial revolution encouraged people to marry and to produce families earlier than in the past, and that they increased the average expectation of life.

7. Arthur R. Schlesinger, "The City in American History," in P. Hatt and A. Reiss, eds., *Reader in Urban Sociology* (Glencoe: The Free Press, 1951), p. 110.

8. John R. Commons has described the process in his classic study, "American Shoemakers, 1648–1895: A Sketch of Industrial Evolution," *Quarterly Journal of Economics* (24 November 1909): 39–84.

9. Joanne E. Holler, *Population Growth and Social Change in the Middle East* (Washington, D.C.: George Washington University Press, 1964), p. 8. Reprinted with permission of the publisher. Other members of the "new middle class" include "the new independent class of intellectuals and specialists recruited from prosperous peasant families and the sons of the rich landowners."

10. United Nations, Economic Commission for Asia and the Far East (ECAFE), *Economic Bulletin for Asia and the Far East*, December 1959, p. 21.

11. United Nations, ECAFE, *Report of the Expert Working Group on Problems of Internal Migration and Urbanization and Selected Papers* (New York, 1967), p. 37.

12. *Ibid.*, pp. 31–32.

13. Louis Wirth, "Urbanism as a Way of Life," *American Journal of Sociology* 44 (July 1938): 9.

14. John Stuart Mill, *Essays on Politics and Culture*, ed. Gertrude Himmelfarb (New York: Doubleday, Anchor Books, 1963), p. 266.

15. Emile Durkheim, *The Division of Labor in Society*, trans. George Simpson (New York: The Free Press, 1964), pp. 336–337.

16. Wilbur Thompson, "The Economic Base of Urban Problems," in N. W. Chamberlain, ed., *Contemporary Economic Issues* (Homewood, Ill.: Richard D. Irwin, 1969), p. 8.

17. Raymond Vernon, *Metropolis 1985: an Interpretation of the Findings of the New York Metropolitan Region Study* (Cambridge: Harvard University Press, 1960).

18. Adna F. Weber, *The Growth of Cities in the Nineteenth Century* (Ithaca: Cornell University Press, 1965), p. 442.

19. Nathan Keyfitz, "Population Density and the Style of Social Life," *BioScience* 16 (December 1966):869.

20. "The village within the city of Calcutta or Madras may well have its own temple and traditional service occupations: sweepers, watchmen, priests, headmen. Some physical production by village methods goes on, and there are tanners, potters, and makers of bullockcarts—but very few farmers. Each compressed village in the city may have some residue of the administrative structure of the village its inhabitants have left, and village factionalism need not be forgotten on the move to the city." *Ibid.*, p. 872.
Another observer comments that most of Calcutta's poor are distributed among locales or areas each of which is "more like a village—one whose fields have been devoured by locusts—than a typical urban slum." Joseph Lelyveld, *New York Times Magazine*, 13 October 1968, p. 62.

21. Holler, *Population Growth and Social Change in the Middle East*, p. 46.

22. Karl Polanyi has dealt with this aspect of western society in *The Great Transformation* (New York: Rinehart, 1944).

23. Weber, *The Growth of Cities in the Nineteenth Century*, p. 432.

24. George Simmel, "Die Grossstädte und das Geistesleben," *Die Grossstadt* (Dresden: Theodor Petermann, 1903) quoted in Wirth, *American Journal of Sociology* 44 (July 1938):53.
Nathan Keyfitz has commented similarly: "Each of us as city people has contact in a day with as many individuals as the villager meets in the course of a lifetime; this includes store clerks, bus conductors, taxi drivers, students, colleagues, theatre ushers, not to mention those we pass as we walk or drive along the street. It would destroy us if we had to react to every one of them as people. We want to know about each of them only enough to cover his particular relationship with us." *BioScience* 16 (December 1966):870.

25. *Time*, 18 July 1969, recalled the incident and reported on research being conducted into the causes of such social—or asocial—behavior. A team of two (John Darley of Princeton and Bibb Latane of Ohio State University) concluded that inaction by some induces inaction by others. Leonard Berkowitz of the University of Wisconsin believes that those weighing the possible risks of intervening are concerned about losing their "freedom."

26. Alfred Kazin, "The Writer and the City," *Harper's Magazine*, December 1968, p. 127.

27. *New York Times*, 20 April 1969. Zimbardo's comment, "Conditions which foster deindividuation make each of us a potential assassin," seems either exaggerated or truistic, but Jules Pfeiffer's play, "The Little Murders," offers him literary support.

28. Professional police forces in the United States date from the 1840's, when they were organized "to restore order to America's large cities." Sam B. Warner, Jr., "Population Movements and Urbanization," in Melvin Kranzberg and Carroll W. Pursell, eds., *Technology in Western Civilization* (London: Oxford University Press, 1967), 1:544.

29. Alexis de Tocqueville, *Democracy in America* (New York: Alfred A. Knopf, 1945), 1:299-300.

30. This proposition has been supported by, among others, former Senator Paul A. Douglas, Chairman of the President's Commission on Civil Disorders and a former president of the American Economic Association. *New York Times*, 18 July 1968.

31. From a study undertaken by Patricia Leavey Hodge and Philip M. Hauser, *The Challenge of America's Metropolitan Outlook—1960 to 1985* (Washington: National Commission on Urban Problems, 1968), Ch. 4.

32. James C. Coke, "The Lesser Metropolitan Areas of Illinois," *Illinois Government* (November 1962), cited by Norton E. Long in L. Schnore and H. Fagin, eds., *Urban Research and Policy Planning* (Beverly Hills, Calif.: Sage Publications, 1967), p. 251.

33. Holler, *Population Growth and Social Change in the Middle East*, p. 4.

34. It has often been pointed out that Marx relied on the urban proletariat to overthrow bourgeois society, but that revolution actually came, when it did, in largely agricultural Russia. Nevertheless, revolution in Russia was not a peasant undertaking but chiefly one of urban workers. One need not argue that urban masses will always revolt: they may be quite passively contained. Or that rural groups will never be induced to seek social change: they may coalesce around a superior leader. The only point is that cities provide the arena in which pressures for change are most likely to be felt, and in which forces for change are most likely to be organized.

35. Joseph Lelyveld, *New York Times Magazine*, 13 October 1968, pp. 77-78.

36. Thus from the 1967 *Report of the Expert Working Group on Problems of Internal Migration and Urbanization* of the United Nations' Economic Commission for Asia and the Far East (ECAFE), pp. 42-43, referring to the problems of all the countries in that area:

> Heavy flows of urbanward migration and the resulting concentration of population have serious social and economic implications. In the last ten years many urban areas in the region have doubled their population and some of them are expected to double their population again by 1975. Concern was expressed about overcrowding, spread of slums and shanty towns; difficulties of waste disposal; juvenile delinquency; transport problems; housing shortages; education facilities, etc. It was pointed out that overcrowded parts of urban centres which often lack recreational facilities may well be the breeding ground of extreme elements, juvenile delinquents, criminals, etc. Further, large scale rural-urban migration may also convert rural underemployment into a problem of urban unemployment, thus adding to social unrest in urban areas.
>
> The health of city inhabitants is endangered by inadequacy of pure water supply and sewerage systems. Migrants from rural areas have mostly no

experience of the problems of city living or knowledge of urban hygiene. Improving transport facilities, increasing education facilities, and constructing additional housing units are some of the major problems of rapid urbanization. . . .

37. *Report of the National Advisory Commission on Civil Disorders* (New York: Bantam, 1968), p. 398.

38. Marshall Wolfe, "Some Implications of Recent Changes in Urban and Rural Settlement Patterns in Latin America," in United Nations, *World Population Conference* (New York: 1965), 4:457–460.

39. Warren C. Robinson, "Urbanization and Fertility: the Non-Western Experience," *The Milbank Memorial Fund Quarterly*, July 1963, quoted in United Nations, ECAFE, *Report of the Expert Working Group on Problems of Internal Migration and Urbanization*, p. 133.

40. Kingsley Davis, "The Urbanization of the Human Population," *Scientific American*, September 1965, p. 49. Davis adds: "The only rivals in an earlier day were the frontier nations, which had the help of great streams of immigrants." I have drawn heavily on this excellent article by perhaps the foremost student of urbanization.

41. *Ibid.*, p. 50. The study by Robinson referred to in note 39 has also explored this question of the relative fertility rates of country and city. His findings, using data for selected underdeveloped countries, were to the effect that the pattern differed. In some countries, the traditional fertility difference occurred, chiefly because of the lower incidence of marriage among urban females. But in other countries, in accordance with Davis's conclusion, when allowance is made for differential infant mortality, virtually no fertility difference between village and city is discernible.

42. *Ibid.*, p. 51. "In the 19th and early 20th centuries the growth of cities arose from and contributed to economic advancement. Cities took surplus manpower from the countryside and put it to work producing goods and services that in turn helped to modernize agriculture. But today in underdeveloped countries, as in present-day advanced nations, city growth has become increasingly unhinged from economic development and hence from rural-urban migration. It derives in greater degree from overall population growth, and this growth in nonindustrial lands has become unprecedented because of modern health techniques combined with high birth rates" (p. 52).

Some experts still maintain that rural migration is a major cause of city growth in the underdeveloped countries. Myrdal, for example, argues this for South Asia. *Asian Drama: An Inquiry into the Poverty of Nations* (New York: The Twentieth Century Fund, 1969), 1:470–471. But the United Nations, ECAFE *Report of the Expert Working Group on Problems of Internal Migration and Urbanization* (1967), tends to support the view that it is more overall population increase than rural migration that is adding to the growth of cities.

"Considering the fact that there is no evidence of significant differences in rural-urban fertility in many Asian countries (in view of the absence or extremely limited use of contraception this is but natural), *a more basic problem of urbanization is likely to be posed by the accelerating rates of population growth than by the phenomenon of rural over-population pushing millions of people into the cities.* Under conditions of rapid population growth, 'push' is everywhere—both in the rural areas *and* in the urban areas" (pp. 100–101, italics in the original).

CHAPTER 5

Population and the Forms of Government

SINCE the time of Plato there has been a recurring philosophic concern with the influence of the size of a population on the form of its government. Rather than undertake a chronicle of such thought, we shall let Jean-Jacques Rousseau serve as the principal spokesman and build our discussion around his views. Set forth in *The Social Contract* in 1762, Rousseau's is perhaps the most penetrating analysis on this subject that has yet been made, whether or not one is disposed to agree with his conclusions. Because of its careful precision, we shall have to summarize it at some length.

Rousseau

Every member of a society enters into a "social contract" simply by the act of his being and remaining a member of that society. That contract calls into existence a "collective moral body" made up of all citizens, who jointly exercise sovereign power. Each individual thus functions in a dual capacity, on the one hand as sharer in the sovereignty of the state, on the other as a subject of the state.

Sovereignty expresses itself as the will of the people, the General Will. It is not necessary for it to be unanimous to be general. "What is necessary is that every voice be taken into account," and that there be no systematic exclusion of any person or class. "Laws are nothing more nor less than the terms of association of civil society."[1] Even if designated men of superior wisdom serve as legislators, they do not exercise sovereignty; their drafts of laws are invalid unless approved by the citizens as a whole, exercising their collective and inalienable sovereignty.

Laws are general, not particular. Their application to particular situations is not an exercise of sovereignty but an executive act. To apply the law, a government is created, which can be defined simply as an intermediate agency between the people collectively in their sovereign capacity and the people individually in their role as subjects. This is the sole function of government, whatever its form, whether hereditary king or elected official. The legitimacy of any government rests on its consonance with the General Will.

Now enters the factor of size, both as to territorial extent and numbers of population. A state can be too small in area to survive by its own efforts. It must have a sufficient geographical base to permit it to establish a kind of equilibrium with the other states to which it is contiguous. It can also become too large to be governed well, since administration is less efficient when conducted over great distances, and the costs of administration increase excessively. The government of a larger state tends to move more sluggishly. Its far-flung subjects feel less of a common interest. Their dissimilarities which spring from the customs of their particular locales have a divisive effect. As far as the man-land ratio goes, there cannot be too small a population to defend its territory or to make economic use of its resources, just as there cannot be too large a population for the resources at its disposal.

But these are simply the practical considerations underlying the more fundamental effect of population size on people's liberty. We have seen that an individual functions in two capacities, one as part of the collective sovereign, the second as subject. If, says Rousseau, a state had a population of 10,000, then the sovereign is to the subject in the ratio of 10,000 to one. But suppose that the population increases to 100,000. The status of the individual as subject remains as before, but he now exercises only a hundred-thousandth of the collective sovereignty. His vote, his influence over the General Will, has been reduced to a tenth of what it formerly was. ". . . each increase in the state's numbers means a proportionate reduction in the amount of liberty."[2]

But this is not all. The more people—and therefore the more heterogeneous—who compose the General Will, the greater the likelihood of divergence between it and the private will of each subject. The more repressive must laws become to insure compliance. As a population grows, then, the government must become stronger for effective execution of the laws.

How does a government increase its strength? Not by increasing the number of its officials, since that would simply lead to a greater need for internal governmental coordination. Indeed, the government becomes less effective as the number of its officials increases. Its only means of strengthening itself is by becoming more compact:

as a population increases, the government must become concentrated in fewer hands. For the largest states, a single supreme magistrate, monarch, or prince is needed.

This principle, that the powers of government should be concentrated in fewer and fewer hands as a population increases, relates only to the effectiveness of government. But something else is happening as the government becomes entrusted to a smaller number of officials or to a single chief executive. A government is legitimate only insofar as its actions coincide with the General Will, but the fewer the people in government, the more it will surely reflect the private wills of the executive. There is thus a conflict between the need for governmental strength and the government's legitimacy; as one increases, the other declines. The growth of a population drives it almost inescapably (chance events aside) in the direction of a stronger, more concentrated, but less legitimate government. The requirements of governmental effectiveness and legitimacy must thus always be brought into some balanced relationship with each other, and that balance, determining the form of government, is a function of the size of population.

A direct democracy is impossible. That would require that all the people not only function in their sovereign capacity, in making the laws of their association, but also would function collectively in administering them, which is clearly impractical. No population large enough to defend itself and work the economy would be small enough to meet constantly to discharge the public business. And the moment they set up administrative agencies, direct democracy would be lost.

For Rousseau, the most desirable form of government is an elected aristocracy, by which he really means a representative form of government. It is more efficient than democracy, but because it involves a number of officials rather than one it is not so concentrated that the vital distinction between the General Will of the sovereign people cannot be maintained against the private will of those entrusted with government. At the same time, Rousseau recognizes that in fact governments tend to be a blend or mixture of forms. Even a direct democracy, if it could function, would need some headman if for no other purpose than to assemble the people and to moderate their meetings, and even a single ruler must have subordinate officials.

But if Rousseau accepts a form of representative government, he is firm in his refusal to accept any representative exercise of sovereignty. Only the people in their collective sovereignty can make a law valid. That may conceivably require cumbersome and expensive procedures, but there is no way out unless people are willing to make themselves slaves to someone else. And in the light of this severe requirement, Rousseau concludes that a sovereign people can retain the powers that belong to it only if they restrict their numbers to the size of a small city. Nor did he believe this was at all impractical. He apparently had in mind that such small sovereignties should insure their own survival through some form of confederation.

Rousseau was following the position of Plato and Aristotle in concluding that only in a political unit the size of a city was good government possible. Aristotle, in *Politics*, had written:

A state then only begins to exist when it has attained a population sufficient for a good life in the political community; it may indeed somewhat exceed this number. But . . . there must be a limit. What should be the limit will be easily ascertained by experience. For both governors and governed have duties to perform; the special functions of a governor are to command and to judge. But if the citizens of a state are to judge and to distribute offices according to merit, then they must know each other's characters; where they do not possess this knowledge, both the election to offices and the decision of law suits will go wrong . . . Clearly, then, the best limit of the population of a state is the largest number which suffices for the purposes of life, and can be taken in at a single view.[3]

Aristotle reflected the institutions of Athens, whose number of participating citizens was perhaps about 40,000. Rotation of public office was frequent, and each citizen had an equal opportunity to serve a short term. Certain offices were filled by lot, a tradition which has persisted into our jury system, as a kind of institutional commitment to the proposition that in important respects all citizen members of the community can be viewed as equal. Athens has always been considered the classic example of a direct democracy, although (as Rousseau pointed out) it could not do without representative procedures, and so fell short of a "pure" democracy in which all citizens function as the executive government. In his words, "The sharing out of executive power is thus always a matter of degree—of a larger number of officials or a lesser."[4] Athens took its place far to the left of the spectrum, with a larger number of citizens serving as executive officials.

Closer to Rousseau in point of time and of a similar view as to the relation between the size of a population and its form of government was Montesquieu, whose *Spirit of the Laws* influenced political thinking in the formative period of the United States.

> It is natural for a republic to have only a small territory. In an extensive republic, the public good is sacrificed to a thousand private views. . . . In a small one, the interest of the public is more obvious, better understood, and more within the reach of every citizen. . . . The natural property of small states is to be governed by a republic; of middling ones to be subject to a monarch, and of large empires to be swayed by a despotic prince.[5]

Liberty—Ancient and Modern

The view that the size of a population was a major determinant of the form of government was clearly well established by the close of the eighteenth century. So too was the view that this relationship demonstrated the desirability of a state sufficiently limited in size to give effect to the sovereignty of the people, without undue loss of that legitimacy of government which Rousseau had demonstrated diminished as a population grew. But now we encounter a related philosophical issue which gave a quite unexpected turn to the discussion.[6] With Rousseau, as with the classics, "liberty" had been identified with the citizen's participation in the functions of sovereignty, above all with the making of laws and decisions as to war and peace. But that sovereign participation carried with it, *as corollary*, the complete subjection of the individual to the exercise of collective sovereignty. The social contract reduces to a single stipulation: "the total alienation to the whole community of each associate, together with every last one of his rights."[7] How else could the citizen share in *sovereignty* unless he, like everyone else, were completely *subject?* ". . . The essence of political society lies in the coincidence of obedience and freedom, and . . . the words 'subject' and 'sovereign,' whose meanings are brought together in the word 'citizen,' are correlative and inseparable."[8]

A people's liberty lay in its own exercise of sovereignty. Anything else would be subservience or slavery. But liberty thus interpreted likewise implied the total subjection of the individual to the sovereign collectivity, Rousseau's General Will.

As Benjamin Constant observed in his celebrated lecture in 1819, "The Liberty of the Ancients Compared to that of the Moderns":

Thus among the ancients, the individual, while he was habitually sovereign in public affairs, was a slave in his private affairs. As citizen, he decided on peace and war; as private man he was circumscribed, spied upon, repressed in his every movement. As a part of the collective body he interrogates, dismisses, impeaches, despoils, banishes, condemns to death his public officers or superiors; as subjected to the collective body, he may in turn be shorn of his status, stripped of his dignities, banished, put to death by the discretionary will of the whole to which he belongs.[9]

But to Constant and to his "moderns" such a conception of liberty was deficient. Having observed the excesses of the French Revolution and the succeeding Napoleonic era, he could write: "When you assert that the sovereignty of the people is unlimited, you create and fling into human society a power which is in itself too great, and harmful in whatever hands it falls; entrust it to one, to several, to all, you will find it equally evil."[10]

The rising tide of liberalism and laissez-faire was having its effect. The conception of liberty held by the "ancients," and by Rousseau as well, no longer seemed the only guarantee against slavery. As the notion of individualism, a concept of very recent origin, began to take hold, liberty was regarded in a different light, as a protection of the individual against the intrusion of others, however "sovereign." Tocqueville, as late as 1840, could write:

Individualism is a novel expression, to which a novel idea has given birth. Our fathers were only acquainted with *egoisme* (selfishness). Selfishness is a passionate and exaggerated love of self, which leads a man to connect everything with himself and to prefer himself to everything in the world. Individualism is a mature and calm feeling, which disposes each member of the community to sever himself from the mass of his fellows and to draw apart with his family and his friends, so that after he has thus formed a little circle of his own, he willingly leaves society at large to itself.[11]

If the term "individualism" was of such recent origin, the conception had been slowly forming for more than a century, with its roots in England. There a combination of urbanization, industrialization, and a rising middle-class insurgency had found its philosophic expression in John Locke, its economic expression in Adam Smith, and its political expression in Jeremy Bentham. The Swiss economist and historian, Simonde de Sismondi, acknowledged the English contribution by saying that "up to the eighteenth century, the liberty of the citizen was always thought of as a participation in the sovereignty of his country, and that it is only the example of the British constitution which has taught us to think of liberty as a protection of the security, the happiness and the independence of daily life."[12]

The contrast between these two conceptions of liberty—one as the exercise of sovereignty, the other as immunity from that exercise—is sharply etched by Rousseau himself, who took issue with the "English" individualistic view. "The English people think itself free, but it is badly mistaken. It is free only during parliamentary elections; once the members of Parliament have been elected it lapses back into slavery, and becomes as nothing."[13]

Constant, unlike Rousseau, had greater sympathy with the new and rising conception of liberty, but at the same time he recognized its adverse effect on the exercise of sovereignty. "Among the moderns . . . the individual, independent as to his private life, is, even within the freest commonwealths, sovereign only in name. His sovereignty is a power almost ever in abeyance; and if, at some infrequent and fixed moments he is allowed to exercise this sovereignty, in a way that is carefully specified and limited, it is only to commit it to others."[14] It is not that Rousseau was wrong in logic: to the extent that the private life of individuals is immunized from intervention of the state, to that extent is the sovereignty of the state (the people as a collectivity) reduced.[15] But to the moderns, he was wrong in the conclusions he drew, the values he tried to preserve. Liberty in the sense of the people's sovereignty was not as important as liberty in the sense of the individual's "bill of rights."

The American Dilemma and Its Resolution

The significance of this fundamental philosophical controversy for our interest in the influence of population on governmental form is very great, and nowhere did it have greater impact than in the United States. There, the philosophically minded founding fathers were conversant with both the French (Montesquieu-Rousseau) and English (Locke-Smith) sides of the argument and were intellectually drawn to the wisdom of both positions. On the one hand, they entertained a fear of the effect which large and dense populations would have on the quality of government; they were concerned with the danger of despots and demagogues. Pure democracy, the New England town meeting, was the desideratum, and if not on a national scale, then a representative government that came close to Rousseau's "elected aristocracy." On the other hand, they had written the rights of the individual into the constitution, and were strongly motivated by the enterprising spirit of laissez-faire which, to the extent it was successful on a new continent, was bound to lead them into an expanded geographical area and a growing population, and hence require a strong central government. Ambivalence between these two points of view characterized the first half century of the new nation.[16]

Indeed, the conflict between these two positions endangered adoption of the Constitution in 1787. The fear that the new federation would embark on a path of empire, undermining the republican form of government to which the original states were committed, engendered a strong reluctance among some delegates to the Constitutional Convention to any strengthening of the ties among the states. It was important to find philosophical justification for guiding the rising star of democracy along a path which some of the greatest minds of the past had said would inevitably lead to tyranny and despotism. It was James Madison who provided the resolution.[17]

Madison compared a pure or direct democracy with a representative government, to determine which is preferable. The two major distinctions between them are that, first, the republican form delegates the governmental function instead of exercising it directly, and second, the republican form embraces a larger population and a larger territory. What, he asks, are the effects of these differences?

The effect of the delegation of government is to "refine and enlarge the public views, by passing them through the medium of a chosen body of citizens." This is likely to mean that decisions will be more carefully considered than if reached by the electorate as a whole. Nevertheless, the opposite result is always possible: intrigue or corruption among the representatives may betray the interests of the people. However, the fact that the republic embraces a larger population than a democracy is in its favor in this respect, since it will include a larger number of able people capable of filling the representative role, and since unworthy candidates will experience greater difficulty in misleading a larger constituency.

The second difference between the two forms of government lies in the larger population and territory of the republic over the pure democracy. But, and this was Madison's trump card, this very size "renders factious combinations less to be dreaded." Madison was much concerned over the danger that factions might develop which could control the powers of government in their own special interest, abusing the rights of others. This danger would be lessened by the larger size of a representative republic.

The smaller the society, the fewer probably will be the distinct parties and interests composing it; the fewer the distinct parties and interests, the more frequently will a majority be found of the same party; and the smaller the number of individuals composing a majority, and the smaller the compass within which they are placed, the more easily will they concert and execute their plans of oppression. Extend the sphere, and you take in a greater variety of parties and interests; you make it less probable that a majority of the whole will have a common motive to invade the rights of other citizens; or if such a common motive exists, it will be more difficult for all who feel it to discover their own strength, and to act in unison with each other.

Now Madison moves on to clinch the argument which was intended to be persuasive of the advantage of federalism over state autonomy and which was later turned to the support of westward expansion: ". . . the same advantage which a republic has over a democracy, in controlling the effects of faction, is enjoyed by a larger over a small republic—is enjoyed by the Union over the States composing it."

The influence of factious leaders may kindle a flame within their particular States, but will be unable to spread a general conflagration through the other States. A religious sect may degenerate into a political faction in a part of the Confederacy; but the variety of sects dispersed over the entire face of it must secure the national councils against any danger from that source. A rage for paper money, for an abolition of debts, for an equal division of property, or for any other improper or wicked project, will be less apt to pervade the whole body of the Union than a particular member of it; in the same proportion as such a malady is more likely to taint a particular county or district, than an entire State.

The Madisonian thesis carried the day. Despite recurrent misgivings, the future lay with individualism (liberty in the newer sense) and expansion. Jefferson, in his second inaugural address in 1804, gave wholehearted support to Madison's thesis in justifying acquisition of the Louisiana Territory. "Who can limit the extent to which the federative principle may operate effectively? The larger our association, the less will it be shaken by local passions."

In fairness to Madison it should be noted that he did not believe in indefinite extensibility of representative government. ". . . The natural limit of a republic is that distance from the center which will barely allow the representatives to meet as often as may be necessary for the administration of public affairs." At the same time he was optimistic in believing that "intercourse throughout the Union will be facilitated by new improvements," so that presumably the frontier would be a constantly moving one. And even this proviso said nothing about population density as a limit to effective representation.

The effect of both English liberalism and its American justification was to remove population expansion as a barrier to effective representative government. Even a large society could preserve its representative institutions from degenerating into tyranny by the few over the many. It remained only to make a terminological modification to sanction the altered perspective, and it was not long in coming. The term "democracy" was loosened from its customary reference to government by the people as a whole and applied equally to government through representatives elected by the people as a whole. It is not wholly clear how this change came about. In part, perhaps because of the extension of the ballot to larger numbers. In part, perhaps because of the identification by Tocqueville, and others of his persuasion, of democracy with equality, and of America with democracy in this sense.

In any event, the conviction that had come down through the centuries that a populous society could be governed only by *undemocratic* governments was largely laid to rest. It was agreed that the possible forms of representation were various. Burke had argued that representatives need not even be elected in order to be truly responsive to the best interests of their constituencies. Mill, fearful of the dominance of majorities over minorities, expressed his approval of proportional representation. The Progressive Movement in the United States sought to recapture some element of representative responsibility and even direct democratic action by espousing the initiative, the referendum, and the recall. Among countries following this swing to representative forms of democratic government, practices have differed widely as to the representative-constituency ratio, the manner of election of representatives, and their powers in office. Through all this diversity of thought and practice, there remains a modern belief, certainly in the western world, in the democratic character of elective representative governments, whatever their form, when coupled with respect for the rights of individuals.

Marxism and Nationalism

In conceptualizing the relation between a population and its government, the Marxist countries have followed a different development,
whose line travels from Hegel through Marx to Lenin. Rousseau's
notion of the General Will comported perfectly with Hegel's belief in a national spirit. Hegel agreed that direct democracy was
possible only in "states which do not much exceed the compass of
cities."[18] Only in such small units are citizens' interests sufficiently
homogeneous, and can the inhabitants, seeing each other daily,
enter into a democratic life with their whole personalities, not only
with their votes. This is manifestly impractical in contemporary
society. The English solution is unacceptable, since representative
parliament is not the embodiment of the national spirit but of special
interests. What is needed is a class of representatives who are national or universal in their outlook, detached from and impartial
toward the social and private interests which they regulate. This
Hegelian view had its influence on Marx.

To Marx, as to Lenin after him, government always represented
the ruling class. That was its function, indeed, its legitimate function.
It is the institutionalization of force or violence by one part of the
population against another part of the population. It was to be expected that government in the age of industrialization should represent the interests of the middle class or bourgeoisie as against the
excluded proletariat. It was also to be expected that when the proletariat came to power it would use the force of government to
liquidate the old institutions and install the new. But once that was
accomplished and the very notion of differentiated classes had been
wiped out, so that no part of the population sought to exploit another part, the need for government itself would vanish. The spontaneous will of the people would be the only authentic political
force.

This rather mystical conception was never given an analytical
elaboration, but it clearly is closer conceptually to the classical
version of democracy. It would make the people sovereign. Presumably a representative government would be needed for administrative purposes, but its actions would coincide in intent with the
sovereign will. Where it departs is in believing that this can occur
spontaneously and without respect to size of population.

It thus appears that philosophical concern with the size of population as influential over the possibility of democratic government ends on the one hand with Locke and Madison and on the other hand with Hegel and Marx. When democracy is equated with either representation and a bill of rights or with the disappearance of economic classes and the dictatorship of the proletariat, the issue of the effect of population size on the state disappears.

This prestidigital phenomenon has been further strengthened by the rise of nationalism in the present century and particularly since World War II. Wherever it appears, nationalism has almost invariably been characterized as "democratic," whatever the form of government propelling it forward. Tocqueville's justification could probably be given for using the term, since in most instances nationalistic governments are for greater equality among the citizenry and for a reduction of the privileges of the elite. They generally seek a redistribution of authority and the social advantage which runs in part to their own interest but which uses economic development and an improvement of the lot of the masses as its vehicle. But once again use of the term in such a manner eliminates the classical concern with the size of population on the form of government.

Population Effects Again

Unfortunately, Rousseau cannot be pushed aside so easily. However little we may accept his recommended policies today, we cannot avoid confronting the issues he raised. For one thing, the meaning of representation is wonderfully ambiguous. When is a person represented or not represented? Is it necessary that his representative be conversant with his views and private interests? If conversant, must he be responsive? In what way? Must the individual be in a position to influence his representative's judgment? Does his representative have the privilege of using his own best judgment, perhaps trading-off certain constituents' interests in order to serve the interests of others when this seems desirable? How weigh the public good, if that is to be served, against constituent welfare? And how effective does the representative have to be in legislating in order to be considered representative? If he is one of so large a number that his voice counts little, may it be that he himself requires representation to a second degree? If the issues to which he addresses himself are so numerous and complex that he cannot himself form an opinion but must rely on experts, has he not already delegated the citizen's vote a second time? Would a citizen be represented if his country were run by a single official but he had a vote in the choice of that official?

Whether these questions are raised in a purely hypothetical or in a politically urgent way depends to a significant extent on the effects of population size. If these questions are meaningful, so too is the issue of the influence of the size of a society on its form of government.

Tocqueville urged that equality of treatment of every citizen is the essential ingredient of a democratic society, whether or not possessing a democratic government in the classical sense. Even if we accept his formulation, to have equality of treatment there must also be equality of representation. And how shall we define that? Does it require that all electoral units be equal in size, so that one man's vote in a given constituency weighs the same as another man's vote in any other constituency, in arriving at a collective decision, as the United States Supreme Court ruled, within certain limits, in *Baker* v. *Carr?* Does it require some control over political campaign expenditures, so that special interests are not enabled to buy their candidate his office and thereby benefit disproportionately from his representative function, as the Congress sought rather weakly to accomplish in the Hatch Act? Does it require special assistance to the poorly educated and special protection to the exploited, as Congress attempted to encourage in civil rights and poverty legislation? Does it require certain definition or redefinition of electoral units so that some minority groups are not always disenfranchised even though technically possessing and actually exercising the right to vote?

All these questions are affected by population distribution and density and the composition of a society's people. They raise the fundamental issue of whether equality of representation is ever feasible, or whether representation, like the social advantage, is not inevitably unequally apportioned. If so, its distribution and redistribution is, as we have already seen, at least partially and certainly importantly, a function of population change. Different constituencies, involving different representation, would lead to different results in the apportionment of both benefits and disadvantages.

The most crucial question is whether a large population, waiving the subsidiary question of just what that means, does not require a more centralized government. The answer, as Rousseau and his classical predecessors saw, would seem clearly to be in the affirmative, but it is a more complicated answer than a simple affirmative suggests. We shall be dealing with its complications for the remainder of this chapter.

Briefly, as the number of people expands, the number of special interests which have to be made compatible with each other increases. The cohesion which in a smaller society comes with greater naturalness out of common traditions and beliefs has to be contrived and engineered when a society becomes larger and more heterogeneous. There is a parallel here between the problems engendered by the heterogeneity of the city as against the village or small town; the populous society is the city writ large.

Size and Regulation

In the larger society the powers of the government to induce or compel actions on the part of constituent groups must be augmented, or it will be unable to carry off satisfactorily its bargaining relation with such groups and still possess enough authority to initiate those actions which appear needed if the society is to meet the changes which it cannot avoid, changes in both its internal and external environments. The fact that it is an elected government, and therefore in some sense representative, does not alter the fact that its authority increases relative to those who elect it and relative to the governments of the smaller units of which it is composed, and must increase if it is to do its job.

The denser a society becomes, the more need for the regulation of its individual members in the interests of all. Matters which in a simpler setting could be left to the individual become the concern of the group. An individual's health is more than a personal matter when it can have repercussive effect on others, or when one's actions, but multiplied many times over, can have a deleterious effect on others' health. A youngster's education might be left to the family in a smaller society where social pressures contained the illiterates and incompetents, but in a large industrialized and urbanized society the education of its members is of importance to all, and cannot be left to the family.

We have already encountered this interdependency effect in discussing the growth of cities. "In the country, a man might construct his own home, build his fire, erect his privy, and dispose of his rubbish without thought for the well-being of his neighbors, but in town these things become objects of community concern and gradually of city ordinance. In the country a man might be little affected by the poverty or wrongdoing of others, but the towns soon discovered their civic responsibility in the combatting and control of these social evils."[19] As population increases, the impact of town on town, of city on country, of suburb on city likewise manifests itself; interdependency extends beyond the relations internal to the denser city and embraces the relations internal to the denser country. How a city or town disposes of its sewage and rubbish, obtains its water supply, and controls its crime become issues of importance to areas outside its boundaries.

But we can go much farther. How *individuals* conduct their affairs in one part of the country affects individuals in other areas. The businessman who markets adulterated or injurious drugs, contaminated foods, or dangerous products cannot be controlled by the social pressures of his neighbors when his dealings are principally with people with whom he never comes in contact. The promoter who exploits the wilderness in developing natural resources can be regarded quite differently in a thinly settled community, where wilderness is plentiful, than he is in a more densely settled country where wilderness is becoming rare. The businessman who invests, or does not invest, when other businessmen are doing the same thing may be quite innocently contributing to inflation or recession. We could extend almost indefinitely the catalogue of such interdependency effects, increasing with population density.

To cope with these relationships, government must intervene with regulation. Ironically, the consequence is to diminish both liberty as conceived by the ancients and liberty as conceived by the moderns. The government acts without the direct consent of the people, at best through representatives however far removed from their constituencies, and liberty in the sense of the active participation in the exercise of sovereignty is necessarily sacrificed. Liberty in the sense of an inviolable area of personal privilege is likewise eroded when the need for regulation in the interests of all intrudes on the sphere of individual rights. The effect of density on free speech was noted by Justice Holmes when he said that a man did not have the right to yell "Fire" in a crowded theater. With an expanding population, the country at large becomes the equivalent of the crowded theater, and a number of private actions previously considered as rights become the equivalent of yelling "Fire."

The government's regulatory powers are not only repressive, however. They must include as well the capacity to induce private actions which are affirmatively wanted: the businessman's investment, the child's education, the employment of members of minority groups, the supply of minimum nutritional needs to the impoverished, and, above all, the financial contributions of citizens through a variety of taxes. The number and importance of such needed affirmative actions on the part of private individuals and institutions increase with the increase in population, and along with the increase in need goes a concomitant increase in central government authority so that the need can be met.

While all this is occurring, there also takes place an increase in knowledge and in technological innovation. The subjects of control and the means of regulation become increasingly technical and complex. (This too, we may recall, is related to population growth.) With greater complexity the government must rely more on expert advice. More and more the experts tend to substitute for the elected representatives. The tendency was noted by Senator Fulbright on the floor of the Senate a few years ago, when he called attention to the way in which military experts virtually dictated decisions which nominally were Congress's to make.[20] The same tendency was the occasion of a bitter all-night debate in the French Assembly at the time of adoption of the Fourth Plan, when members repeatedly complained that they were being confronted with a master plan so technically coherent that they were advised that to tinker with any part would destroy the whole.[21]

Once again, the effect is to concentrate greater power in the hands of the central government. A large representative legislature cannot collectively act on technical expert advice; it can only accept or reject it. Its function becomes more and more reduced to that of delay or veto. Initiative passes into the hands of the executive office. Rousseau's sovereign powers are delegated to that which should be subordinate to sovereign power. And the result is generally approved by the "progressive" elements in a society, since only in this fashion can action be taken on the problems which are pressing—problems which as often as not have their origin in the growth and composition of population.

The Design of Systems

I would speculate at this point, though somewhat hesitantly, that even the evident tendency for social scientists to become increasingly "scientific" in their studies springs in part from this population effect on the practice of government. Of course there are more influences at work than this; for one thing, the increased specialization that comes with the advance of knowledge. Nevertheless, it seems to me an entirely tenable hypothesis that the effort to "scientify" the study of human relationships rises in some degree from the fact that when numbers of people get sufficiently large they must be *controlled*, we begin to study people as objects with governmental support and subsidy.

In any event, integration of people into a functioning society becomes less and less the function of primary social institutions—the family, the school, the church, the work group—and more and more the function of social engineers and systems analysts. The system is contrived, and the individual and group find their place within the expertly designed system. As the system is changed, so too are the functions of the individual, who must adjust (be "retrained") or find himself excluded from the system; provided for but unneeded. If this exaggerates the present state of affairs in the most industrialized economies, it does so only slightly.[22] The system is fashioned by experts, who must work with human material which is not as malleable as might be desired but which, with increasing knowledge of human behavior, can be reasonably well controlled. The individual finds his place in the system; he may change roles, but always within the system context.

One may write regretfully (romantically regretfully) of this development, but it is hard to see what other course is possible with a large population. A dense population may develop its institutions in a spontaneous or evolutionary fashion, but this cannot be relied on. It becomes necessary to "improve on nature" by artful contrivance. Institutions must be consciously built, and individuals must find their roles within such institutions: *this* is the organizational revolution. A few may escape the need, at least for a time—the "hippies" of the late 1960s, for example, or academic people in the period just prior to that. And some may be excluded from the opportunity: the long-term unemployed, an increasingly older "youth" category, and an increasingly younger "old age" category, for example. For most of the population, however, institutionalization of their activities is essential. The question is only how far such institutionalization need be carried, the extent to which the efficiency concepts characteristic of systems engineers and economic experts should be allowed to control.

The consciously organized aspect of large populations has its inevitable impact on our conceptions of individualism. Professor Ward has described with great felicity the shifting content of this term in the United States, from its earlier connotation of ebullient and aggressive action on the part of the rugged individual (as typified by Andrew Carnegie) to its present meaning of the individual's finding that place within the institutional design where he can best contribute to the organizational objective (as typified by Frederick Taylor).[23] In such an institutionalized society, the government's role as over-all organizer and controller of the system to which all other units are subsystems is inescapable. The only questions are of the degree, quality, and explicitness of its control.[24]

Centralization and Decentralization

Tocqueville believed that centralization of governmental functions comes naturally to a democracy. The stress on equality under the law encourages the idea of a single and central government over the whole of the country, affecting all equally. The rise of a middle class, which democracy promotes by giving rein to private actions, means that large numbers of the ablest citizens will be preoccupied with their own affairs and disinclined to take part in public business; they prefer to leave that to an elected government. With a propertied and numerous middle class comes also the desire for a strong central government to preserve law and order. Thus everything predisposes a democracy toward the support of a centralized administration.[25]

Although Tocqueville confidently believed that the American population would grow to a hundred million within the century, an expanding population was not one of the causes which he identified as making for centralization of government. We have seen how the need for coordinating decision-making units which, when of smaller size, could be given greater autonomy inevitably drives a growing society toward concentration of governmental authority, adding its weight to the influences mentioned by Tocqueville.

Such concentration may come in fact even if not provided for in law. Smaller jurisdictional units may cede their nominal authority to a central government which provides the funds and expertise for the solution of local problems. The number of elected representatives may prevent their effective participation in government, along with the increasing technical complexity of the issues which must be confronted, so that they defer to executive initiative. No formal change in government will have taken place, but the seat of sovereignty will have moved from the cumbersome legislature to the compact executive.

But this is no one-way movement. If more and more problems were channelled up to the executive office it would become glutted with matters awaiting action. The advantages of executive speed and decisiveness in contrast to legislative initiative would be lost. At the same time, the assertion of central authority in a given field, however necessary or appropriate, does not guarantee that local problems will be satisfactorily met. There are always special circumstances that require specialized information and differentiated action, and guidelines laid down by a distant authority sometimes impede or prohibit adaptive solutions. These two considerations dictate that as a central government draws more authority to itself in some areas, it releases authority to subordinate governmental units in other areas, and that in administering policies which apply unevenly to local areas, it permits considerable local discretion.

These movements of centralization and decentralization need not occur simultaneously; their timing is in large part related to the rate of population growth and urbanization. An expanded population may require centralized administration of educational policy, for example, at one point in time, to achieve equality of standards and opportunity among localities which are markedly dissimilar in their school programs. But, at a later period, the further growth of population and its concentration in metropolitan areas may necessitate decentralization of educational policies, within broad over-all guidelines, so that subpopulations which are markedly dissimilar may be more equally treated by means of programs geared to their specific needs.

If a central government fails to decentralize when this is called for, either or both of two consequences will ensue. The program in question may become more inefficient and ineffective, falling farther and farther short of its objective. In time, it is likely to evoke sufficient popular protest so that reform is forced on the government. This appears to be the situation in France today, where a centralized administrative structure going back to the Napoleonic era is showing less and less capability of confronting current problems. On the other hand, just as centralization may take place de facto, without provision in law, so may decentralization. Local administrations may find the means of modifying central programs to their own specifications; popular movements on a local scale may take initiative into their own hands, with the central government overlooking their mutinous action to avoid any direct challenge to its authority. This appears to be the situation in the government of the Catholic Church today, as local churches interpret central doctrines according to their own needs.[26]

Growth of a population, then, along with its urbanization, clearly drives a society in the direction of centralizing more of its functions in the national government. But just as clearly, the growth and urbanization of a society also require decentralization of certain functions which previously had been centrally controlled, in order to make them conformable to the special needs which have developed in certain large sectors.

This is by no means a balancing kind of two-way movement in which centralization is matched by decentralization. For one thing, decentralization of central government operations, when looked at from the point of view of the local government to which they are delegated, involves an expansion of local government, so that its functions, when looked at from the viewpoint of local institutions and groups, will have grown. Thus population growth is likely, over time, to force an increase in governmental coordinating and regulating functions at all levels. The fact that some central activities must be decentralized is simply a fresh proportioning of relative central and local functions so that these do not become either excessively concentrated or excessively dispersed for operational effectiveness. But over-all, over time, as a population expands and its cities become more densely settled, an increase in governmental functions is inescapable. And whatever the political unit, whether city, state, or nation, the governmental function is increasingly an executive, that is, centralized exercise.

An increase in population thus has its effect on the form of government by forcing greater centralization, in a dual sense. More problems are forced to the central, that is, national level of government, because of the need for system coordination. And more problems are forced to the central, that is, executive office, as the system of representation proves too cumbersome to deal with problems grown complex because of their scale and the possibilities of technical solution.[27]

Popular Government

Increasing numbers of people and a more concentrated form of government, coupled with improved means of communication (television and radio in particular), are a recipe for popular government, but not for democratic government. In the United States, for example, city bosses once could deliver enough votes, on the basis of deals, to put over a political candidate, but that possibility ended with World War II. Now the relationship between a candidate and the masses is more direct and immediate. In consequence, all the arts of mass communication are employed to merchandise a candidate like a new product. In the same way public policies are given an advertising appeal. This consciousness of the mass and of the necessity of winning its favor has its effect on the kinds of programs a candidate and a government propose. Louis Wirth made the assessment thirty years ago, with respect to urban society, and increasing urbanization now makes his comments applicable to a national "mass society."

When large numbers have to make common use of facilities and institutions, an arrangement must be made to adjust the facilities and institutions to the needs of the average person rather than to those of particular individuals. The services of the public utilities, of the recreational, educational, and cultural institutions must be adjusted to mass requirements. Similarly, the cultural institutions, such as the schools, the movies, the radio, and the newspapers, by virtue of their mass clientele, must necessarily operate as leveling influences. The political process as it appears in urban life could not be understood without taking account of mass appeals made through modern propaganda techniques. If the individual would participate at all in the social, political, and economic life of the city, he must subordinate some of his individuality to the demands of the larger community and in that measure immerse himself in mass movements.[28]

Given mass society and an expanding population, public programs designed to satisfy the "average person" might not appeal to "particular individuals," but they are politically inevitable. *The Wall*

Street Journal, discussing the impact of population pressure on the use of recreational areas, cites certain suggestions of Roger Revelle, Director of the Harvard Center for Population Studies:

> To accommodate this increase, he says, not only must more land be set aside for parks and similar facilities but we need to find new patterns of use that will allow the number of visitors to be greatly increased. Among the possibilities suggested by Mr. Revelle—some of which might admittedly detract a bit from the charms of the wilderness—are wear-resistant footpaths through forests; electronic guide systems and fences that would keep crowds of hikers from tripping over each other; staggered visiting hours; and a rationing system that would allow each family a certain number of park visits per year.[29]

One can readily sympathize with Dean R. L. Predmore of Duke University, a humanist, when he says that "Under such conditions as these, that 'tonic of wildness' so passionately prescribed by Henry David Thoreau for modern man would surely turn into a regurgitant."[30] Nevertheless, if the popular demand runs in this direction, what political candidate seeking the votes of mass society could deny it access to the national parks under as favorable conditions as can be engineered (including popular evening entertainment, as Yosemite Park in California, initiated some years ago)?

The fact is that mass society creates par excellence the conditions for a modern demagogue, either moderate or radical in temperament, as the occasion requires. It creates a political elite, that is, a leadership group, which can maintain its eliteness only by satisfying the many, and provides it with the communication facilities to make its link to the many effective. It was for this reason that Plato believed in a government by philosopher-statesmen. Democratic government presented the too real possibility of coercion by the popular will, an "authority of the poor," unmindful of "virtue." Aristotle, too, had his qualms about an urban democracy, which he feared would open an arena to the demagogue.

If one rejects a nonelective government with power to impose its conception of the public good, there is little alternative in an expanding society to the focussing of mass public opinion on an increasingly centralized public administration, a formulation which is not without its dangers. A government's willingness to respond with policies which are popular with the average person does not necessarily mean, however, that everyone therefore shares in the social advantage equally. The trend may be in that direction (less inequality of treatment), as Tocqueville so firmly believed, but inequality cannot be eradicated. Popular policies may, in fact, be one means of containing pressures for redistribution of the social advantage in more fundamental respects. The soothing effects of bread and circuses were known by the Roman emperors long before their rediscovery in modern times.

The elected government of a large population must be responsible to the average person, but it cannot wholly ignore special interests. The existing authority structure, with which any government must work, supports the present distribution of the social advantage, in which many if not most people have a stake. There is thus an inbuilt tendency to conservatism. The more middle class a society (that is, the higher the proportion that has a significant share in the social dividend), the more conservative is it likely to be.[31] Popular governments can skim a little cream from the top of the income distribution, and distribute a little gravy to those at the bottom, without disturbing the basically conservative attitude of its mass constituency. They can ignore the welfare of a few to satisfy the desires of the many (as in the demolition of housing for highways), within an appeasing formula of "due process," without disturbing the social structure.

Law and Order

Even with the assistance of a generally conservative disposition and the aid of mass communications media, however, the containment of dissident groups within an expanding population is not a simple matter. We earlier observed how an increase in population density affects groups and subpopulations differently; some scarce factor, such as space, cannot be increased proportionately, so that some (the already disadvantaged) are likely to experience a reduction in their social portion. The possibilities for unrest and protest increase.

Tocqueville had a further reason for believing that larger populations and urbanization presented governmental dangers. "Great wealth and extreme poverty, capital cities of large size, a lax morality, selfishness, and antagonism of interests are the dangers which almost invariably arise from the magnitude of states."[32] The only way that a representative government could counter these tendencies is through commanding the support of a majority. But, this, Tocqueville thought, was a more difficult process where "the people are more diversified by the increase of the population." The number of dissidents increases, interests become fragmented, and "the difficulty of forming a compact majority is constantly augmented."

This was precisely the problem which Rousseau had confronted: can a government impose order on a large population without repression? and he had concluded in the negative. As a population expands, the government must itself become more compact, more centralized, capable of acting swiftly and of exercising such strength as is needed. Madison had reversed this formulation by arguing that the diverse minorities would be swallowed up in a larger population, making it easier for a government to put together a majority which was uncontrolled by special interests. In a sense, Madison had rested his position on the belief that pluralism would sufficiently fragment a society to make governmental control more feasible, not less. Presumably the rise of mass communications would strengthen his case by making it easier for a government to popularize its programs.

But Madison's optimism does not appear wholly justified by events. In a large society, made increasingly interdependent by specialization and increasingly dependent on integration by design rather than by custom, a minority group, if determined enough, can disrupt and obstruct the functioning of society. As one political analyst has observed, "Much has been written since the Constitutional Convention about 'the tyranny of the majority,' but wherever we look today willful minorities seem to be dominating public affairs and even prevailing by force over the majority."[33]

Without passing on the prevalence or success of strong and violent factional actions, we can note their presence in other industrialized countries than the United States. Whether the minorities are based on a language-culture differentiation (as in Canada, Belgium, and, to some extent, India), or on a racial distinction (as in the United States), or on radical student groups (the world over), or on other economic, social, religious, or political divisions, if they are determined to the point of decisively rejecting the prevailing structure of authority, they present the government with an intolerable dilemma. How can it countenance such direct and extralegal, if not illegal, actions and yet maintain its legitimacy? But how can it contain direct action by large groups?

If the rejection of authority is persistent enough, the dissident group can be contained in only one of two ways—by concession or by force. Either involves a realignment of authority. "When authority is lost . . . the only way it can be restored is by a change in the actual distribution of political power." When the institutions of government "cannot gain acceptance of their authority among substantial minorities who have the power to resist any possible good they can do, at that point, I think we have to consider new forms of organization. . . ."[34]

The government which faces a determined minority challenge must place greater reliance on force and repression, the path which Rousseau expected it to follow, or it must relax its authority and show greater permissiveness toward the group pressing for change. This latter approach may be successful if the concessions made can be portrayed as peculiarly needful and overdue, so that they do not constitute a pattern for other dissident groups to follow, and if the concessions, once made, succeed in reintegrating the challenging group. The challenge by organized labor in the United States during the 1930's provides an excellent example. But if the challenges become repeated and frequent, then the route of greater permissiveness can only lead in time to the disintegration of society into warring factions, the gradual dissolution of a recognized authority structure.

Even without such confrontations of authority with direct action, however, it appears that Tocqueville was more nearly right than Madison. A growing society experiences greater and greater difficulty in holding together the groups and interests which compose it. In effect, the social contract becomes a more and more complicated process of bargaining, with the central government attempting to fashion a series of workable compromises among many interests. It cannot rely solely or even principally on force or compulsion to maintain social integration; the component parts of the grand system must be induced and persuaded as well as coerced into performing their roles.

As a society becomes larger and more heterogeneous, the fashioning of the complex of necessary bargains becomes more and more difficult. The concessions it must make to secure the wanted involvement of certain groups offend the sense of equity on the part of others. The effort by some interests to maintain the status quo, in which they hold a disproportionate advantage, prevents adjustments which are needed to satisfy others who are convinced that they are disproportionately disadvantaged. The more difficult the adjustments, the more likely that government will resort to force and coercion, but without solving the fundamental problem. The level of agreement at which diverse interests can be brought together becomes increasingly general, pushing the consequential and immediate issues to lower governmental levels or leaving them unresolved. Decentralization takes place in fact, if not in form. At some point the degree of decentralization becomes indistinguishable from local autonomy.

Once again we observe the dual process at work. With growth in population, there is a centripetal movement of power to the center to hold the system together. But, with increasing growth, there is also a centrifugal movement of power (discretion) toward the periphery, lightening the strain on the center by reducing the need for control. Past some point in size, the demands on the center become less and less significant relative to the power diffused to the periphery. The centrifugal effect overcomes the centripetal effect. The fate of all empires is dissolution.[35]

The difficulties of coordinating a larger and for that reason more heterogeneous population of interests is thus the ultimate limit on the growth in size of a society, at least within a specific political unit. Past some point the problem of contriving an effective integrative system becomes unmanageable. The larger system breaks down into smaller, more homogeneous units.

Tocqueville posed the problem and gave his own pessimistic conclusion with respect to federal government in the United States. Writing in 1835, he foresaw that within a hundred years the aggregate population would have reached a hundred million, and the number of states would have expanded to forty. He assumed that these would all maintain an interest in preserving the Union. Nevertheless, "I still say that, for the very reason that they are a hundred millions, forming forty distinct nations unequally strong, the continuance of the Federal government can be only a fortunate accident."[36]

The fact that Tocqueville's prophecy has gone unfulfilled may cast some doubt on the validity of the analysis presented here. Still, one may point to the fact that the union was preserved only through Civil War (the coercive force), and that there is no analytical basis for assuming a specific timetable of change. Moreover, appropriate changes in governmental form, in social organization, up to a point permit a larger and larger unit, so that the "ultimate limit" is in part a function of the degree of organizational ingenuity on the part of a people. Nevertheless, if the analysis of this chapter is accepted, then the effect of continued population growth is to force a change in the form of government, at first toward centralization, then in time toward decentralization (with centralization continuing, but now within the local unit) and ultimately (at some uncertain point) toward a reconstitution of political units. The local governments become more autonomous in most spheres of activity. A central government may and probably will continue to perform certain coordinating and integrative functions in a few delimited spheres, such as those relating to the preservation of peace among its constituent units, but its regulatory role diminishes greatly.

Summary

Classical philosophic thought tended to the view that as a population grows, government must become more centralized. Democracy requires small political units. With this went a conception of liberty as the exercise of popular sovereignty. But popular sovereignty also implied the total subjection of the individual to the collectivity, a position unacceptable to the rising school of liberalism and individualism, which defined liberty as the inviolable rights of the individual. This redefinition led to acceptance of representative forms of government, capable of embracing large populations without loss of liberty as long as individual rights were preserved. A belief that a large population could more easily contain factions, which otherwise might dominate a small society oppressively, facilitated this change of view.

In Marxist ideology, the only legitimate sovereignty lies in the spontaneous will of the people. In developing economies, democracy has been associated with nationalism and with economic planning in the interests of all, thus adapting Tocqueville's identification of democratic society with egalitarianism. In these cases, too, the effect has been conceptually to dissociate forms of government from the size of population.

But the relationship remains in fact. As a population expands and includes a wider spectrum of special-interest groups, the need for stronger central government increases. As the economic functions of a growing society become more specialized and coherent, the need for governmental regulation becomes greater. Issues become more complex, not only because of the scale factor but also because of the concomitant increase in knowledge and its technical applications. The representative function becomes more attenuated, as a compact executive government, aided by experts, initiates more and more actions, subject only, if at all, to delay or veto by the larger and more cumbersome legislative body. With size, the social and economic system cannot be left to natural social evolution, but must be consciously contrived and designed. The individual finds his place within that system, and the concept of individualism itself undergoes modification, stressing more the character of his performance within system constraints than his unconstrained and independent actions. Thus, liberty in the sense of participation in sovereignty and liberty in the sense of a privileged area of private rights are both eroded.

The centralization of governmental functions that comes with an expanding population involves a dual movement—toward national government in contrast to local, toward executive in contrast to legislative government. But decentralization accompanies centralization. As the size of a population increases, its subunit characteristics become more divergent, requiring the special knowledge and greater attention that can only come at the local level. Thus, a growing population spins certain problem areas upward as the need for regulation increases, and it also spins them downward as the need for special consideration increases. Or certain aspects of a given problem may require central coordination and other aspects of the same problem local application.

As industrialized societies increase in size, the combination of a knowledgeable, urbanized mass society and an elective government promotes a populist orientation. Public programs are conceived which appeal to the average person, or, as some have phrased it, there begins the era of the common man. This means a more egalitarian society in some respects, even though not necessarily the fundamental ones. The industrialized mass society is also a middle-class society, with a high proportion of its population having a significant stake in the existing distribution of the social advantage, always alert to supporting marginal modifications which benefit their positions but unreceptive to radical changes which would endanger their sizable share. This basically conservative attitude conduces toward greater social stability, but if there are substantial subpopulations with a disproportionate disadvantage, their lot will become worse in such a status quo-oriented society, creating conditions for potential unrest or explosion.

If significant minorities reject the existing authority structure, and are sufficiently determined and persistent in their course of action, the central government can reply only by using force or by making concessions. By either route the authority structure is altered. Force, however, does not resolve the basic problem of the dissident minority, unless it is carried to the point of extermination (as in Hitler's

Germany) or physical confinement (as attempted in South Africa). If the resistance to authority continues, and other groups develop imitative behavior in self-defense, a society moves toward dissolution into more homogeneous groups. Limited functions may remain at the center, to coordinate the relations of the now-autonomous units.

A later need for integration may reverse the process and even create higher (international) levels of coordination, as we shall explore in a later chapter. The distribution of authority is never static in the face of change, including population change. Concomitant changes in knowledge, technology, and the spread of education also affect the process, interacting with population change.

If a minority group is distributed throughout a population (as Negroes are in the United States), the satisfaction of the determined minority becomes all the more difficult, since there is no defined political unit to which authority can be decentralized. In this case pressures may be generated, in a socially unconscious way, to redistribute the minority group itself in such a manner that it coagulates in political units capable of self-government. It is conceivable that "the Negro Problem" in the United States will approach some solution only when Negro density in selected major cities has reached a point where it represents a high proportion of the population of those cities and, at the same time, that it constitutes a high proportion of the total Negro population, permitting effective decentralization of authority to this group.[37]

NOTES

1. Jean-Jacques Rousseau, *The Social Contract*, trans. Willmoore Kendall (Chicago: Henry Regnery, 1954), pp. 35, 55.

2. *Ibid.*, p. 87.

3. William D. Ross, ed., *The Works of Aristotle*, Vol. 10, *Politica*, trans. Benjamin Jowett (Oxford: The Clarendon Press, 1913), p. 1326.

4. Rousseau, *The Social Contract*, p. 117. Athens was not the only close example of direct democracy. Rousseau makes quite a case for Rome, and other Italian cities of ancient and medieval times had highly participatory forms of government. New England's town meetings are a more contemporary instance, interesting, too, in that as some New England towns grew too large to accommodate all voting citizens in a single meeting room they moved to establish *representative* town meetings.

5. Montesquieu, *Spirit of the Laws*, trans. Thomas Nugent, rev. J. V. Prichard (London: G. Bell and Sons, 1914), 1:130–131.

6. I am deeply indebted to Bertrand de Jouvenel, whose penetrating essay, "On the Evolution of Forms of Government," in B. de Jouvenel, ed., *Futuribles I* (Geneva: Librairie Droz, 1963), especially pp. 99–102, called my attention to this changing conception of liberty.

7. Rousseau, *The Social Contract*, p. 19.

8. *Ibid.*, p. 143.

9. Quoted in de Jouvenel, *Futuribles I*, p. 100.

10. Benjamin Constant, *Principes de Politique* (Paris, 1815) quoted in de Jouvenel, *Futuribles I*, p. 102.

11. Alexis de Tocqueville, *Democracy in America* (New York: Alfred A. Knopf, 1945) 2:104.

12. Simonde de Sismondi, *Histoire des Republiques Italiennes du Moyen Age*, 1840, quoted in de Jouvenel, *Futuribles I*, p. 101.

13. Rousseau, *The Social Contract*, p. 149.

14. Quoted in de Jouvenel, *Futuribles I*, p. 100.

15. ". . . if the individual retained any rights whatever, this is what would happen: There being no common superior able to say the last word on any issue between him and the public, he would be his own judge on this or that point, and so would try before long to be his judge on all points. The state of nature would thus persist; and the association would necessarily become useless, if not tyrannical." Rousseau, *The Social Contract*, p. 19.

16. William Appleman Williams has shown this with analytical brilliance in *The Contours of American History*, paperback edition (Chicago: Quadrangle Books, 1966).

17. *The Federalist Papers*, No. 10. All quotations from Madison are from this source, which has been reprinted in R. Bendix and S. M. Lipset, eds., *Class, Status and Power* (Glencoe: The Free Press, 1953), pp. 21–26.

18. G. W. F. Hegel, *The Philosophy of History*, trans. J. Sibree (New York: Dover Publications, 1956), p. 255. The translation is of lectures delivered by Hegel in 1830–1831.

19. Carl Bridenbaugh, *Cities in the Wilderness* (New York: Alfred A. Knopf, 1955), p. 93. Similarly from Adna F. Weber, *The Growth of Cities in the Nineteenth Century* (Ithaca: Cornell University Press, 1965), p. 435: "I may enjoy playing a cornet during the cool summer evenings; but that is not to the interest of my neighbor who has to go to work early in the morning and so needs early sleep. It may be greatly to my interest to build a tannery on a vacant city lot that comes to me cheap; but it is not the interest of people who have fine residences on adjoining property."

20. "Unless we become a nation of statesmen-scientists, we can kiss goodbye to our whole traditional constitutional system for responsible power. It will be done for, because only a handful of experts will make decisions for the rest of us, and we will have no exact basis for knowing whether they decided well." Reported in *The New York Times*, 22 August 1958.

21. The event is described in my *Private and Public Planning* (New York: McGraw-Hill, 1965), pp. 214–215. The same phenomenon was repeated in Belgium only a short time later.

22. Robert Boguslaw has written entertainingly of this tendency in *The New Utopians* (Englewood Cliffs, N.J.: Prentice-Hall, 1965) and Jacques Ellul more ominously in "Western Man in 1970," in de Jouvenel, *Futuribles I*, pp. 27–64.

23. John William Ward, "The Ideal of Individualism and the Reality of

Organization," in Earl Cheit, *The Business Establishment* (New York: John Wiley & Sons, 1964), pp. 77–112.

24. We shall examine this aspect again in Chapter 6. I have tried to analyze this relationship between system and subsystem, between government and private business in *Private and Public Planning*, written, however, before I became conscious of the pervasive significance of population changes.

25. De Tocqueville, *Democracy in America*, 2:306–313. John Stuart Mill likewise believed that the representative form of government had encouraged centralization in post-revolutionary France: "A political act, to be done only once in a few years, and for which nothing in the daily habits of the citizen has prepared him, leaves his intellect and moral dispositions very much as it found them; and the citizens not being encouraged to take upon themselves collectively that portion of the business of society which had been performed by the privileged classes, the central government easily drew to itself not only the whole local administration, but much of what, in countries like ours, is performed by associations of individuals." *Essays on Politics and Culture*, ed. Gertrude Himmelfarb (New York: Doubleday, Anchor Books, 1963), p. 229.

26. Edward B. Fiske provides an excellent analysis of this movement in "The Pope's Difficult Decision," *New York Times*, 1 August 1968. Among his observations: "Bishops are finding that survival means the adaptation of liturgies and policies made in Rome to local conditions."

27. The representative function may languish and government become more concentrated in another way. If the apportionment of representatives is by geographical unit, with the number of representatives held constant, then with an expanding population the ratio of representatives to constituents declines, diluting the representative function. The legislature may be able to operate more effectively—in any event, no less effectively than in the past—but the ties to its constituencies will have been attenuated and in this sense government will have become more concentrated. It is still likely that because of the increasing technicality and complexity of issues, its functions will devolve more and more on the executive.

28. Louis Wirth, *American Journal of Sociology* 44 (July 1938): 58. Copyright 1968 by The University of Chicago Press.

29. *Wall Street Journal*, 8 December 1966.

30. *BioScience* 16 (July 1968):692.

31. This is not the same thing as saying that a largely middle-class society (for example, the United States) will be highly conservative, but only that it will be more conservative than a society with less of a middle class. And obviously the upper-class element of a generally middle-class society will be more conservative, on the whole, than the middle-class component of that same society.

32. De Tocqueville, *Democracy in America*, 1:167.

33. James Reston, "The Tyranny of Minorities," *New York Times*, 20 September 1968.

34. Nathan Glazer, "For White and Black, Community Control Is the Issue," *New York Times Magazine*, 27 April 1969, p. 49. Glazer is especially concerned with what he believes to be a minority push for decentralization of government throughout the world, taking Negro demands for community autonomy in the United States as one example of many.

35. I first developed this thesis in *A General Theory of Economic Process* (New York: Harper & Brothers, 1955), pp. 149–153, at a time when my interest was more specifically in the relationships among bargaining units. The same

interest led to a related analysis, "Determinants of Collective Bargaining Structures," in Arnold Weber, ed., *The Structure of Collective Bargaining* (New York: The Free Press, 1961), pp. 3–19.

36. De Tocqueville, *Democracy in America*, 1:413–414.

37. Some suggestion for representation along this line has been made by Roy Innis, national director of the Congress of Racial Equality, in "Separatist Economics: A New Social Contract," published in W. F. Haddad and G. D. Pugh, eds., *Black Economic Development* (Englewood Cliffs, N.J.: Prentice-Hall, 1969), pp. 50–59. Innis argues for the separation and self-control of black-populated urban areas. "They must become political sub-divisions of the state, instead of sub-colonial appendages of the cities. . . . in such a society the control of goods and services flowing through a distinct geographical area inhabited by a distinct population group would be in the hands of those indigenous to the area." This plan of action would presumably break up metropolitan areas into a number of racially independent or ethnically homogeneous groups. This course seems less likely to me than the political control of the large cities themselves which is likely to fall to Negroes simply with the passage of time.

CHAPTER 6

Population Effects and Organizations

A MORE populous society requires a change in the scale of its organizations. As a society becomes more dense with people, the small organizations which served it can no longer do all that is needed. Replication is not enough. The social infrastructure, to use the currently popular term, must be rescaled in proportions more appropriate to the larger society itself.

Size

One can see why this must be so. For one thing, small organizations cannot accommodate specialization in the performance of their functions. An expanding organization achieves economies of scale in each particular of its operations. By segmenting its functions, it can redesign each of them on a larger scale in whatever way is technically superior.

There is a second consideration. Since the infrastructure is society's way of organizing itself, of relating people to each other in a coordinated and coherent fashion, for some purposes at least large organizations are necessary to achieve the social effect which is wanted. In the area of political organization, numerous small discrete elective units within a large city, each the size of a neighborhood, would hardly result in the over-all political cohesion which is necessary to concerted action on a variety of fronts. In the area of economic organization, numerous small proprietorships, each completely independent of the other, would not permit the effective organization of a society's productive and distributive activities. Some functions of a growing population could not even be carried on by small organizations. The provision of water and electricity to a city would be impossible on the basis of thousands of separate suppliers. A populous society simply could not function under a regime of pure competition, with each unit so small it has no effect on the market. The organizational problem would be too enormous.

As a third consideration, small organizations make little impact on a large society. As social issues move from a local to a national scale, so must the scale of an organization which is involved in those issues. Local societies of workers are sufficient when communities are largely self-contained, but when towns and cities begin competing and cooperating with each other worker interests can only be effectively represented in a national organization. Even as this is written, news media carry the story of merger negotiations taking place within the Lutheran Church in the United States, now fragmented into a number of separate units. If these can be brought together, it is said, the resulting organization of nine million members following a common creed will give this church a special influence, occupying as it would a place between the monolithic Catholic Church, on the one hand, and the multiform Protestant churches, on the other.

When a population expands, then, so does the size of its organizations. Among the most important of these are the business unit (the corporation, in western society), the trade association, the labor union, the political party, and a variety of educational, religious, and cultural institutions. Some of these may be public, others private.

Structure

An increase in the scale of organization is not accomplished by simple multiplication of all its parts. There is a necessary change in proportions and in structure, in part because the possibilities of economies of scale are realized for the several parts of the organization at different points of growth, in part because growth permits the introduction of entirely new technological forms, and in part because the problem of managing or coordinating the organization requires new solutions.

At one time it was believed, following Alfred Marshall, that it was the managerial factor which would impose limits on the growth of an organization such as the business firm. Management was the fixed factor, insuring that, as capital and labor increased relative to it, at some point diminishing returns would set in. The inability of a manager's mind to comprehend an ever increasing complex of operations would call a halt to expansion. That view is no longer so widely entertained. Edith Penrose has effectively made the point that management is not a person but a function, and a reorganization of the function permits expansion without necessarily diminishing returns to scale. In particular, decentralization of some activities permits the concentration of central management on a limited number of especially vital areas. There is, then, no optimum size of organization as long as structure is modified to accommodate growth, which is a matter of invention and innovation, just as much so as in the case of technology.[1]

Nevertheless, there are some ultimate limits to growth in the size of organizations, even if these cannot be precisely identified. As an organization increases its size, it accumulates larger and larger numbers of people, often combining into specialized units and cliques, each making its own demands on the organization both with respect to the adoption of operating policies and the disbursement of organizational benefits (a distribution of the organizational advantage comparable to the distribution of the social advantage). The one ineluctable function resting on management is to satisfy all these demands sufficiently to retain the adherence to the organization of all those on whom it depends (or on replacements for them). But as the number and variety of such demands increase and overlap, it becomes increasingly difficult to satisfy this requirement. At some point the problem becomes too difficult for solution, whatever modifications of structure may be introduced. Further growth (requiring bargains with additional individuals or groups which do not conflict with bargains already struck with present personnel) is impossible. The individuals whose services are sought can strike better bargains elsewhere, with organizations of lesser size. Indeed, it may prove impossible to retain the services of some already within the organization, as these find it to their interests to spin off and start their own independent activity or join with another organization. We have already encountered this limit on growth in the previous chapter, in examining the limits on the growth of a population within a given political unit. At some point the problem of governing such an expanded population, of satisfying the increasingly heterogeneous interests, becomes unmanageable. An organization is like a population, its management is its form of government, confronting the same problem of coordinating diverse interests, though with respect to a different set of issues. And like the government of an expanding population, at some point the management of an organization comes up against a barrier to further expansion. Otherwise, we should face the possibility that the whole world might be embraced in a single organization.[2]

The existence of such indefinite ultimate limits to expansion is probably less important, however, than the principle of organizational change to facilitate growth. The reproportioning of a society through its organizational structure is of central significance. The growth of a society *necessitates* a change in the size and form of its organizational constituents, sometimes in ways that are not always recognized as such. The *need* for organizational change is not contrived, even though organizational change itself is likely to be (an example of the kind of system design we encountered in the last chapter). Major organizational changes may be greeted with suspicion and not recognized as responding to needs arising from population growth.

It seems to me entirely possible that the rise of the conglomerate form of corporate organization (just as the rise of the international corporation, and the rise of the national corporation before that) may be just such an unconscious effort to restructure an industrialized society in a way that meets the needs of a still expanding population. What we may be witnessing is less the efforts of aggressive managements to expand their own organizational frontiers than an invitation extended by a growing society to introduce new organizational forms conducive to its present and future growth. It is at least conceivable that the economy of the advanced countries some decades from now may be built around a number of major conglomerates.

To suggest this as a possibility is not to imply its probability, and in any event other novel forms of organization may contend for preference. For example, the system of prime contracting by government in the United States is a recent social invention of the first importance. By means of it, organizations of great size and complexity can be created ad hoc for particular needs, and disbanded when the needs are met. The prime contractor assembles a system of subcontractors (already existing firms, some larger than it), relating each in a functionally coherent manner, its central authority recognized by all for this specific purpose only. This organizational form can obviously be adopted for a variety of purposes. Conceivably it too may be one way in which a society is experimenting with a new organizational infrastructure to meet the needs of its expanding population.

Still another example of the organizational restructuring of a growing society is provided by the increasing use of business corporations to supplement the educational sector. The learning needs of an expanding population, particularly in the face of the concomitant expansion of knowledge, creates a more urgent need for continuing ("lifetime") education. This has imposed a burden on the existing educational establishment which it cannot effectively meet. As a consequence, more and more teaching functions are being provided by large corporations whose personnel, facilities, and finances permit them to engage in such activity. In recent years, such training activities have often been publicly subsidized. Once again, society seeks to restructure its organizations in a way that meets the needs of a growing population. There may not indeed be any explicit realization of that fact, but the response is no less real although not formulated in those terms.

Performance

An expanding population, then, brings with it an increase in the size of its organizations and a change in their structure. It also induces a change in their performance. The functions which its organizations perform on a large scale, with specialized technologies, often differ qualitatively from those they performed on a smaller scale. For one thing, the product or service which was geared to individualistic needs is redesigned for mass production. This is true not only of manufactures but of education, religion, recreation, and services generally. With large numbers of consumers and larger supplying organizations it becomes unfeasible to cater to idiosyncratic wants. Standardization is necessary.

In education, for example, the larger size of institutions and classes imposes the need for new organization (larger administrative units more impersonally administered) and for new techniques (visual aids, television, programmed instruction). Despite the greater impersonality, it is not always clear that the quality of instruction deteriorates; television makes possible, for example, the introduction into the classroom of great minds of the present and recent past in a way that may have tremendous educational impact. What is clear is that the quality changes and, whether for better or worse, almost always in the direction of increased uniformity of treatment.

As we earlier observed, in the advanced economies the middle class tends to become the mass. While an expanding population increases heterogeneity, the common culture which unites so large a mass tends toward the more superficial and has its effect on the standardized offerings, which are pitched to the level of the many, whether this is in the design of cars or of education. Just as mass society leads to popular government, so does it necessarily lead to populist-oriented institutions. "Culture" becomes more a response to popular taste than the molder of taste. Although a rising educational level may improve the taste to which cultural institutions respond, the schools and universities are themselves among the cultural institutions responding, so that their formative influence is diluted.

As higher education falls a prey to the mass, research as well as teaching will be affected. The student will no longer feel his relation to a community of scholarship; he is not concerned about—indeed, is impatient with—the traditional values of university life. He does not look forward to becoming a new man; he expects to retain his commonness and to be distinguished from the multitude only by a certain technical competence. Like his highly specialized professor, his participation is segmental; it does not commit him as a whole man to becoming the bearer and protector of the society's aspirations. In the faculties two new types will become prominent; the technician and the demagogue. Only these will maintain and increase enrollments; more important—the level of enrollment could indeed be steady—only these will earn the plaudits of the student body. The student will become his teacher's judge, sometimes even explicitly so. The result will be a decline in the university's ability to affect deeply the life of the student and concomitantly an increase in the vulnerability of both faculty and student to the stereotyped blandishments of the market place.[3]

There is reason to resist a wholly pessimistic conclusion as to the impact of mass society on culture, however. Granted that a dominant middle class will place its impress on society's institutions, this does not exclude the possibility of a culture which, with that as a base, also reflects the tastes and values of a cultural elite. Unquestionably, however, control of present institutions will pass out of their hands: the university will be reoriented toward the tastes and standards of the average man. Creativity along with discipline, inventiveness along with a sense of style, imagination coupled with refinement of standards and taste will survive in such a setting with greater difficulty. Nevertheless, since heterogeneity of interests is also a characteristic of the larger society there is some basis for optimism that there will be enough recruits to maintain an active cultural frontier.

Control

With an increase in the size of organizations, a change in their structure, and an alteration in their performance, there also goes a change in their control of a rather complex sort. First, there is an upward movement of the hierarchical structure, from local to national, accompanying the expansion of population. We have already taken note of this. W. Lloyd Warner's study of Yankee City provides an excellent example. Over the years, local plants of this shoe-making community became subsidiaries of national corporations which had outlets in numerous other cities and their central office in some distant metropolis. Local associations of mill owners became embraced in national manufacturers' associations. Local labor bodies became chapters of national labor unions.[4]

As a second stage, the hierarchical control of organizations is subjected to challenge from the expanded ranks. Corporate management is challenged by its workers. Union leadership is challenged by its members. The authority of church superiors is subjected to questioning by the lesser clergy and the laity. University administrators are confronted by students. In all cases the demand is for a more representative government of the organization.

In this phase the legitimate organization is faced with the same dilemma which we noted in the case of governments facing a challenge to their authority on the part of substantial minority groups. How give in to such direct action without jeopardizing the whole authority structure? But also how to control direct action on such a large scale? As a British shop steward remarked during a wildcat strike of 8,500 workers at an automobile plant, when asked his attitude toward legislative proposals to outlaw such unauthorized direct actions: "We're not saying we're the bee's knees and nothing should change. But we do say legislation is not the answer. That's nonsense. How are you going to fine 8,500 men?"[5] How fine them indeed? How contain them except by concession or force, with difficulties attending either course of action?

As a third aspect of this shift in control, there is a division within the representative movement. The tendency on the part of most members, except in the face of some precipitating event, is toward apathy. Within the mass society of the now expanded organization there may indeed be the same tendency toward anomie that we observed in the case of the city, or at least a tendency toward dis-involvement. A small number of activists assume control of the organization. Factional contests become resolved, and the leadership becomes intrenched. Michels' "iron law of oligarchy" asserts itself.[6]

Control over the organization thus tends to devolve upon those who occupy leadership roles under the existing authority structure, influenced in their actions by those who occupy leadership positions in opposition groups within the organization. In time the position of the opposition may be legitimized: labor union leaders must be consulted by company managers on matters significantly affecting their constituencies under United States legislation; worker representatives are entitled to directorial positions in the corporation under codetermination in Germany; student representatives are admitted to university councils and even boards of trustees in a number of countries. The tendency is toward formal representation of those participating in mass organizations. The alternative of a nonelective control by a small group over large organizations becomes increasingly difficult to maintain as those organizations expand to thousands or hundreds of thousands and even millions of members. This is true whether the control is exercised by a co-optative board of trustees, a management-controlled board of directors, or an appointed college of cardinals.

The Corporation and the Planning Framework

There is still another change in control which comes as a consequence of expanding populations, though it may come for other reasons as well. The business corporation, the dominant private institution in western societies, is subjected to increasing governmental control within a planning framework. Such control may come principally from dissatisfaction with existing economic performance, as in France and to some extent England. It may come from ideological motivation, as in the socialist countries. But growth in population and increasing density of population are further factors necessitating more systematic management of a nation's resources, including its private institutions.

"Planning" has been a word so ideologically loaded that it elicits instinctive antipathy from businessmen in the United States when used with respect to government, but in their own operations they are among the world's ablest planners. The difference in attitude is not illogical. In the large corporation, planning assists in exercising more effective coordination and control of its increasingly numerous subunits. In the same way, public planning enables the government to exercise more effective control and coordination of the corporations themselves as subunits. It is a safe assumption that no one likes to be coordinated or controlled. The manager of a corporate subsidiary probably feels about his company's central planning the way that top management feels about government planning. One always prefers to be the planner rather than the planned. The same attitudes are undoubtedly to be found in Russia.

The reasons for such attitudes are easily identified in the light of the analysis of the preceding chapter. Planning is a function of sovereignty; it relates to the most fundamental activities of people in their economic roles. But when the numbers involved become large, then direct participation in the exercise of sovereignty or planning is not feasible, either by all those composing the corporation, with respect to corporate planning, or by the population in the nation at large, with respect to public planning. The only recourse is to some system of representation. But this is at best only imperfectly provided for in any system of planning. Within a large corporation, only a few individuals at each level of operations participate in drafting the plans for that operation, within guidelines which are dictated to them by the unit above. Moreover, this handful of individuals, even if representative of larger numbers on their same level, is in no sense elective.

The same can be said of public planning. Even in France, which has made a great show of private participation in the drafting of "le Plan," the number of individuals actually involved is on the order of 3,000, inclusive of corporate, labor, and ministry officials. If this is representation, it is representation by an elite and nonelective aristocracy. The larger the society, the more difficult this problem. This is simply Rousseau revisited.

Perhaps the closest parallel to Rousseauian pure democracy to be found today is in the workers' councils of Yugoslavia, which have aroused such widespread interest perhaps for this very reason. The workers' council, which is the governing body of a company, is elected by all the employees of the company. The body of employees is in fact the sovereign authority which Rousseau had insisted on, and passes on all major actions taken by the workers' council acting as its government, sometimes debating these for hours.[7] Among the issues it must confront are those relating to its own wage scales and the division of profits between reinvestment and worker

bonuses. It also chooses the top management of the company, and its decisions are entirely subject to the authority of the workers' council and, below the council, to the full body of employees.

But the purity of this democracy is already being subjected to the erosion of growing pains, just as Rousseau had feared. The need for quick and decisive actions in competitive and emergency situations has led in some companies to a de facto centralization of authority in the hands of management, who reports less and is endorsed more quickly. And the practice of debating all major issues often at great length, among large numbers, has led to a drain of time on the part of all employees that can only become increasingly burdensome. It would be surprising indeed if in time the employee democracy of Yugoslavia did not go the way of the town meeting in New England.

But however unrepresentative, planning cannot be avoided. It is only a question of its explicitness, its degree, and its quality. Even those who resist its application admit its necessity, even if within limits. There are few businessmen in the United States, for example, who would withdraw from government its powers of affecting the aggregate level of economic activity through monetary and fiscal measures, although they would limit those powers. The welfare of all is tied up in the performance of the economy. Experience with depressions, limping gains in productivity, more unemployment than is socially acceptable; alternating with inflation, a shortage of funds for housing, demands for more and better education; and accompanied by deterioration of environmental conditions and the massive problems of urbanization all underscore the necessity of employing society's resources with organized efficiency, in a unit large enough to take account of economic interdependency. An expanding population reinforces that need.

Planning involves treating the economy as a system, of which government is the manager. From this point of view, the corporation becomes a subsystem within the larger unit. Society poses certain objectives for the economic system, some of a general nature (such as full employment or a rate of growth in GNP) and some of a specific nature (such as the development of a national transportation system or landing a man on the moon). The corporation becomes an instrument in the realization of these social objectives.

How much its discretion is circumscribed by the role ascribed to it depends in part on the prevailing social philosophy ("individualism" versus "socialism") and in part on the degree of importance attached to the social objective. With respect to general objectives, private discretion may normally remain great, induced or coerced

only by such gentle controls as credit availability or interest rates, but in times of distress—such as a severe depression or inflation—the range of controls is likely to become greater and more directive. With respect to some specific objectives, corporate involvement may be left to volunteers (as in accepting a government contract), but with respect to other objectives (such as pollution control or minority hiring), all companies may be conscripted.

A corporation's objectives are obviously not always identical with social objectives; its advantage may be secured only at the expense of the social advantage. If this were not the case there would be little need for regulation. At the same time, the corporation's objectives are clearly not always incompatible with social objectives, or otherwise it would not be permitted to exist at all. Thus the objectives of the corporation (as subsystem) and the social economy (as system) are both partially congruent and partially divergent. The more permissive the planning framework is, the more likely it is that corporate discretion will promote its own objectives at the expense of the system's. If this leakage of system purpose becomes excessive, there is no recourse for the government but to draw the discretionary boundaries more tightly.

Nevertheless, a central government can never totally control corporate decisions, even if it wished to do so in a time of great emergency, such as war. All contingencies cannot be provided for, and private managements must be given latitude to deal with a variety of situations as they emerge, even though the degree of latitude is restricted. The government may tighten or loosen the boundaries of corporate discretion, as circumstances dictate, but there is always some degree of control by each over the other's performance. To the corporation, concerned with its own objectives, the controls of the government may seem imposing and complete, but to the government, concerned with the system's objectives, its powers of eliciting supporting action from the subsidiary organizations on which it must rely are likely to seem weak and ineffective.

With the growth of population and the consequent growth in the size of organizations, then, the need for coordination to secure social objectives becomes greater. Interdependency increases, in part because of greater specialization but in part simply from the pressures of people on each other and on resources. The need for coordination is experienced both within the larger organization and in society at large. Indeed, we can recognize that these two spheres of planning are closely related to each other in the sense that each completes the other; social planning provides a framework within

which subsidiary organizations can plan more certainly and effectively, and organizational planning creates a mechanism for the more effective execution of social directives. Growth in the size of a population creates added pressure for the more explicit refinement of the planning mechanism throughout the whole system.

In the process, as we have seen, control of the large individual enterprise undergoes modification. In addition to the influences generated by its own expansion—the centralization of authority in its national headquarters and accommodation of the pressures for representation of its enlarged constituency—there is also some shift in authority away from it to the managers of the over-all economic system, that is, to the government.

Growth in population creates its own need for a reproportioning of society's organizational structure, inevitably requiring larger subsidiary units for effective administration of its economic resources. These subsidiary units may be public or private; there is no reason why some modified form of the corporation cannot serve the purpose. But the meaning of the term "private" inevitably changes in the process, just as earlier we saw that the meaning of individualism has been subject to change. Increasingly it connotes simply that managers of the private organizations have been chosen by other means than government appointment, and by that fact acquire some degree of independence in the definition and pursuit of their own goals. But it is a matter of degree only, and the old dichotomy between what is public and what is private must inevitably crumble in the case of the larger private organizations.

There is another conclusion which follows from this analysis. Efforts to restrict the growth of private organizations, as notably in the antitrust legislation of the United States, may be misguided or (at a minimum) carried too far. With population expansion comes an imperious necessity for a change in the size and structure of social instruments like the corporation. Prevailing economic doctrine casts suspicion on size, equating it with monopoly. But its supporting arguments are now archaic. It condemns monopoly because it is inimical to the purer forms of competition. Although competition remains a marvelous and for that matter unavoidable means of organizing social behavior, it cannot do the whole task. Neither can government, unless it extends its spheres of activity in the growing society to a degree which western thought, at least, finds unacceptable.

What is needed are organizations which, though private, are nonetheless social, organizations which are nongovernmental but more clearly subject to governmental controls of a planning nature,

occupying a level between central government and private corporate units. It is possible but unlikely that these will spring full blown
from the mind of some system designer, consciously contrived in
the manner we noted in the preceding chapter—unlikely because a
system designer for this purpose would in all probability be a governmental expert and would exercise the predilection of a government official to place authority with the government he serves. The
greater likelihood is that such a new form of economic unit, if it
does emerge, will have its origin somewhere in the corporate sector,
on the part of an entrepreneur or private planner—a system designer
at this lesser system (subsystem) level, who is not consciously concerned with any larger role which his creation may play. A conscious private response to new opportunities for exploitation may
thus constitute unconscious social experimentation, carrying potentials for revision of the economic structure in ways not now
envisioned. It is for that reason that I would urge a more reflective,
more cautious, and probably more permissive policy toward conglomerate firms than seems now to characterize the Congress, without, of course, abandoning a searching scrutiny for potential ills
which they may embody, but which are not essential to their performance.

Summary

Population growth does not leave a society's organizations unaffected, whether private or public. It induces an increase in size in
order to take advantage of possible economies of scale, to improve
productive and distributive arrangements, and to augment organizational impact. As organizations expand, they must alter their structure. In effect, the whole society grows, and this imposes a necessity
on its organizational skeleton to alter its form. Performance, too, is
affected. With the spread of industrialization and education, the
middle class becomes the mass and exercises popular control over
cultural life, tending toward standards acceptable to the average or
common man. There is a standardization of institutional offerings,
geared to the tastes of the many, in all areas, ranging from consumer goods to education.

Control over organizations is likewise affected by their growth in
size, and in the size of the population. Local units are subordinated

to central, usually national, authority. The larger membership or constituency tends to organize and pressure for participation in the making of decisions affecting it. Leadership in these opposition groups tends to gravitate toward a few activists who are formally representative of the larger body.

Change in control of a different sort, of government over the enterprise, arises out of the need for more explicit planning engendered by, among other reasons, a population which is growing and increasing in density. Planning on an economy-wide basis involves treating the corporation as a subunit of the larger system, which has its own objectives. Government, as the manager of the system, employs the corporation as an instrument for the achievement of social objectives, though it can never completely control it, even in periods of emergency.

In the process of growing, a society (just as an organization) must restructure itself. This may require the development of new institutions, which may be private in the sense of nongovernmental, but also social in the sense of being more pivotal in the planning framework than the present corporation now is.

We have been speaking here primarily of the advanced industrialized societies. It is in these that the impact of population growth on organizations makes itself felt most decisively. In the underdeveloped economies, organizational activity itself must be encouraged. A society which, while populous, is only loosely integrated, lacking the economic base for organization, is faced with the need for developing an appropriate infrastructure at a more elemental level. The leadership role falls almost solely to government, out of default, and the pressures for planning largely involve a governmental response. Under these circumstances, the effect of population growth is less on existing organizations than on the kinds of organizations which government must create to fill a vacuum.

NOTES

1. Edith Penrose, *Theory of Growth of the Firm* (New York: John Wiley & Sons, 1959).

2. Actually this is not quite so fanciful as it sounds at first encounter. If one believes, as I do, that some form of effective world government will come in the not very distant future, this would inaugurate a world-embracing organization

or system. Its functions would obviously be limited to certain major kinds of activities, but in these areas its authority would be recognized, and nations would become decentralized units or subsystems within that limited framework, enjoying a large measure of autonomy but not full autonomy. Within each nation its political subdivisions and organizations would constitute a still further decentralization, each enjoying some degree of independence and discretion, but always limited by certain powers reserved to the center. The linkages within such a system might be very loose, but it can nevertheless be conceptualized as a single all-embracing system. For purposes of the present analysis, however, it is simpler to conceive of organizations and nations as constituting the relevant systems.

3. Philip Selznick, "Institutional Vulnerability in Mass Society," *American Journal of Sociology* 56 (1951):331. Copyright 1951 by The University of Chicago Press.

4. W. Lloyd Warner, "The Corporation, the Community, and the Emergent Process," in Philip Olson, ed., *America as a Mass Society* (New York: The Free Press, 1963), p. 137.

5. *New York Times*, 4 June 1969.

6. Robert Michels, *Political Parties* (Glencoe: The Free Press, 1949).

7. I have relied here on Ichak Adizes, whose "Self-Management: The Yugoslav Post-1965 Reform Experience" (Doctoral diss., Graduate School of Business, Columbia University, 1969), was based on participatory observation in two Yugoslav plants over a period of six months.

CHAPTER 7

Population and the Distribution of Wealth and Income

POLITICAL philosophers have generally agreed that democracy is difficult to maintain in the face of substantial economic inequality of classes, and vice versa. Plato was concerned that democracy would lead to the "authority of the poor" and a consequent exploitation of the wealthy and productive. Rousseau, on the other hand, believed that equality was, along with liberty, the cornerstone of a good system of laws. Not equality in an abstract statistical sense, but in the political sense that "no citizen shall have so much wealth that he can buy another, and none so little that he is forced to sell himself."[1] The way in which a state could assure its stability was to narrow the distance between the extremes of pauperism and great wealth.

In similar vein, Madison observed in the *Federalist* essays that "the most common, and durable source of factions has been the various and unequal distribution of property. Those who hold and those who are without property have ever formed distinct interests in society."[2] It was to avoid such factionalism that he sought to devise a political system which, while responsive to the citizenry, would nevertheless impose certain restraints on precipitate action, such as were provided for in the tripartite division of power in the federal government and the bipartite division between state and federal governments. It was also his high hope, as we have already seen, that westward expansion, giving outlet to ambitions for property of anyone dissatisfied with his economic status, would also give rise to an expansive society which would swamp any factional interests.

Aside from the Madisonian solution, which was after all peculiar to a pioneer society, there were two basic solutions to the problem of how to reconcile property imbalance and stable government. If property freed men from a dependence on others as John Locke had so persuasively argued, if in fact the unpropertied were also unfree, then the franchise should be limited to those who were free, that is, to those who held property. This would simultaneously rest government in the hands of a group that had proved itself industrious and capable, and avoid the danger that the votes of some would be controlled by others. For those of this conviction, property qualifications for voting were the obvious answer.

But there was another approach which was equally obvious to those of a different persuasion. If the lack of property made some unfree in contrast with those who owned property, then private property itself should be eliminated, putting all on an equal footing. This was the position of the Levellers, who had their greatest political influence in England in the seventeenth century, and likewise the position of many utopians throughout history, and of Karl Marx. In the United States, aside from the socialist community experiments which failed to muster any lasting following, it was Henry George who came closest to arousing support for such a point of view through his campaign for the "single tax," which, while leaving property in private hands, would have skimmed off most of the economic benefits of land ownership.

Effects of Population Growth on Inequality

The effects of property ownership on inequality are heightened with an expanding population. Property, particularly in the form of land, is fixed and becomes scarcer in relation to the numbers of people dependent on it. Its value rises, benefiting those who hold title, forcing the many who are not so fortunate to pay a higher tribute for its use. Ricardo's theory of rent rested on the bringing in of less and less productive land as a population expanded and pushed on its natural resource frontier, with the older and more desirable land gaining in relative value, the added gain taking the form of rent. Thus growth in a society's numbers was of primary economic benefit to such property holders. This was why Henry George believed that equity would be served by taxing such rent away, as a gain accruing to individuals not through any effort of their own, but simply by virtue of population growth.

But an expanding population benefits not only those who own land. Capital in various forms—buildings, equipment, goodwill, even organization itself—can be increased over time, but in the short run it is fixed, and an increase in the size of the population increases its revenue-producing capacity. To be sure, in neither the case of land or capital is a return guaranteed, but whatever the risks there are in investment, they are lessened by the prospect of a growing population; whatever the anticipated profits, they are increased by an increase in numbers of people.

The nonpropertied suffer a reverse fate. As their numbers rise, they press on the resources which are more or less fixed. Prices rise; in the absence of offsetting effects, their real incomes decline. Inequality increases. The disproportionately disadvantaged are still further disadvantaged. Social cohesion is weakened; class conflict and factionalism are stimulated.

But who are the disproportionately disadvantaged? In industrialized societies they are likely to be small in number and politically ineffective, unless, indeed, there is some significant minority group which has been singled out for discriminatory treatment, such as the Negroes in the United States and the French in Canada. On the whole, the large middle-class sector, if not wholly satisfied with its portion, is generally sufficiently satisfied to give the society a conservative complexion. If a small upper-class group benefits more than it, the difference is not so glaring as to create unrest. Even so, an expanding middle class may press against resources in private hands, leading to dissatisfaction in some specific respect, such as housing, but the consequence is likely to be a push for public action in that one respect rather than any more general class contention.

Still, it is worth recalling that the graduated income tax in the United States, introduced first as an emergency fiscal measure during the Civil War but put on a more permanent basis later, was largely supported by the agrarian and merchant interests (opposed to increased taxes on land and imports) and fought by manufacturers and bankers. Following the Sixteenth Amendment to the Constitution, designed to resolve doubts about the constitutionality of the principle, Congress imposed a mild surcharge on incomes above $20,000. In the debates at the time, Henry Cabot Lodge expressed the opposition view that progressivity constituted "confiscation of property under the guise of taxation," converting the measure "from the imposition of a tax to the pillage of a class."[3]

The division here lay in special interests which would be adversely affected by one fiscal measure rather than another, *some* fiscal measure being necessary, and presumably to a degree the interests of a lower middle class against an upper middle class. But despite some radical propaganda and charges of a socialist conspiracy, the notion of progressivity, embodied as much in the exemption of lower-income groups as in the surcharge on high incomes, probably reflected an implicit belief in the declining marginal utility of money. This was a concept stemming from classical (middle-class) economics, at least as far back as Jeremy Bentham, a body of doctrine which has had a marked influence on western conceptions of equity.

Nevertheless, although innocent enough in its origins, the graduated income tax has the potential for becoming an instrument of income levelling in the face of mounting fiscal requirements to meet particular needs of a growing proportion of an increasingly urbanized population. What was once easily accepted as an evident principle of equity[4] becomes a more contentious philosophy when progressivity involves levelling *down* in greater measure from a larger proportion of the populace, to benefit a "deprived" segment which is also growing proportionately. What is involved is some polarization of economic interests.

In the underdeveloped countries, any pressures for income redistribution have so far been spasmodic and ineffective. In the first instance, farms which are held in peasant hands in those countries where primogeniture is not practiced in the course of succeeding generations are divided again and again among the heirs. In time such small parcels become economically inefficient. In time of crisis, they become security for desperately needed loans. Sooner or later, the security is forfeited, and a process of reconsolidation of landholdings takes place.[5] In addition, simple expansion of population adds to the numbers of the landless. Thus it is the larger and growing mass which is disproportionately disadvantaged by the concentration of ownership in a small elite class.

This is a process not totally dissimilar from the early days of industrialization in western societies. In England, for example, many peasants were dispossessed from their lands by enclosures. Some became hired hands on the larger farms, and others joined the ranks of the rising urban proletariat. Food shortages and rising populations led to recurrent riots among town populations. In Nottingham, in 1792, "a mob of hungry men and women made a bonfire of the doors, shutters and implements of the butchers as a protest against the price of meat. . . ." In 1796, "bakers' shops were looted by hungry mobs, and again in the following year. In 1800 prices were still higher, and 'bread was an article of great scarcity this year'; fierce food riots broke out in April and again in August. . . ."[6]

There are analysts who believe that the political process which led from such large-scale dissatisfaction with the distribution of authority and the social advantage in the England of that day, via extension of the suffrage, to the redistribution of authority and privilege in a later day, will be repeated in the underdeveloped societies. They see a large and exploited population coming into possession of the vote and using it as an instrument for the overthrow of elite control. Confiscation of property may lead to socialist societies; at a minimum graduated taxation will lop off disproportionate advantage and use it for social welfare purposes. The result may not be accomplished in one move, but little by little it will have its effect. Thus, for example, in 1963, in a popular referendum, the voters of Iran approved a law providing that workers should receive as much as 20 percent of the profits of the industrial establishments employing them.[7]

Others are more dubious. Myrdal, for example, expresses his "profound skepticism in regard to the validity of any forecasts about future political developments in the South Asian region, especially those based on such glib notions about the behavior of the masses. Both Marx's theory of the political effect of impoverishment and the amplifying doctrine of a revolution of rising expectations seem unrealistic in the South Asian setting." He sees it as perfectly possible "that the lower strata in the Indian villages would remain supine in their shackles of inequality even if their living standards were to deteriorate still further."[8] Even with his skepticism, however, Myrdal apparently reserves a prophetic escape hatch. It is possible, he admits, that the full meaning of the radical policy pronouncements of dissatisfied intellectuals "will gradually dawn on the masses and that this might lead to their activation."[9] And with respect to "democratic decentralization" in India and Pakistan, which has so far worked to the advantage of the elites, he believes that these procedures may nonetheless be carriers of an ideology which "may be seeping downwards and in time making it more difficult to deny elementary rights to people hitherto regarded as outcasts."[10]

This last view is the one that seems most clearly justified. Of course, it is a matter of time, and of course it is possible that disadvantaged masses may swallow their lot and sit on their vote for an indefinite future. But it is inconceivable that such a process could continue indefinitely. In the face of swelling populations, increasing misery, and a gradual education by radical leaders in the power and use of popular suffrage, it is *only* a matter of time. Military coups may remove democratic rights, containing mass discontent, but again, only for a time. The underlying problem of mass discontent with the distribution of authority, once aroused, cannot forever be restrained by force. Indeed, it is more likely on the contemporary scene that military leaders will set themselves at the head of popular causes.

The consequence is almost sure to be, in time, a radical assault on present ownership systems in the underdeveloped areas. It is quite unlikely that enough time will be allowed to permit the rise of a middle class extensive enough to create political stability. That would first require industrialization, which, as we have already seen, is to a considerable extent inhibited by the fact that it is not *effectively* wanted by those whom it would benefit most, the masses.

These effects of population growth have been portrayed in microcosm by J. E. Meade in his 1966 presidential address before the Royal Economic Society.[11] The island of Mauritius in that year had a population of approximately three-fourths of a million. Its rate of natural increase was about twenty-seven per thousand. There is a sharp division between property owners and workers. In the face of the rapid population growth, an already great inequality in the distribution of income was increasing, as was the rate of unemployment. There were numerous situations where a propitiously lower wage rate would have led to more employment—more labor-intensive practices could have been employed on the sugar plantations, in growing tea, on the wharves, in textiles. But a wage rate which would have been low enough to have encouraged these activities would have led to an unacceptable increase in inequality in the distribution of income. Indeed, in the period 1956–1964 the wage level in Mauritius doubled without a substantial increase in prices. "The development was a very natural one. The political process of extension of the franchise and of movements toward self-government, majority rule and independence in Mauritius [introduced by the British since World War II], combined with the 'wind of change' which is blowing throughout such communities, has made the underdog more aggressive in his claims. Trade unions and official wage boards have developed an upward thrust on wage-rates."[12] But this had its deterrent effects on much-needed employment.

What is the way out of such a box? Meade concludes that as things stand now, "the outlook for peaceful development is poor." It is necessary to develop new forms of social organization which will encourage employment while promoting a redistribution of wealth and income. "There do exist devices which will have this effect, ranging from a radical socialization of private property or measures to redistribute the ownership of private property to less-radical 'welfare-state' measures, such as the taxation of high personal incomes to finance either subsidies on employment or the cost of living or social-security benefits for workers."[13]

The introduction of such sweeping social changes requires tighter political organization than now exists. One of the difficulties is that the population has been splintered into a 5 percent Franco-Mauritian elite (from the pre-Napoleonic period of French occupation) who are the rich plantation owners, a 25 percent Creole group (descendants of the French and their African slaves), a 66 percent Indian labor force, and 4 percent Chinese. In addition, there are religious (Catholic, Hindu, Moslem, Buddhist) as well as language differences. It is only recently that politics has tended to polarize around two parties, one representative of the Indians (both Hindus and Moslems), the other of the Creoles and Catholics, financed by the wealthy Franco-Mauritians. This latter party is desperately striving to avoid "domination of the island by the majority of Indians, who it is feared will job their nephews and cousins into the posts now held by Creoles."[14]

It would be anybody's guess how long the Indian majority will permit the ruling elite to enjoy the privileges which the present authority structure grants it. The Indian division into Hindu and Moslem components weakens its effectiveness. But it would be a rash Franco-Mauritian indeed who would assume that the concentration of privilege and property in the hands of 5 percent of the population will continue for very much longer, whether that means a decade or a generation. In the face of a rapidly expanding population, with the consequent deterioration of conditions for the many, one could safely predict that in this case a radical reorganization of the society is only a matter of time.

Industrialized Societies

Let us return now to the effects of population growth on the distribution of wealth and income in the advanced economy. We earlier noted that with a middle-class base, there is a wider participation in the social advantage, hence more of the population risks loss of some privilege by radical change, inducing a more conservative attitude. But this by no means implies that the status quo is preserved indefinitely. As the numbers and density of the population increase, pressures for social reorganization accumulate and sometimes cannot be contained without greater risk of social disturbance.

This is especially the case, as we have noted, when there is a significant minority group subjected to discriminatory treatment. The Negroes in the United States are an especially evident example, but they do not compose a unique category. In all such instances, a combination of deterioration of conditions, increasing compactness of location, the rise of new leadership, and an ultimate rejection of the oppressive authority system precipitate the condition we noted in a previous chapter. Containment must be by force or concession and, in either event, the authority structure and the distribution of social benefits are altered.

Aside from such identifiable minority groups, there may be a more diffuse population of the disproportionately disadvantaged: the maladjusted, the physically and mentally incompetent, the emotionally disturbed, and those saddled with responsibilities they cannot manage by themselves. It is true that people with these characteristics are to be found in all income and social brackets, but in the lower-income groups they tend to become a charge upon the public, and therefore a special class—the "welfare population."

By their very characteristics, the members of such a population are not likely to be fomenters of radical action. Nevertheless, in a representative society where they, like others, exercise the vote, they cannot be totally ignored. In an expanding population, they are likely to become disproportionately the victims of the increasing relative scarcity of whatever fixed factor is strategic, whether space or schooling or health care. Whether their proportion in the population also rises is likely to be governed by related factors such as the nature of technological change. In any event, with an expanding society the needs of such a group become more pressing. They are more susceptible to the appeals of the politician who seeks their votes. The welfare population becomes a hunting ground for the demagogic campaigner.

By itself the welfare population is weak. As an adjunct to a more determined minority group seeking change, it constitutes a potent ally. Thus in the United States the Negro insurgence of the 1960's evoked widespread protest movements and direct actions among welfare clients, many of them Negro but including whites as well. In this movement, social workers often acted as catalysts and sometimes as leaders.

[New York] budget officials said angry demonstrations this week by slum youths demanding more jobs was part of a "bigger picture" in which the poor see such services as welfare, health, and jobs as "a matter of right," not charity dispensed at the public's pleasure.

This attitude, the officials said, is fostered by antipoverty programs that organize the poor to take political action and inform them of the various programs and services open to them.

In effect, one city agency is helping to create a demand that other agencies cannot fill, the officials said.[15]

Larger cities are at the center of this turbulence. In addition to accumulating the dependents, they exercise a magnetic pull on those who have been loosened from smaller community settings. For whatever reasons labor surpluses emerge, these tend to be concentrated in the unskilled and economically unintegrated members of a society. In an urbanizing population, these are certain either to be already located in or gravitate to the cities in order to establish claims on a subsistence income, either through some service occupation where skill is less needed (in sanitation or custodial work, hotel and restaurant employment) or through welfare. Even if welfare is available in rural areas, there are likely to be more constraint and obloquy on the individual who resorts to it than there is in the impersonal city. In the city, welfare for some becomes not only a right but almost an occupation, and the massing of numbers on welfare insures that they will be accorded political respect.

Once the idea gains hold that such groups, when organized, do in fact wield political power, the possibility emerges for serious confrontation with the city government. It is not that the welfare population has no stake in the existing distribution of the social advantage and therefore no risk in attacking it; indeed, dependent as it is on public largesse, it has a great deal to lose. But it is the very impermanence of its economic position which induces the more aggressive to make demands for their integration (or reintegration) into society by vesting their benefits as rights, and by augmenting them to the level where they provide closer comparability with other members of society. To *demand* public benefits as *rights* in a sense lends greater dignity to the recipients. To fight for such rights, by direct action if need be, is a means of earning them. When confronted by direct action on the part of groups so determined, city governments as well as national are faced with the old dilemma of replying with force or concession, and again, in either case the authority structure and the distribution of the social advantage are altered.

Obviously, the subsidizing of large numbers of people in a society involves a redistribution of income. It is interesting indeed that it is in the individualistic and capitalistic United States that greatest support is to be found for the notion of a guaranteed minimum income for all, regardless of employment, and for the negative income tax, which would involve payments to the poor increasing proportionately with their poverty, whatever the reasons for it. These programs have won the support of a number of prominent businessmen. This is a long push forward toward the goal of equality for all which Tocqueville hypothesized as at the end of the road down which society has been traveling for centuries. It may also be viewed by some among the system's present beneficiaries as a method of retaining more of the existing distribution of authority and privilege, in the somewhat longer run, than would be possible simply by resting resolutely on the status quo.

Social Control of Private Property

Even without pressures from dissatisfied minority groups or a welfare population, growth in numbers and density of people will have a more certain effect on property rights. We previously noted how the urbanization trend, by bringing people into closer contact, obliges governments to regulate people's activities more closely. It likewise drives them to regulate the use of property, imposing negative limitations or affirmative requirements which affect the value of property. The heavy tax load on urban real estate is one example of this. Another now in process of being formulated is aimed at forcing owners of rental buildings to maintain them in a condition conforming to desirable housing standards. "Such proposals for effecting urban maintenance involve the redefinition of property rights. They would transfer some of the rights of the landlord to the tenant and to the public—to the urban community as a whole."[16]

Regulatory actions of this sort, designed to serve the many, will override the material rights of the wealthier few. Popular governments will have little recourse but to respond "in the public interest," even in a conservative middle-class society—not with the destruction of property rights, which would almost certainly be unacceptable, but with specific limitations imposed bit by bit (just as the public regulatory actions on private rights generally are piecemeal reactions to specific "felt needs of the times").

A still more pervasive form of limitation on private property rights comes with the resort to more explicit public planning procedures, along the lines we noted in the preceding chapter. The private corporate unit is more firmly integrated into the economic system, given its role to play in the achieving of social objectives. Its discretion in the use of its resources is thereby restricted; its own objectives are subordinated, in some degree, to those of the larger society.

Particularly is it true of the large corporations that their social role is given increasing weight relative to their private interests. This steady transition is more easily effected because of what Schumpeter referred to as the "evaporation of the material substance of property."[17] To owners of the corporation, "property" is no longer factory buildings and machines; it is a dematerialized parcel of paper shares. This fractionalization of real substance "takes the life out of the idea of property. It loosens the grip that once was so strong—the grip in the sense of the legal right and the actual ability to do as one pleases with his own. . . ."[18]

In place of material substance, it is conceivable, as Charles Reich has argued, that a new form of property is in process of being created. This is the right to certain government benefits, whether these are in the form of social insurance (which substitutes for household savings), or a government contract (which replaces a businessman's asset of goodwill in continued private customer relations), or a license to practice a profession or operate a television station (which is more valuable than any capital equipment which is involved). Valuables like these "are steadily taking the place of traditional forms of wealth—forms which are held as private property. . . . The wealth of more and more Americans depends upon a relationship to government."[19]

Reich foresees that such "new property" will assume even greater importance with the further expansion of the welfare population. In addition to this source of growth, however, it would appear that we will see, increasingly, a mingling of the old and new forms of property. Only through government license—"license" in its elemental sense of consent—can private material property be used, in ways conforming to standards designed to protect the public interest. And this trend will be difficult to resist precisely because the expanding numbers of an urbanizing population emphasize the public impact of private ownership.

The individual's stake in the social system—his income, status, function, rights, and privileges—will loom larger and more worth protecting than any bundle of material wealth for most people. His relative share in the whole social complex will become more important than the small private area around which he still seeks to build a fence. The result, in time, is more likely to approximate socialism than to resemble what we have associated with capitalism in the past, though there is no reason to believe that its western expression will be similar to the communist states of Eastern Europe today. But, with greater numbers and density of people, it will be increasingly difficult to carve society up into privileged and private preserves. Even if property titles remain in private hands, they will be subjected to tighter public control, and the taxation imposed on their use will make them expensive enjoyments.

Here again it is likely to be the influence of the young which will play a special role in effecting this deprivation of property. The young can be expected to be more receptive to change, more impatient with the past, and without opportunity to have accumulated any personal property to defend, if they were so inclined. From generation to generation, in the face of population growth, we can expect a cumulative erosion of the sanctity of property rights, just as we can expect a leveling effect of taxation on incomes.

Summary

Inequality in wealth and income, always a potential threat to political stability, increases with population expansion. Land is fixed, and some forms of capital are relatively fixed in amount. The value of these rises as they become relatively scarcer, and this, in private hands, leads to greater concentration of wealth. The nonpropertied suffer a relative and sometimes absolute deterioration of economic position unless political actions are taken to offset the effect.

In underdeveloped areas, this disadvantaged group is in fact the mass of the population. A question that has interested numerous observers is whether the grant of popular suffrage (which in fact is occurring or has occurred quite widely) will lead the masses to support radical policies for a redistribution of wealth or even the nationalization (socialization) of land and industry. The apparent apathy of the masses has caused some to conclude that such a political upheaval will require extensive preparation. Nevertheless, it seems a reasonable prediction that, given the positive effect of population increase on inequalities of wealth, it is only a matter of time before the requisite populist political action will be forthcoming.

Even in industrialized societies, with a large middle-class constituency, an expanding population makes incursions on concentrations of private wealth. This may come about through the determined actions of a grossly disadvantaged minority group, whose disadvantage increases as population presses on fixed resources, or through the political activity of a welfare population concentrated in the cities. But perhaps even more important than such direct pressures is the more pervasive necessity of limiting the rights of private property in the public interest, as people crowd each other more closely. More explicit forms of public planning serve to control still further the discretion of owners and managers of private enterprises, as they become more tightly integrated into an economic system managed by government in the pursuit of social objectives. This is especially true of the large corporations, which even now are not viewed as private property in the traditional sense of a concrete object of ownership by an individual.

With continued growth in numbers and density of people, then, it will be increasingly difficult to defend the rights of private property against the demand of public interest. Property may be left in private hands, but it will be increasingly subject to regulation. Incomes may remain greatly unequal, but taxation to raise the revenues needed for social welfare programs will weigh more heavily and certainly on the wealthy, even more than now, having a leveling (Tocqueville would say "democratic") effect.

NOTES

1. Jean-Jacques Rousseau, *The Social Contract*, trans. Willmore Kendall, (Chicago: Henry Regnery, 1954), p. 76.
2. James Madison, *The Federalist*, No. 10 (New York: The Heritage Press, 1945), p. 57.
3. Sidney Ratner, *American Taxation* (New York: W. W. Norton, 1942), p. 331, quoting from the *Congressional Record*.
4. "The adoption of a scale augmenting the rate of taxation upon incomes as they rise in amount, although unequal in one sense, cannot be considered oppressive or unjust, inasmuch as the ability to pay increases in much more than arithmetical proportion as the amount of income exceeds the limit of reasonable necessity." From the Report of the Secretary of the Treasury, 1864, p. 15, quoted in E. R. A. Seligman, *Progressive Taxation in Theory and Practice*, 2nd ed. (Princeton: Princeton University Press, 1909), p. 102.
5. Gunnar Myrdal, *Asian Drama: An Inquiry into the Poverty of Nations*

(New York: The Twentieth Century Fund, 1969), 2:1047–1052, describes the process in South Asia. "Land thus tends to pass mainly to wealthier persons, whether in the village or elsewhere, that is, to those who draw most of their income from nonagricultural pursuits" (p. 1050).

6. J. D. Chambers, "Three Essays on the Population and Economy of the Midlands," in D. V. Glass and D. E. C. Eversley, eds., *Population in History* (London: Edward Arnold, 1965), p. 347.

7. Joanne E. Holler, *Population Growth and Social Change in the Middle East* (Washington, D.C.: George Washington University Press, 1964), p. 29.

8. Myrdal, *Asian Drama*, 2:796.

9. *Ibid.*, p. 781.

10. *Ibid.*, 1:300.

11. J. E. Meade, "Population Explosion, the Standard of Living and Social Conflict," *Economic Journal* 77 (June 1967):233–255.

12. *Ibid.*, p. 250.

13. *Ibid.*

14. *Ibid.*, p. 244, Meade notes: "Recently in the discussions about political independence for the island (which the Creoles and the Franco-Mauritians fear as meaning their surrender to the Indian majority) there were disturbances which led to the sending of a small body of British troops to the island to maintain order."

15. *New York Times*, 12 July, 1968.

16. Philip Hauser, *Population Perspectives* (New Brunswick: Rutgers University Press, 1960), p. 148.

17. Joseph A. Schumpeter, *Capitalism, Socialism, and Democracy* (New York: Harper & Row, Torchbook, 1962), p. 142.

18. *Ibid.*

19. Charles A. Reich, "The New Property," *Yale Law Journal* 73 (April 1964): 733.

CHAPTER 8

Population and
International Relations

WE almost take for granted that the nations of the world should display a tremendous diversity of geographical and population size, on the one hand, and of national wealth and per capita income, on the other. But what is it that determines a nation's well-being? Obviously it cannot be size alone. Little Sweden boasts a per capita income almost as high as the United States, certainly better than the USSR and vastly superior to populous and sprawling China and India.

Indeed, one can easily conclude that the absolute size of a population, taken by itself, has nothing to do with a nation's prosperity. Yet nations clearly *are* concerned with the absolute size of their populations: some want a larger one, as in the case of Canada, Australia, and even Russia; others have undertaken state-sponsored birth control programs in an urgent effort to slow the rate of population increase, as in the case of India, Pakistan, and Turkey. We are thus led to the further conclusion that the desirable size of a population must be regulated by other factors.

The Demographic Matrix

We have already been informed by Rousseau what one of those other factors is. He stressed the extent of the natural resources relative to the people: a well-endowed country can support a larger population than one which nature has treated niggardly. Indeed, a rich and extensive country may require a larger population if it is to be properly exploited. The economic law of proportionate returns suggests that when the number of people is small relative to their resources, an increase in their number increases the marginal return. At some point, however, a further increase in population cannot be put to equally good use relative to the fixed resources, and production enters into the phase of a diminishing marginal return. Thus population must be proportioned to resources to achieve the best economic effect.

To speak of resources so abstractly obscures a second important consideration, however. Resources may be given by nature but their exploitation is a social phenomenon. Even the identification of something as a resource requires a degree of acquired understanding. The "iron age" began when the Dorians, who had discovered for themselves that iron was a resource, overran the Cretans and Achaeans, who had not. All resources, whether fossil fuels, minerals, or food itself, become resources only as a result of prior discovery and the subsequent refinement of knowledge. All technological developments, by means of which resources are worked, from the simplest primitive tools to the most sophisticated examples of modern engineering, are likewise social products. It is unnecessary to elaborate further the complex social structures by which resources, once identified as such, are sought, recovered, allocated, distributed, and stored; we are interested only in the simple fact that resources are not a fixed factor except at a moment of time, in the short run; over time resources expand with social development. The resources available to a country now are not the same resources which will be available to it fifty or a hundred years from now even if its geographical boundaries remain unchanged.

In addition to the influence of natural endowment, then, the appropriate size of a population is partly determined by its institutional vitality, which gives rise to its systems of scientific and technical development, of education, of production, distribution, and a variety of other related activities. Included among these institutions, at some stage of development, are large-scale organization of agriculture and manufacturing units. So important is this development to the economic welfare of a nation that we are entitled to single it out for special attention, under the rubric of industrialization, and to say that the degree of a country's industrialization (as one, but a major, aspect of its institutional vitality) is a principal determinant of the size of population which is economically appropriate.

So too is the degree of its urbanization. It is only at the stage when social organization permits a continuing release of people from the soil *and* their absorption into industrialized communities that the functional process of urbanization gets under way, which has been so generative of innovation through specialization. If we think of the city as a social institution and not just a geographical location for numbers of people, then we realize that, like other institutions such as universities and corporations, it is not enough to ask whether a country has or does not have them but how effectively they function. The city as an institution, with specific social and economic functions to perform, performs those functions less well in the underdeveloped than in the developed countries. Their institutional life is in this sense less vital, and therefore less capable of supporting a larger population.

Still another determinant of the appropriate level of population is a country's culture. This includes attitudes which it induces toward work and the accumulation of wealth; how it interprets personal success; the forms of education it encourages. This is a disputed and contentious area, which we shall not take time to explore here. Suffice it to say that unquestionably a society which sees dignity in any occupation, stresses utilitarian education on a widespread basis, believes in principle in equal opportunity for all, regards material gain as a sign of social accomplishment, and places its religious imprimatur on hard work is more likely to cultivate its economic garden than a society which condemns manual labor, directs its educational resources to the dilettante pursuits of an upper-class group, restricts admission to occupations by caste or status, and regards the extirpation of wants or desires as the higher good. This does not require or warrant judging the relative superiority of cultures on other bases than economic; it says only that the first type of society will sustain a larger population at a given standard of living than will the second type of society. (Even in this limited formulation, it does not say that a larger population is better than a smaller population. Presumably, whether a high rate of natural increase is—in the abstract—to be preferred over a low rate is itself a cultural matter.)

As a final consideration, the appropriate size of a people is partly dependent on its political stability. Again going back to Rousseau and the classics, we can recall that for all their fondness for the small state they recognized that it must be large enough to defend itself, to enter into a kind of political equilibrium with neighboring nations. But if numbers are required to achieve political stability, it is also the case that political stability affects the size of the population that can be effectively integrated into a cohesive social and economic system. A weak or inept government gives rise to diversive internal forces, that factionalism which Madison so feared.

China is an instructive example in this respect. In the nineteenth century it was torn internally by rebellion and local feuding. The continuing disturbances contributed to social disorganization and disruption, exacerbating the effects of recurrent drought and flood.

Indeed, the political turmoil made impossible any effective attack on such natural problems. Whatever one's attitude toward the present Communist regime, it has introduced a measure of political stability which will unquestionably permit a larger population than would otherwise be the case.[1]

We have identified a number of determinants of the size of a population which is appropriate if the maximum economic well-being of its people is a nation's objective: the extent of its natural resources, its institutional vitality, which includes the degree of industrialization and functional urbanization, its cultural values, and political stability. Rather than leave these as a "laundry list" of facilitating conditions, let us recast them within the conceptual structure developed in preceding chapters.

The maximum economic well-being of a people calls for a social organization (including functional urbanization) adequate to the population's size and density, and an authority structure and a distribution of the social advantage which is generally enough accepted to insure political stability, all in the light of the prevailing culture. What we have now is more than a laundry list. We have a set of interdependent functional relationships.

As a population grows, its organizational requirements are modified. Since any change in social organization is likely to affect the existing authority and privilege structure, it may meet resistance from those who prefer the status quo. If the effect of this containment is to deteriorate the social performance, it will build up opposing pressure. In time this pressure must have some outlet either through peaceful accommodation or explosive action. We have observed too how population size interacts with social organization in affecting the extent and use of knowledge, with consequences on the acceptability to rising new groups of the existing distribution of authority and advantage. We have seen how a people's culture affects its effective wants, and thereby its social organization. Other relationships could be added.

All these relationships are subject to change, at different rates of change. The rates and directions of change affect the size of the population which can be accorded a given level of economic well-being. We are thus dealing with nothing that is fixed but with elements that are fluid or viscous in different degree: some are more "fixed" than others. And it is in this sense, not just the simple Malthusian sense, that population presses on fixed resources. In some situations, the factor which is relatively fixed and which therefore creates the population problem may be a society's institutional vitality; in other instances, its authority structure or the distribution of the social advantage; in still others, the culture.

Whatever the mix of these ingredients within a country at a point in time, we shall refer to it as the demographic matrix. A different blend of these ingredients, which would improve the economic well-being of a given population or increase the size of a population enjoying a given standard of living, constitutes a preferred demographic matrix. Obviously there can be more than one preferred demographic matrix, depending on how the ingredients are blended. Ideologues have their own preferred forms of social organization, systems of authority, and distributions of privilege, for example. Equally obviously, all preferred demographic matrices need not result in the same appropriate size for the population. It is for this reason that I refrain from using the term which is often employed, "the optimum size of population."

Advantaged and Disadvantaged Nations

Whenever a country's demographic matrix is out of kilter, in that it creates a condition of internal unrest so that dissatisfied groups, whether reformers or exploited minorities, seek a change to some preferred demographic matrix, we have the type of situation that we analyzed in Chapter 2. If the pressures are insistent enough, presumably some action will be taken to remove the impediment preventing movement to a preferred matrix. But this may not be possible, even with the best of intentions on the part of those in authority. For example, if cultural values are the relatively fixed factor, this may be too sensitive a matter for the government to act on effectively. Such an effort could lead to more internal chaos than is tolerable, threatening political stability even more than do existing dissatisfactions. Or the time required to make the adjustments which seem indicated may be too long to be politically acceptable: the building of social and economic institutions, for example, cannot be accomplished overnight. Thus a country, even when it is motivated to take some action to improve its demographic matrix, may find itself impotent. The only moves it can make on its own initiative may be too feeble to be effective.

At such times there may come an overthrow of government and the installation of a new regime. But if the latter only inherits the same basic problems, perhaps buying only a little time, the role of impotence is simply transferred to a different set of actors. In time, the government—whatever government—is driven to seek solution in resources that only others outside its borders can supply.

It is here that our analysis of the dynamics of the effects of population change on a society can be brought to bear simply by making their application to a larger political unit. The same concepts which apply on the national scale apply on an international scale. We confront a structure of international authority, the product of past military, economic, political, and even religious relationships among nations. That authority structure supports an unequal distribution of the social advantage among nations. Both are based upon a prevailing system of social organization in the world at large, including international political bodies, monetary and banking systems, organized markets, ownership rights, and knowledge institutions.

The nation which finds itself locked into an unsatisfactory demographic matrix from which escape through its own unaided efforts seems impossible is in the position of a dissatisfied minority group within a society. It sees an improvement in its position as dependent on its ability to induce others to act. An assertion by other nations that it should face up to its own internal problems or pull itself up by its bootstraps gets as receptive a hearing as the same injunction offered by whites to the Negroes in the United States. Unable to effect a substantial enough improvement on its own, it feels boxed in by the property rights, political power, intrenched economic position of others—all gained by them at an earlier time when it was perhaps repressed or exploited by the very peoples now enjoying the fruits of that exploitation.

On the international scene, then, just as within any society, there are those who benefit disproportionately from the existing structure of authority and the distribution of the social advantage. This is not to cast any opprobrium upon such peoples: their advantage was often gained, as such advantages commonly are, by the seizing of an opportunity at the right moment. Thus the British seized the opportunities presented by an age of maritime exploration and their subsequent industrial development to colonialize half the world, the nineteenth-century phase of that movement accomplished not so much through military power as through the export of institutions: free trade, a gold-based system of exchange, transfers and protection of private property, all leading to the economic dependency of others but receiving theoretical justification in the doctrine of comparative economic advantage, which proved that *both* the superior and inferior trading partners were better off.

It is not surprising that the present-day legatees of such enterprise should be reluctant to give up their advantages won. Just as within a nation, so are there champions of an international status quo, reluctant to revise the authority structure which supports their present advantage. Clearly the United States is pre-eminently in this position on the world scene today, and its foreign political involvements testify to its availability as a tacit or actual ally to those groups most likely to maintain a favorable attitude toward the status quo.

As in the case of individual societies, so is it the case internationally that there are devices for containing pressures for changes in the present distribution of authority and privilege. These range from external force, at one extreme, through a middle range of support to friendly internal groups, to concessions at the other extreme. For all the goodwill that clearly accompanies most foreign aid, for example, from one point of view such a redistribution of income can be regarded as a modest means of relieving pressures for more extreme adjustments.

The kinds of adjustments which may be sought by the dissatisfied nations obviously depend on their internal circumstances. Some may seek freer access to foreign markets from which they are now effectively, if only partially, blocked, as in the case of Japan. (The fact that Japan may protect her own domestic markets from others is not precisely relevant, since she is not looking for symmetry in the application of a rule but for her own path to a preferred demographic matrix.) Another country may look for additional lands to exploit, particularly if there is some shade of illegitimacy of present title. Thus an Indian writer asserted shortly after World War II: "The Pacific is, to a large degree, an Asiatic Ocean, and the islands, large or small, including the subcontinent of Australia and New Zealand, may be said to belong to a panAsiatic system. In this part of the globe, which is largely uninhabited, the doctrine of Asiatic Lebensraum cannot be dismissed offhand nor the doctrine of the White Man's reserve taken for granted."[2]

Still other nations may seek direct economic assistance from the wealthier peoples, permitting some internal improvement in income distribution without requiring an overhaul of the authority structure. Such international charity is distasteful, however, and, as in the case of the welfare population within a society, efforts are sometimes made to convert it into a right. Proposals have thus been made for international acceptance of a form of graduated income tax, which would effect a redistribution of income from the wealthy nations to the poor. Other proposals have urged international price supports for the primary raw materials and foods so often supplied by underdeveloped nations, in the way that price supports have sometimes been used within a nation to redirect income in favor of the farm population.

International and Confrontation Politics

It is easy to see why nations which find it difficult to escape from the confines of an adverse demographic matrix would call on other nations for assistance. It is less easy to see why other nations should respond, but there are at least four good reasons. It will facilitate thinking about these if we continue to keep in mind the parallel with pressures generated within a society by dissatisfied groups seeking to bring about a change in their circumstances.

1. A nation seeking to improve its demographic matrix may engage in military adventures. This is the equivalent of direct action on the domestic scene.

The population expert, W. S. Thompson, has been one of the most articulate spokesmen for the view that population pressure has been a major cause of war.

> . . . The changing rates of population growth in different nations help to create changes in the pressure of populations on the resources available to them and . . . as these changing pressures come to be felt more and more they are almost certain to lead to violent attempts to effect new adjustments more favorable to the growing peoples. Moreover, the tensions thus created are likely to become greater as the industrial power of these growing peoples increases and as their political organization enables them to act in a more unified manner to undertake to enforce what they come to feel are just demands for a larger share in the world's resources.[3]

Thompson believes that World War II was in large measure the product of disregard by the satisfied nations of the growing population pressures on the Axis aggressors accompanied at the same time by rising military might. He takes the case of Japan to illustrate his point. Although its population was expanding only moderately, it was enough to press on food supply. Measured by number of persons per square mile of arable land, Japan is the most densely crowded country in the world (3,575 per square mile in 1950, as against 293 in the United States, 511 in France, 2,551 in the United Kingdom). With the depression of the 1930's, Japan's ability to acquire food through trade declined. Given the discrimination it faced in world markets, its future looked bleak. An outright assault on the coterie of western nations controlling the international system seemed the most effective way out of this demographic trap, at least to the military clique which had seized power. Thompson believes that Japan's problem of a preferable demographic matrix has not yet been solved.[4]

One need not accept this interpretation of the seeds of World War II, nor need he *justify* resort to war as a means of remedying the demographic problem, in order to recognize *objectively* that war constitutes one escape for nations who believe they are boxed in by the past. One need not even sympathize with such a nation's aspirations in order to recognize, again objectively, their explosive force. The same could be said, for example, about direct action by Negroes in the United States in the 1960's. The violence precipitated by extremist black groups need not be justified, and Negro demands need not be endorsed, in order to appreciate that direct action was being used effectively to restructure authority and redistribute social advantage.

But all this creates a basic problem in social organization. Rising nations like Japan demand to be permitted a larger share in the system of international benefits and a more influential voice in international arrangements. Because it demands, should it be accommodated by the satisfied nations like the United States? The answer does not necessarily hinge on equity, though that may be involved, as we shall see, but perhaps chiefly on whether the satisfied nations can prevent a rearrangement of power and benefits if they would, and at what cost. How can Japan be frozen out of an expanding share if there is to be any semblance of international stability? Should the status quo be defended even if the result is war?

Thompson poses the problem with respect to a specific locale. "The Australians and New Zealanders have a hard choice to make. They must embark very energetically upon a program of immigration which will steadily dilute the Britishness of their people or they must face the expansion of the Asiatic peoples with a population so small and so weak militarily that they will have no chance in the struggle that will ensue."[5] But it is also the case that this poses a hard problem for the elite nations, the larger powers. If a struggle does ensue, what role should they play? Is the status quo always to be defended against military action, simply because it is the status quo, or simply because military action is involved? Or should the Asiatic pressures be allowed to have their way in the struggle which Thompson foresees, either because that would represent a small concession on the part of the elite powers which would serve to maintain more of their existing advantage than would any other course they might follow, or because the Asiatics might be viewed as having equity on their side by virtue of Australian resistance to Asiatic immigration?

The Power of Weakness

The nations which can embark on military actions to improve their position in the international authority structure and in the distribution of the international advantage will of necessity require a substantial industrial base. They will not be among the countries usually included in the category of the underdeveloped. They are likely to be countries which have already made sufficient advance that they feel their present limited share in the world's power and resources is inconsistent with their actual status and their still larger ambitions. Their determination coupled with military capability means that they have to be taken seriously.

But what of the underdeveloped nations themselves, comprising most of Asia and virtually all of the Middle East, Africa, and Latin America? Their economic position improves slightly from year to year, in absolute terms; for most of them, per capita income rises slowly and unspectacularly. Even this accomplishment masks the abject poverty of the masses, since per capita income is a statistical abstraction, a simple average, and within many countries the distribution of the slowly rising GNP is such that the economic position of the average worker may change imperceptibly, if at all, over a decade. *Relative* to the industrialized nations, the position of the underdeveloped countries worsens; the gap between the "haves" and the "have-nots" widens.

In short, many underdeveloped countries are barely managing to maintain their present demographic matrix and few are capable of achieving a preferred matrix. If the lot of the masses is a subsistence standard of living, if the size of the masses is growing at a rapid rate, if urbanization too is proceeding apace and increasing the volatility of a people, there are strong pressures building up which can lead to explosion. Under the circumstances it is understandable that countries in this position should turn to the industrialized world for assistance. But unless they come simply as supplicants, asking for charity, what if anything gives force to their appeals for aid?

2. *The impoverished nations seeking to improve their demographic matrix may capitalize on the danger which their political instability poses for the major powers.*

The explosive situation within the populous underdeveloped nations may conceivably be contained by their governments for some time to come, as Myrdal pointed out. In the face of increasing extremes of wealth and poverty, however, abetted by improved means of communication for the spreading of ideas, we have that historical recipe for political unrest which we noted in the preceding chapter, to which philosophers such as Rousseau and political analysts like Tocqueville have testified. From time to time a spark sets off the explosion in a particular country, as Mao in China and Castro in Cuba. At such times there is always the fear or hope, depending on the point of view, that the virus of revolution can spread to other populations in similarly depressed circumstances.

The significance of such internal unrest to the developed nations is that it constitutes a threat to the stability of the international status quo, from which they benefit. That threat expresses itself in several ways. For one thing, the large powers have important economic investments in countries around the world; the expropriation of their property interests would be something of a blow to their asset position. But that aspect of the matter is often overstressed. Much more important is the fact that the whole system of world trade—the flows of goods and materials and services and credit—has been structured in the interests of the dominant powers. Overseas economic investments are a significant part but not the whole of the structure of international relations. Insurgent nationalism constitutes a major threat to the international *order*, which is to say, to the present system of economic and political arrangements.

That threat is heightened by the fact that the major powers are disputants among themselves. The ideological rivalry between the bloc committed to socialism and that committed to liberalism, and the fear by each that the other constitutes a threat to its own survival, has tended to polarize the world. Russia has succeeded in dividing the world and in establishing within its sphere its own international system. Led by the United States, the western powers are left to enjoy their hegemony in the largest part of what remains.

But each serves as a possible refuge to the satellites and allies by which the other is surrounded, so that each lives in a state of constant alert. Instability in any country, whether Czechoslovakia or Egypt or Brazil or India, threatens the composition of the competing blocs either through the detachment of an adherent or the addition of a supporter. If a movement or trend developed in either direction, it could leave the other of the two major powers isolated and threatened. The stakes are great.

In this situation, political unrest is both a threat and an opportunity, depending on the country involved. Unrest within a country which is oriented toward one bloc is a threat to that bloc and an opportunity for its rival. Unrest within a country which is still unaligned is simultaneously a threat and an opportunity to both blocs. It is within this context of power politics that an underdeveloped country's appeal for assistance in the face of an adverse demographic matrix about which it can do little or nothing acquires some force.

The response can take several forms. Simplest is the provision of food and necessities with which the receiving government can pacify its dissidents. Military assistance can help to maintain a friendly government in power by giving it the means to put down insurgency from within or incursion from without. Technical assistance and the provision of capital look to a more distant future and are of value only if they can produce results soon enough to forestall serious internal challenges. The terms on which any such programs are conducted have to be bargained out between the recipient and donor countries, but the very fact that the terms are a bargainable matter underscores the fact that indigent countries are not without bargaining power. The irony and the paradox are that their power derives from their very weakness; it is the threat which their internal instability poses to international stability which is the source of their ability to claim external aid. All such assistance programs can be looked on, from the vantage point of the donor country, as a means of containing the pressures for radical change in a country whose internal stability is important to their own advantage.

This does not rule out the possibility that the recipient and donor governments may not see eye to eye. The donor country may be convinced that only with certain, perhaps major, concessions to internal pressures can stability be maintained. Perhaps it believes that a program of land or tax reform is necessary to satisfy the forces of discontent. From the viewpoint of the incumbent government, however, such programs may mean a collision course with the elite groups it represents or with whom it seeks accommodation. To force the issue might endanger its survival, in the short run, even more than the discontent of the masses. The donor country may be willing to sacrifice elite interests in the recipient country in order to preserve its own (elite) interests in the larger world context. To the recipient government, revision in the distribution of world authority and resources is desirable, but the internal authority structure is (not always, but often) something largely to be preserved, since after all the government—unless it is a revolutionary government —achieved power within that authority structure.

At times the reverse may be true. A nationalistic government, seeking economic advancement even at the expense of intrenched interests, looks to the outside for support. A donor country, most concerned about the recipient's internal stability and afraid of precipitating a violent clash as the local elite resist assault on their privileges, may decide against the government. It can do this either by the terms of its aid or by sub rosa encouragement to a more like-minded successor government.

The significant consideration is not that a donor power is always on the side of reform or always on the side of privilege, but that its judgment as to what cause it shall espouse, if any, is based upon its own perceived needs within the world context.

Population growth and urbanization within the underdeveloped countries thus have their impact on the demographic matrix. At this point in time, the effect is to worsen the matrix, generating internal pressures for social change. For reasons we have explored at some length, these pressures cannot be ignored forever; sooner or later they have their outlet, in one form or another, not easily predictable. It is the realization of that fact, or at least the fear of its possibility, that pushes the wealthier countries to provide assistance. Not military might but desperate weakness constitutes the threat behind the claims by the poorer countries for a share in the wealth of the mighty. It is in this sense that one can understand Babeuf's insight that the unhappy are the really important powers of the earth.[6]

The Moral Imp

In marked contrast to such political realities is a third influence inducing a shift in the distribution of world power and income. This is the element of morality.

3. Nations which are locked into an adverse demographic matrix which threatens their welfare are likely to be the beneficiaries of a gradually developing ethical sense among peoples and nations.

It may seem quixotic to introduce this factor in an age which has given rise to genocide and total war. On the other hand, it would be a gross error to omit it from the calculus. If it is hard to identify its specific impact, in view of intercorrelation with the political factors just discussed, it is none the less real for that fact.

What accounts for the evolution of such a social (in contrast to religious) morality is likewise problematical. Tocqueville envisioned a kind of centuries-long movement toward increasing equality among men, without satisfactorily explaining the cause of such a tendency. The concepts of communism and socialism which in their purest form appeal to a sense of the common family of man have had their adherents throughout history, and have shown their power in the contemporary world. Even in western culture, antithetical though it is toward systems which would undermine the position of the individual in society, the principle of the welfare state has won acceptance. It seems entirely possible that the growth and urbanization of populations have had their own influence, by bringing people into closer contact and making less tenable the extremes of wealth and poverty thus revealed and by permitting the quicker spread of ideas, and their reinforcement in being held by larger numbers.

Possibly also influential in the western world today may be a belief in the perfectability of society. The accomplishments of science and technology have encouraged a conviction that once we have identified a problem—including hunger and disease and even population control—all that is needed is to mount the right kind of attack on that problem in order to solve it. "Now it can be said that it is possible to achieve almost anything we want—so great is the effectiveness of technology based on the experimental method. Thus the main issue for scientists and for society as a whole is now to decide *what* to do among all the things that could and should be done."[7] In the light of such a view, those with the resources to solve the pressing problem bear the responsibility for its solution.

Whatever the cause, the consequence has been a rise in an ethical feeling of the oneness of people and a concern for the welfare of others. The misfortunes of others are felt more keenly as misfortunes to ourselves. We are less able to withdraw into our own world, isolating ourselves from involvement in the real world beyond. Few programs launched by President Kennedy had more appeal than the

Peace Corps, in whose service hundreds of thousands of young people found personal satisfaction in serving others. Whatever other influences may have been present, one major source of student unrest in the United States in the late 1960's was a desire of the rising generation to dissociate itself from what seemed the callous disregard of its predecessors for the plight of the underprivileged and discriminatorily treated. (In both these instances, the role of the young as the carriers of the "new" morality is worth noting.)

This slowly evolving secular morality is almost certain to have an expression in the form of programs which will become institutionalized and accepted as desirable—desirable because morally "necessary." We may still be a considerable distance from that result, as witness the difficulty which administrations in the United States have experienced in securing congressional appropriations for foreign assistance. But this reluctance is probably explainable on other counts, such as the drain on the treasury of the war in Vietnam and the fact that the foreign assistance program itself has fallen into disrepute on programmatic grounds. It is my belief that with the end of hostilities and with the rationalization of foreign aid programs, the compulsive power of equalitarian ethics will make itself felt both on the domestic and the international scene. In time the notion that the greater wealth of certain nations should be used to improve the position of the less favorably situated will be accepted only somewhat less readily than the notion that the greater wealth of more fortunate individuals should be drawn on, through a graduated system of taxation, for the benefit of those less advantaged.

The Political Imperative

4. The increasing need for a system of international government, however limited, will give rise to a more effective instrument for the relief of nations suffering from an adverse demographic matrix which they cannot adequately correct in the short run.

A great deal could be said on this subject, but I shall restrict myself to restating a view which I have set forth elsewhere.[8] For half a century there has been strong sentiment on behalf of some form of world government. The reluctance of the major powers, in particular the United States and Russia, to give up any significant national sovereignty has lessened the effectiveness of the two attempts so far made in the League of Nations and the United Nations. Now, however, a new element has entered the picture: the development of weapons of such power that they literally threaten the destruction of existing civilization. Nuclear energy coupled with delivery systems such as missiles and space platforms of increasing sophistication mean that the world will continue to survive only on the sufferance of those few who possess the discretion to unloose the attack.

This "sword of Damocles" type of existence will in time become unacceptable and intolerable, to the large powers no less than the smaller ones, to the developed nations no less than to the underdeveloped. Sentiment will develop, as indeed it already has, for effective arms control, and given a minor disaster or two (hopefullly on small enough a scale that it teaches a lesson rather than puts an end to the class) that sentiment is likely to have its effect. An arms control program will then be instituted under the aegis of an international body, the United Nations or a successor organization. In contrast to past maneuvering to exclude China from the community of nations, every inducement will be offered to secure its membership.

Once such a program comes into existence, world government acquires a new and special authority. No nation of any size could leave the organization without jeopardizing the arms control program and restoring a world which survives only at the will of those holding discretion over the massive weapons systems. The same reason that brings nations together in a world government capable of controlling all arms would hold them inside that world government. In that situation, the disadvantaged nations would be in a position to use their larger numbers to induce the world government to adopt programs aimed at the alleviation of their distress and the more rapid development of their economies, through a redistribution of the world's resources and income.

The wealthier nations would be in little position to resist such programs, except in detail. All that it would cost them would be some small portion of their national incomes, while the alternative would be perpetual jeopardy of their very existence. Moreover, the equity principle involved would be one which would be difficult to contest: the concept of a graduated income tax for the redistribution of wealth has been accepted domestically, and there is no clear justification for refusing its application internationally. The new secular morality will give support to the use of world government for such ends.

This does not, of course, rule out a lot of hard bargaining over the shape and content of international welfare programs. A world government would face all the problems of reconciling divergent interests and accommodating pressures for social change, without radical readjustment of the authority structure, which now face national governments. Nevertheless, the existence of a new and higher seat of government which is both the focus for pressures and the coordinator of the necessary bargains would mark a long step forward toward the peaceful resolution of the problems arising from shifting demographic matrices, differing as among nations.

These are four reasons, then, why countries which feel themselves disproportionately disadvantaged in the distribution of world resources and world authority can bring pressures for a redistribution: by threat of war on the part of those with rising industrial capability; by threat of internal instability on the part of those with deteriorating prospects; by trading on the equity of a situation, which is to say by appeals to a new morality stressing greater equalitarianism; and by virtue of a world government which can mediate the pressures for change.

Clearly none of these influences is certain, but that is not the issue. Changes in the distribution of world power and advantage do take place. We have been concerned only with identifying the role of population pressures in the redistributive process, and the mechanisms through which such population pressures operate.

The Seats of the Mighty

Which are the nations which rise to positions of greatest influence on the world scene? We are now in a position to say that they are those with a favorable demographic matrix relative to a large population. The country whose natural endowment, social institutions (including industrial and urban structures), cultural values, and political stability support a population of considerable size at an advanced material standard of living becomes a candidate for a seat among the mighty nations.

Obviously this is not a precise formulation, since the demographic matrices of nations cannot be ranked unequivocally. For one thing, what constitutes a superior standard of living remains a judgmental matter even after we specify a material standard. Per capita GNP is at best a rough guide. As a second consideration, within limits which are uncertain, numbers of people and standard of living constitute tradeoffs in the calculus of power. A nation with a larger population and a somewhat lower material standard may claim and be granted equality alongside a nation with a somewhat smaller population and a higher material standard. A third uncertainty is introduced by the impermanence of certain of the ingredients of the demographic matrix, notably political stability. A country with a strong government may acquire greater influence than another which is larger and more prosperous but given to recurrent political turmoil.

Even with such uncertainties, however, we can conclude that world power falls only to those countries which possess a relatively large population, living on a relatively high plane of material comfort, and with relative strength in the elements composing their demographic matrix. On this basis we can feel certain, to take but two instances, that Taiwan China is not now and will never be a great power, despite its permanent seat on the Security Council of the United Nations, and that mainland China, while not now a great power, may well become one.

Summary

The size of the population which a country can support at a given standard of living is the product of four major influences: its natural endowment, socially defined; its institutional organizations including the degree of industrialization and functional urbanization; its culture; and its political stability. These can be related to each other by a formulation which uses the analytical concepts we have developed. The appropriate size of a country's population depends on the maturity and vitality of its organizational life, as these both define and create its resources, and on the acceptability of its authority structure and distribution of the social advantage given the composition of the population, as these determine its effective wants. The greater the socially defined resources, and the more stable the political system, and the more materialistic the culture, the larger the population that can be sustained at a given standard of living.

We call the particular blend of these elements attributable to a country its demographic matrix. If a different blend would produce a more desirable result we refer to it as a preferred demographic matrix. Obviously a country's demographic matrix changes over time, and there can be a number of preferred positions each with its appropriate population, rendering suspect the notion of some optimum size.

The elements composing the demographic matrix are all more or less fixed and fluid at a point in time. When we speak of a population as pressing on fixed resources, it is the *relative* fixity of these several constituent resources of a country which we should have in mind. When a country which faces an adverse demographic matrix finds it impossible to move to a preferred matrix because of the fixity of one or more of these elements, its only recourse is to seek a solution outside itself.

An industrializing country so situated, hemmed in by the past, may come to believe that only through military action can it push its way up in the world's authority structure and secure a redistribution of benefits appropriate to its position. The more favorable, or less adverse, its present demographic matrix, the greater is its military capability. The more adverse it expects its future demographic matrix to become, the greater its incentive to undertake the risk of war now, before its military capability is drained away. There is thus, for a nation in this position, a question of timing—of delaying action until industrial strength seems adequate for the venture but not for so long that population pressures force a diversion of resources. Nations which prefer the existing international distribution of advantage then face the dilemma of whether to seek to preserve the status quo by force (counter military action) or to make concessions sufficient to preserve the peace.

Underdeveloped countries with an adverse demographic matrix and confronting some fixed element which prevents their moving to a preferred matrix are seldom able to capitalize on any military capability. Their greatest asset in inducing the wealthy nations to come to their aid is their very weakness. Their internal political instability constitutes a threat to the existing international order from which the more powerful nations derive their benefits. The more populous the country in difficulty is, the greater the threat which its instability poses, hence the less instability required to bring it the support which it seeks, and the greater the support the greater the instability.

Two other influences making for a possible redistribution of income and authority among nations are in process of development, but remain largely in the future. These are an evolving secular morality whose stress is on equalitarianism, and a stronger world government, necessitated by arms control, which can also serve as the instrument for mediating the effects of population pressures.

In the concert of nations, greatest influence is exercised by those possessing populations which are relatively large, enjoying a relatively high material standard of living, with both these characteristics supported by a demographic matrix which is relatively strong in its constituent elements of natural endowment, social organization, cultural values, and political stability.

NOTES

1. W. S. Thompson has argued this point effectively in *Population Problems* (New York: McGraw-Hill, 1953), pp. 355–359.
2. Radhakamal Mukerjee, *Races, Lands, and Food* (New York: Dryden Press, 1946), p. 7.
3. W. S. Thompson, *Population Problems*, p. 349.
4. *Ibid.*, pp. 342–343, 351–355. Thompson argues that the situation facing Japan differs markedly from that earlier confronting England who also had to feed her expanding population through trade. Japan lacks the natural resources available to Britain; Britain rose to industrial pre-eminence at a time when the rest of the world was still largely agricultural; Japan has no large body of nationals residing abroad who prefer its products, in contrast to the English-speaking peoples around the world; capital and management are now more mobile, increasing competition; Japan faces greater export restrictions in foreign markets than England did, and England had accumulated vast overseas investments which helped to earn her food.
5. W. S. Thompson, *Plenty of People*, rev. ed. (New York: Ronald Press, 1948), p. 129.
6. Quoted by Edmund B. Wilson, *To the Finland Station* (New York: Doubleday, Anchor Books, 1940), p. 74.
7. René Dubos, *The Dreams of Reason* (New York: Columbia University Press, 1961), p. 62.
8. *The West in a World Without War* (New York: McGraw-Hill, 1963).

CHAPTER 9

Summary
and Conclusions

WE have covered a good deal of territory in the preceding pages, from the effects of population changes on forms of government and the process of urbanization to their relation to technological change and the rise of new organizations. Now it is time to retrace our journey not simply as a way of refreshing our memories of what we have witnessed but more importantly to sort our impressions and to reorganize them into a more integrated statement.

Population Effects within a Society

The social organization of a people—how it organizes itself economically, politically, socially, religiously, the institutions it constructs to facilitate the conduct of its daily affairs and to provide continuity to social relationships over time—tends to create a complex network of superordinate and subordinate relations and a body of customs, rules, and regulations. This structure of authority both gives rise to and supports the apportionment of social status, political position, and economic benefits among the people, something which can be referred to in the aggregate as the distribution of the social advantage. Obviously shares in the social advantage are distributed unequally, but most individuals have some perquisites of value which they would not like to have taken from them. Even the feudal serf received certain benefits from his lord as a matter of right.

Fear that radical change in the social organization might deprive them of their allotted advantage, however small that may be, gives rise to a basic conservatism in most people in a society, giving a stability to their relationships over time, so that social cohesion and organization are not simply imposed by a strong few on the many weak but arise out of a general will that present forms shall be preserved—always with the proviso, of course, that most constituent groups in a society have grievances that they would like corrected, marginal adjustments in the distribution of the social advantage for which they press and plead, but would not disrupt. Whenever a society does not have this degree of stability it is, by definition, ripe for radical action and even revolution. A society may possess such stability in the main but encompass a minority group or groups which feel sufficiently disadvantaged in the distribution of benefits that they feel little adherence to the existing order.

To give somewhat sharper focus to the analysis, let us begin our generalization with western industrial society since the late nineteenth century. We introduce the assumption of growth in the size of the population and ask what follows from it. The most obvious effect it creates, in time, is an urgent need for changes in the social organization.

That need for change in social organization will, however, be resisted by those elites who benefit most from the existing distribution of the social advantage, since with any significant change in social organization comes alteration in the authority structure and benefit system. Their adherence to the status quo impedes the effective functioning of society by the continued use of outdated institutions to meet the needs of added numbers. The resulting hardships, like the social advantage, are distributed unequally. At some point the buildup of pressures becomes too great to contain any longer, and some modification in the social organization takes place. This was the effect, for example, of nineteenth-century control over social institutions by an aristocratic elite with a local orientation and manorial temperament, who resisted the large-scale industrialization which threatened to rob them of control and the trend to urbanization which sacrificed style to function, manners to popularity, stability to diversity, and diminished the importance of their local seat of authority.

What, then, are some of the changes in social structure which population growth would necessitate? Since an increase in numbers would also imply, almost certainly, an increase in density due to urbanization, people would press more closely on each other, necessitating more governmental regulation of individual and organizational activity and the provision of a greater range of governmental services.

Simultaneously there would be an increase in the size of nongovernmental organizations—business firms, labor unions, political parties, universities, religious bodies—so that these could function effectively within the larger context. With an increase in size would come as well a necessary change in their structure in the form of centralization of authority on a national basis, an alteration in their performance toward standardization of the goods and services they provide, and a shift in their control in the direction of according a greater degree of representation to their expanded constituencies, whether employees, members, or students.

With growth in the size of total population, in the scale of cities, and in the scope of organization, a trend would develop toward the centralization of governmental powers, in two respects: the national government would exercise stronger coordinating and controlling powers over subordinate units, and the executive authority would acquire greater powers of initiative relative to the legislative authority because of the need for prompt action in complex situations often requiring the advice of experts.

These direct effects of population increase on the need for social reorganization would generate a further chain of effects:

The market for, and profitability of, certain economic goods and services would increase relative to others, channeling the flow of inventive activity in their direction. Technological developments would be oriented toward what society stamped as most urgent or most wanted in an effective sense, in the sense, that is, of rewarding most highly those whose activities contributed to meeting those wants. The reward might conceivably be social rather than pecuniary, but in western society the pecuniary reward has been peculiarly effective.

Urbanization with industrialization would increase the degree both of specialization in the production of goods and services and of specialization in the kinds of goods and services produced. The concentration of people in cities would also create a demand for the large-scale provision of food, leading to the mechanization of agriculture. The desire by rural families for the specialized goods of industry, along with mechanization of the farm, would lead to the increasing commercialization of agricultural production and the migration of unneeded farm families to the cities. With an increase in the population, particularly in the metropolitan areas, there would be an absolute increase in the number of creative people and in those contributing to the knowledge base, with further effects on invention and innovation.

The consequence of these chains of linked events is to create new opportunities, which are seized on by a relatively small number of ambitious and aggressive individuals, around whom new classes of interests tend to develop. Incapable by themselves of winning changes in the authority structure and the distribution of the social advantage which they believe appropriate to their role in the modified social organization, they make alliances with others whose numbers or influence are more equal to the task. Where suffrage is general, political alliances are among the most common.

In contrast to those who reap rewards from the social changes induced by growth in the population are certain subpopulations which are disproportionately disadvantaged. The added numbers of the subpopulation tend to press on certain resources—social no less than physical, including available housing, recreational areas, occupations to which they are restricted by the authority structure —more than is the case with other groups. There is a special kind of density effect here, density of people within a social space which is relatively fixed within the over-all social structure. The tighter and more constraining these limitations become in the face of increasing numbers, the greater the explosive potential. All that is needed is determination on the part of the group and effective leadership.

The leadership may come from within the group or from outside. Outside leadership may come from radical reformers who are idealistically minded or from one of the rising interest groups which seeks an alliance to increase its own strength. In this kind of action, young people are likely to play a particularly important role, in part because of their lesser stake in the status quo, in part because of youthful idealism and impatience with the past, in part because of the disproportionate growth in their numbers when a society is expanding.

Determined minorities pose a dilemma for any society. They can either be contained by force or by concession. Difficulties attend either course of action. The need for continued repression of any group itself changes the authority structure, heightening the police powers of the state but without solving the basic underlying problem. Concessions to an aggressive dissident group invite imitation by other groups, particularly those out of sympathy with the first, threatening the authority of the state and, again, obliging it to move further along a path either of force or concession.

The necessity for coordinating stronger group interests adds to the need for centralization of governmental power. As heterogeneity increases with the more extensive scale of society, some decentralization of functions and authority becomes necessary to insure that local and specialized needs are met and to reduce the potential for conflict between government and group. The centrifugal effect of decentralization thus opposes the centripetal effect of centralization. At some point in the growth of numbers and density, the forces making for a high degree of local autonomy can be expected to restrict the center's role to a more limited number of coordinating functions.

"Decentralization" is a term of relative meaning, however, for the functions which devolve from the center to the lesser units are centrally performed there. With increasing numbers, smaller systems run through the same process of centralization cum decentralization as is true of larger units. And even in the case of central national governments, the pressing need of an expanding world population for coordination of its increasing contacts spins power upward to supranational bodies and ultimately to a world government.

An industrialized and urbanized society gives rise to a middle-class culture which originates in the cities but blankets the society. If individualism (along with alienation) is characteristic of the urban centers, so too is mass popular culture, which has the effect of standardizing social, intellectual, artistic, and recreational expression at the level of "average" taste, in a kind of cultural levelling. Conservative in fundamental social relationships, mass culture tends to impose a populist imprint on the activities of governments and organizations.

There is a levelling influence as well with respect to wealth and income. This arises not from radical ideological programs of redistribution but from gradualist welfare programs which depend heavily on a graduated income tax for financing. It is also due to the need to regulate the uses of private property in a society whose expanding numbers require increasing attention to the public effects of private actions. This need reaches its most systematic expression in the greater reliance on explicit forms of planning, with the decisions of private economic units shaped not so much by their own objectives as by the role which they are to play in the larger social system.

Population Effects in an International Setting

Many of these same population effects which we observe within a national society also operate within the larger international unit. Nations become special interest groups within a heterogeneous world society.

The appropriate size of a country's population for a given standard of living depends upon its natural resources, as these are socially defined; its organizational development and vitality, including the degree of its industrialization and functional urbanization; the cultural values which shape its attitudes and responses; and its political stability, which depends on how acceptable are its authority structure and distribution of the social advantage. We refer to the blend of these at any point in time as the country's demographic matrix. None of these elements is fixed, but all vary or can be made to vary at different rates. If the size of the population cannot be managed to conform to what the demographic matrix permits, then a given standard of living can be maintained only if the demographic matrix can itself be managed. This means moving to some new and preferred matrix—preferred in the sense that some change in the underlying conditions, even if not wanted for its own sake, is wanted in order to make possible the same or a higher standard of living. To adhere to the prevailing conditions of the demographic matrix in the face of an expanding population would mean acceptance of a deteriorating standard of living.

A country facing or anticipating a population increase, or seeking to move to a higher material standard of living may be able to manage the less fixed elements of its demographic matrix effectively enough so that they do not constitute limiting factors in the economic growth process. Resources, institutional momentum, cultural values, and the distribution of authority and social benefits may, one or all, be fluid enough to keep a society moving forward. But if this should not be the case, then additional population can be accommodated only at the price of a reduction in standards or by resort to an outside solution.

In this latter situation, a nation becomes a "disadvantaged minority" which seeks a change in the international structure of authority and distribution of the social advantage. Its ability to induce change may stem from its capability of engaging in direct (that is, military) action or from its incapability of maintaining internal political stability, endangering the international status quo. In either case the existing world power structure is confronted with the same basic dilemma as a determined minority poses to a national government: either it must resist with force or it must make concessions. In either event, changes in the existing authority structure are certain to follow. The status can never again be quo ante.

Population Effects and Morality

In the world at large, as well as in its component political parts, the effect of population change is thus to pose problems for a new morality. Like all social phenomena, morality too is not static but must remain fluid to be effective, even if the degree of its fluidity bears a functional relationship to other phenomena, so that it cannot be treated as a blank page to be written on each day according to the inspiration of the moment.

The disparate rates of population change among nations, accompanied by equally disparate capabilities of managing their demographic matrices, create one type of moral dilemma, as we have seen. But the need for a more encompassing morality also lies closer to home, among peoples generally, as the closeness of contact of larger numbers of people creates new problems concerning the relationship of the individual to society.

The fact that private actions can have polluting effects, not only of the air and water but also of the social environment, becomes a more serious matter with increasing density. Governmental regulation of the individual seems daily more necessary on a wider front. Self-regulation by each individual of his own behavior seems more imperative if people are to live in some semblance of harmony.

The problems do not stop there. Increased knowledge creates a new potential for improving the lot of the individual. It becomes possible to provide him with a superior education, to minister more effectively to his health needs and even to extend his life span, to improve the quality of his surroundings. But the pressure of added numbers raises difficult choices. Who, among the many, shall benefit from these potentials? The answer can be dichotomized by the application of elitist or equalitarian philosophies. In a society whose growing numbers emphasize a mass and populist orientation, the tendency will be to move toward an increasingly equalitarian solution. The standardizing and levelling effects which we noted earlier will apply as well to the distribution of these benefits.

Even so, choice problems remain. Even an equalitarian society does not extend benefits and distribute hardships equally to all, but excludes certain categories from certain privileges and liabilities. Thus the young are deprived of rights of suffrage, older groups are immune from military service, free public education is extended only to those showing some minimum level of intelligence or educability, drugs or liquors or tobacco may be foreclosed except to those with specific medical need or of an age considered socially appropriate. In all these cases the question is one, as the United States Supreme Court has said, of "reasonable" classification. In the case of health, to take but one obvious and difficult area, should the benefits of new medical knowledge be extended equally to all, or is there some basis for a reasonable classification which emphasizes certain needs more than others?

One aspect of the issue was posed by a British physician speaking at a congress of the Royal Society of Health in 1969. He urged that the present medical practice of keeping alive every individual who could afford attention, regardless of the incapacitating infirmities of old age, was no longer supportable.

> . . . in a community which can no longer adequately nurse all its chronic sick and where beds are so blocked by the aged that younger people requiring surgical and medical treatment cannot be admitted, we can no longer avoid the issue of medicated survival, which as so successfully practiced is surely one of the cruelist hazards to which we can be subjected.[1]

The age problem is only suggestive of other problems which would also be encountered in the allocation of scarce social resources in a society given to an equalitarian sentiment. But perhaps most fundamental is the issue raised by René Dubos as to whether a populist orientation in the use of resources at some point may not have a blighting effect on the quality of the life we seek to preserve.

> We must beware lest we create the illusion that health will be a birthright for all in the medical utopia, or a state to be reached passively by following the directions of physicians or by taking drugs bought at the corner store. In the real world of the future, as in the past, health will depend on a creative way of life, on the manner in which men respond to the unpredictable challenges that continue to arise from an ever changing environment. . . .
>
> It must be realized, furthermore, that the attitudes of the physicians who are practicing the medicine of today and the efforts of the scientists who are creating the medicine of tomorrow are influenced—and to a large extent directed—by the beliefs and wishes of the culture to which they belong. If the social atmosphere puts a great premium on techniques and products designed to minimize effort, to relieve pain, and to increase the selfish enjoyment of today, these goals will be given priority by medical practitioners and research scientists. To a very

large extent, this is what is happening today—in my opinion, at the sacrifice of higher values.[2]

If the distribution of the social advantage and the authority structure comes out of the social organization—the institutions which are needed and the people these place in positions of influence—there will always be some elite enjoying some protected advantage, as we noted in the preceding chapters. In this sense, no society will ever answer the question of who gets what with a completely equalitarian version of *who*. But this is likely to be a much less important question than the *what*, which involves the output of the social organization.

The qualitative performance of the social organization is shaped by both the forces of effective demand and effective supply. We have accepted Schmookler's thesis that invention tends to follow effective demand, extending that formulation to include social invention. We come back, then, to the fact that the qualitative performance of the social organization is basically a matter of effective demand: the wants which people desire with enough strength to provide direction to the creative minds among them.

The determinants of effective desires are obscure. There is a persisting tendency to ascribe these to education, but if this is so it is not likely to be the education of formal institutions, or at least not only that. We can only fix upon, however abstractly, the value-positing and value-creating characteristics of an epoch, whatever these may be. They are not necessarily the same for all societies, either in point of time or place. They inevitably involve a people's morality, whether religious or secular, as that which gives strength and reason (purpose) to whatever it values.

Whether a mass society gives rise, then, to a kind of arithmetic equalitarianism in its social organization or adopts a more calculated basis for distributing the benefits of its increasing knowledge among its increasing numbers is, in the last analysis, a moral problem to which we have no analytical solution.

Population Effects and the Future

Let us return to the case of the underdeveloped nations. It is conceivable, as some have argued, that their present rate of population growth is a temporary phenomenon. With the passage of time, a quickening pace of industrialization, and increasing urbanization, their rate of increase conceivably will slack off enough to produce a sustainable and even an improving standard of living, given their demographic matrix. Irene Taeuber has argued to that effect. "Given the technologies and the basic values of the twentieth century, both population growth and the ultimate slowing of that growth are predictable consequences of the industrial and urban transformation of agrarian cultures."[3]

Even if this should prove to be the case, some differential rates of population growth and differential abilities to accommodate them will always remain, setting in motion, somewhere in the world, the chain of effects which we have examined. Social changes (technological, educational, cultural) can likewise be expected to have their impact on the need for change in social organization within a particular society, with the consequences suggested by the preceding analysis. But, beyond these certainties, it is by no means clear that the reduction in rates of population increase will follow so predictably from industrialization and urbanization as some, like Miss Taeuber, have maintained, for at least two reasons.

First, it is not evident that industrialization is wanted by these societies so effectively as to produce the population effects envisaged on a large enough scale, and soon enough to constitute any solution. This would require acceptance of a different life style marked by, among other things, a loosening of family ties, a greater degree of individual initiative and personal responsibility for results, including a personal responsibility for organizational effectiveness as measured by competitive performance, a discipline of time and place and impersonal organization, a heightened sense of scientific objectivity and materialistic specificity (in distinction to what is subjective and philosophically abstract), and an overriding objective of worldly gain. In general, it would call for a willingness to accept the risk of losing one's toehold, however insecure it may be, in a social system which is, after all, familiar, by having to scramble for a new stake within a set of institutions which is forbiddingly strange.

Japan could achieve a remarkable social transformation in many of these respects (though not in all, as the continuing importance of the family concept attests). Other countries may achieve a social reconstitution under duress, as in the case of Communist China. Conceivably other forms of social organization than those familiar to the West will serve the purpose of industrialization. In general, however, it is by no means clear that enough people are willing to substitute a new set of values for those to which they are accustomed, and they are not convinced that that is the only means by which an improvement in their condition can take place.[4] It is for this reason that I am less sanguine about the effective management of the demographic transition under representative governments; it seems more likely that frustration or desperation will drive one country after another into military or one-party socialist solutions, or some combination of the two.

A second reason for doubting that the population problem of the underdeveloped countries will be solved with the passage of time is that for urbanization to have its effect of reducing the rate of growth in population and increasing the rate of economic growth, it must be functional urbanization. This means that it must perform the functions of integrating people into industrial organizations, of stimulating specialization of activity and the growth and dissemination of useful knowledge, of sparking ambitions and setting new cultural standards. The kind of urbanization which consists largely of village huddling replicated to a point of urban density is quite a different thing.

If the situation confronting the underdeveloped nations is a bleak one, it is not because, or not only because, of a fear that Malthusian remedies to excessive population will manifest their inexorable presence. It is as much because the pressures generated can explode a Pandora's box of political effects which will not leave the West untouched. The international authority structure is under attack. The international distribution of the social advantage is being protested. It is not the West which is attacking and protesting; the West is on the defensive. And the one most certain and salient fact is that of all the possible or feasible outcomes of present forces, the least possible is the maintenance of the status quo. Population pressures are having their effect, and even with the greatest of optimism as to how such pressures can be contained or released, they are in process of creating a new world, in which possession of the moon will not guarantee possession of this earth. Or, if it did, we would not want to be part of it.

NOTES

1. Dr. Kenneth O. A. Vickery, as quoted in the *New York Times*, 30 April 1969. Dr. Vickery suggested eighty as the age past which doctors should forego the practice of "resuscitating the dying." Obviously any age, suggested or legislated, would be subject to revision in the face of changing circumstances.

2. René Dubos, *The Dreams of Reason* (New York: Columbia University Press, 1961), p. 96. It is interesting to note how the second paragraph supports Schmookler's thesis (see Chapter 3 of this book) and applies it as well to the creation of knowledge.

3. Irene Taeuber, "Population Increase and Manpower Utilization in Imperial Japan," in J. J. Spengler and Otis D. Duncan, eds., *Demographic Analysis* (Glencoe: The Free Press, 1956), p. 737. In the preceding sentence she writes that "experience within the East corroborates the hypothesis deducible from Western experience: substantial increase in the size of the total population is a correlate of industrialization, but the social and psychological transformations implicit in industrialization result eventually in a lessened rate of reproduction and a slowing growth."

4. The kind of social reorganization and cultural value reorientation which may be needed to achieve any kind of population stability, either in developed or underdeveloped countries, may prove to be of a very radical nature. Judith Blake has suggested the need for a further reduction in the role of the family, a modified conception of what constitutes normality in sexual relations, a marked revision in the place of women in society (not simply in their working but in having available to them a richer, more varied, more *equal* occupational fare). Judith Blake, "Population Policy for Americans: Is the Government Being Misled?" *Science* (May 2, 1969), pp. 522–529. Miss Blake is addressing herself to the American scene, but her strictures have wider applicability. It is her belief that considerable progress can be made simply by lifting penalties—social, political, economic—on those whose own preferences run in these directions, though it seems evident that positive inducements would be needed as well. But changes of this nature, if they are to be introduced in countries where most needed, would be the most difficult to effect.

Index